URBAN CULTURE

URBAN CULTURE
Exploring Cities and Cultures

ALAN C. TURLEY
University of New Orleans

PEARSON
Prentice
Hall

Upper Saddle River, New Jersey 07458

Library of Congress Cataloging-in-Publication Data

TURLEY, ALAN C.
    Urban culture: exploring cities and cultures/Alan C. Turley.
        p. cm.
    Includes bibliographical references and index.
    ISBN 0-13-041694-0 (alk. paper)
    1. Sociology, Urban. 2. Cities and towns. 3. Culture. I. Title.

HT151.T87 2005
307.76—dc22   2003065603

Publisher: Nancy Roberts
Executive Editor: Chris DeJohn
**Director of Production
    and Manufacturing:** Barbara Kittle
**Editorial/Production Supervision
    and Interior Design:** Rob DeGeorge
Copyeditor: Sylvia Moore
Prepress and Manufacturing Buyer: Mary
    Ann Gloriande
Cover Director: Jayne Conte
Cover Design: Bruce Kenselaar
Electronic Art Creation: Mirella Signoretto
Senior Marketing Manager: Marissa
    Feliberty

Marketing Assistant: Adam Laitman
Editorial Assistant: Veronica D'Amico
Image Permission Coordinator: Nancy
    Seise
Cover Image Specialist: Karen Sanatar
Interior Image Specialist: Beth Brenzel
Manager, Rights and Permissions: Zina
    Arabia
Director, Image Resource Center: Melinda
    Reo
Composition: Lithokraft II
Printer/Binder: Courier Companies, Inc.
Cover Printer: Coral Graphics
Text: 10/12 Palatino

Credits and acknowledgments borrowed from other sources and reproduced, with permission, in this textbook appear on appropriate page within text or, in the case of photographs, on p. 238.

Pearson Education LTD.
Pearson Education Singapore, Pte. Ltd
Pearson Education Canada, Ltd
Pearson Education—Japan

Pearson Education Australia PTY, Limited
Pearson Education North Asia Ltd
Pearson Educación de Mexico, S.A. de C.V.
Pearson Education Malaysia, Pte. Ltd

10 9 8 7 6 5 4 3 2 1
ISBN 0-13-041694-0

*To Marian, for her help,
and to Judy, for her support.*

Contents

Preface

This book illustrates the effects of the urban environment on the production of culture. It covers music, art, writing, and deviant culture production from the perspective that the urban landscape and urban structure impact the groups of people living in the city. City life has an effect on production and consumption of culture and literally defines where culture can take place. Using urban theory to talk about culture reflects a new approach to a field that hasn't witnessed many new teaching innovations. A book that covers cultural topics together with urban theory and methods will reach modern students in a way in which they haven't before been challenged. Students grasp modern culture better than they grasp any other type of knowledge, so by combining elements of what they know of their world with the theory and methods of urban sociology and anthropology, this book presents pedagogy in a way that is more accessible to students. Applying urban sociology's main theories to new challenges—like examining culture—should make this book more accessible to students of all ages.

This book is a text for courses in urban sociology or urban anthropology; it can also be used as the primary text in an urban culture class. Though some of the culture discussed is from ancient times, the text attempts to engage students to apply the urban theories to which they are exposed to the cultural topic being discussed. Hopefully, this will provoke readers to apply these theories on their own, and this is the goal of any urban course—enabling students to use the theories, not just read, memorize, and forget.

The first chapters explain the major theories in urban sociology by using culture production in the urban environment as the recurrent theme. Then we will examine music, writing and theater, architecture and fashion, and photography and film as examples of ways to see urban theory in action as well as to get students to use urban theory in new and novel ways. No special artistic knowledge is needed for these chapters; again, the goal is to get students to use urban theories and apply them to culture (something with which they are more comfortable and familiar than with demographical tables or maps). If I have committed some oversight and the artistic explanations are not detailed enough, please contact me at the following address: Department of Sociology, University of New Orleans, 2000 Lakeshore, New Orleans, LA 70148.

I wish to thank the following reviewers for their helpful comments and suggestions: Brian Aldrich, Winona State University; Henry Lee Allan, Wheaton College; Walter F. Carroll, Bridgewater State College; Joe Feagin, University of Florida; W. Richard Goe, Kansas State University; Earl Smith, Wake Forest University; and Renee T. White, Central Connecticut University.

URBAN CULTURE

CHAPTER ONE

A Definition of Urban Culture

Urban culture has two levels of meaning for us in this text. One level of urban culture is how the city has impacted its citizens, businesses, social organizations, spatial organization, and artistic production, just to give a few examples. Culture is anything that humans make or use in their environment, everything from hammers and nails to a house that these materials construct are all culture. These are examples of what we call "material culture," but there is another kind of culture that a city can impact that we call "nonmaterial culture." All of the ideas, laws, beliefs, songs, poetry, religious thoughts, art norms, and folkways in a society are nonmaterial culture. A lawbook is an example of material culture in that it was constructed out of blank paper, ink was printed on the pages, and it was physically bound together to make a book. It is *also* an example of nonmaterial culture, because the laws and ideas in the book are not the ink on the page, but exist in the collective consciousness of the society. Finally, a lawbook could be an example of urban culture if perhaps it was a collection of municipal laws and codes for that city. Obviously, the city impacted these laws and codes, because they pertain only to that city, and they are part of the urban culture, because the city influenced their production.

The second level of urban culture is how the citizens, businesses, social organizations, spatial organization, and art affect the city. For an example, we will turn to Green Bay, Wisconsin, and the effect one particular kind of sports culture has on the city. Few football fans are as loyal or devoted to their NFL franchise as the urbanites in Green Bay are to the Green Bay Packers. The fans, called "cheeseheads" have supported this football franchise to Super Bowl wins and through losing seasons, and they have put Green Bay on the urban map of America, despite its small size of about 120,000. The citizens' devotion to the football team, even though it is the smallest city with an NFL team and insists on playing in an outdoor stadium through the brutal winter months, have spawned businesses devoted to the team and to creating fans that have required urban road and airport modifications to accommodate home games, making the city's stadium a holy relic of urban football culture. These citizens and the culture that they have produced have definitely had an impact on the city.

THEORIES OF THE CITY

Our first assumption in this book is that the city matters, that there is something unique about living in the city: (1) the city affects the individual and (2) groups of these individuals in turn change the city. Just as the natural environment influences what grows and survives in the wild, the city influences the patterns of growth and association of its citizens; but the difference is that citizens can change their environment and the city. How these forces work to make the city and the city's culture unique is the focus of this text. To understand the city we should start with the various theoretical perspectives sociology has developed to analyze the city. There are four main urban theoretical perspectives that can illustrate the effects the city has on the development of culture:

1. *Urban Conflict Theory*—Engels and Marx, followed by John Logan, Harvey Molotch, and Manuel Castells
2. *Urban Ecology Theory*—Robert Park, Ernest Burgess, Amos Hawley, then improved upon by Walter Firey
3. *Urban Anomie Theory*—beginning with Georg Simmel, then Louis Wirth
4. *Urban Culturalist Theory*—Herbert Gans and Howard Becker

Urban Conflict Theory

Certainly one of the first theorists to acknowledge the importance of the city was Frederick Engels, longtime writing partner of Karl Marx. Called Conflict Theorists today, Marx and Engels focused on the disproportionate power that the different classes have in society (working, middle, and upper) and the changes to society that occur when these classes wield that power. They felt that the working class *made* the wealth of the upper class, but because of the upper class's control of social and political power, the working class was denied their share of the society's resources. Engels was attempting to find a way to visualize for his readers the plight of the working class, whose cause both Marx and Engels devoted their lives to champion.

He found his illustration in the slums of England's cities, like Manchester and London. He described the wretched urban existence of the people who had been thrown off their land in the rural districts surrounding London and were now the cheap wage labor of the industrialists in the 1840s. Compared to the opulence of how the aristocracy and capitalist class lived in Manchester, the working class's conditions were appalling. (Few apartments were more than closets, constructed like wood shacks with planks as sidewalks to keep pedestrians from the mud, no pavement for roadways, no running water, no waste service, no sewage, no gas or electric lights, and only small coal stove heaters for warmth that often as not were responsible for terrible fires that killed whole housing blocks.) It was clear from Engels's descriptions that not only did the city function as a warehouse for cheap labor, it also housed a disparity of infrastructure from the policed and paved avenues, private gardens, estate grounds, and parks of the rich to the squalor of the shantytowns, rooming houses, slums, and pubs of the working class. Marx's own work regarding the city shows the urban environment is like a theater stage set for class conflict with little special about the city, save the density of workers needed for the revolution. The work of Engels shows his improvements on Marx's urban theater analysis, and Engels's inflammatory writing becomes the precursor of a journalistic style of writing that will change America's view of its cities.

Jacob Riis pioneered investigative journalism and social commentary with his descriptions and pictures of the city in the 1890 book *How the Other Half Lives*. In fact, his work literally created a new kind of urban culture, which is the journalistic examination of the darkest places in our cities and the lowest classes in the cities. While critical of the urban conditions, Riis wasn't advocating a Marxian revolution. He was, however, informed by the Marxian tradition of class analysis that the lower classes were living a wretched life that wasn't their fault. This brand of journalism was labeled "yellow journalism," because of its association with satirical cartoons of the day, which were illustrated with yellow print colors. While not sociological theory, Riis's work informed the mass of citizens about the disparate social conditions of the different social classes and was an extension of Engels's work on the urban working class.

Max Weber (1921) was also influenced by the work of Marx and Engels, but being more concerned with methodological rigor he wanted a more coherent way to analyze the city than previous European Marxists. Weber's examination of the city led to four main points of distinction for urban areas.

1. Economic relations are paramount in the city. Rural areas have the capacity to sustain themselves by growing food, while urbanites have to base their lives on commercial transactions.

2. Cities are connected to larger social institutions that act upon cities in their environment. These social institutions, like governments and international economies, are able to shape and influence cities.

3. Social networks and associates in the city combine to form an interrelated association that distinguishes urban life. Weber felt that the networks and processes in the city could help the civilization process.

4. The city is an autonomous and self-sufficient unit: legally, politically, and militarily. From this autonomous state, the urbanite develops a loyalty and allegiance to the city.

These distinctly urban elements were part of Weber's analytical model. Class and status would be a part of Weber's analysis as a concept he called "life chances," which incorporated economic, social, political, and educational variables. The city would be a component of an individual's life chances, but unlike Marx and Engels this wasn't Weber's first priority; Weber was attempting to develop a methodology to study the city.

Urban Ecology Theory

Another urban perspective we will examine in depth is called urban ecology, which came from the Chicago School of sociology. These theorists were the first to develop a new systematic way to analyze the city that was different than the previous work by European sociologists like Tönnies, Marx, and Weber. Beginning at the University of Chicago in the 1920s, Robert Park and Ernest Burgess were the sociologists that developed and first noticed the effect of greater numbers of people living in the city. Before this time cities were a minor phenomenon of interest in America social science, since 80 percent of the United States and an even greater percentage of the world's population lived outside of cities; when cities were examined, their significance was only thought of as a *container* of social or historical occurrences. Few sociologists or anthropologists felt that the container or arena that social groups or classes existed in was important to understand, but the sociologists of the new sociology department at the University of Chicago did feel it was important. They began to notice social patterns in the city and found that the city's residents were unique. An example of one of the uniquely urban cultural patterns that urban ecologists discovered was a common vernacular usage—blue-collar and white-collar workers.

They discovered this urban cultural phenomenon by doing old-fashion qualitative research observations . . . they stood on a street corner. By observing the workers go by on their way to work they noticed that those workers with blue shirts, blue collars, and name plates most often worked in manual, working class jobs and those that wore a white shirt, white collar, and a tie worked in management positions in office buildings. So, an urban culture phenomenon was chronicled by these sociologists, and it was unique to the urban environment, since most rural employment didn't necessitate these clothing distinctions between workers and managers.

Human ecology analyzed the city in an almost biological fashion, in which the city was viewed as an organism that processes raw materials from the surrounding area to reproduce what it needs to sustain and expand itself. Like an organism, the city will grow in a predictable fashion with specific features or organs, i.e., a central business district, transportation arteries, and

FUNCTIONALISM AND MICROSOCIOLOGY

The competing sociological perspective to Conflict Theory in sociology is Functionalism, which fits into the framework of Urban Ecology Theory, but is not exactly the same. Influenced by the earliest fathers of sociology, August Comte and Emile Durkheim, Functionalism believes we can know and classify group behavior completely with enough quantitative study. That societies tend toward order and equilibrium, and that groups are composed of individuals who are making rational choices in their life to increase their pleasure and decrease their pain. Crime, riots, violence, poverty, and so forth are temporary fluctuations in society's balance as people make "irrational choices" temporarily. For cities, the ordered, efficient planning of streets and services makes sense to Functionalist theorists, who feel that urban problems are just temporary symptoms of urban areas that aren't working, but that do work most of the time. Cities function as a social unit, not because the elite classes exercise some draconian power to make them work, but because most citizens want the city to work. So, society is not held together by naked aggression and power, but by a degree of consensus from each class level.

A third perspective in sociology ignores the "Grand Theory" debate between Conflict and Functional Theory about class, power, and consensus and instead concentrates on the social psychology of small groups. Microsociology or Symbolic Interactionism, as it is sometimes called, focuses on how we construct meaning and identity in the small groups (family, friends, coworkers) we interact with every day. George H. Mead is one of the key theorists in this perspective, and his work illustrates how all the symbols (language, actions, and gifts) and identities (our work role, family role, friend role) we use every day combine to produce the reality we call "the city." Symbolic interactionists maintain that these symbols and identities are much more meaningful to our daily lives than the amount of power or consensus that is exerted over our work lives. Cities then become arenas of complex and overlapping identities and symbols that make urbanites "different" in the way they react to and process social stimuli, *because* of the influence of the urban environment. The unique way that urbanites deal with these symbolic interactions is *urban sociopsychology*.

workers' housing. As the city grows in a region, a hierarchy of cities develops with certain cities performing specific functions in the environment and the most dominant city performing the *key function* or dominant function. The key function is the ability of a city to be dominant in some industry or service in the region, usually this is because of the size or location of the city. A city that can direct and coordinate an industry or service, and is dominant

This white-collar worker is wearing a "uniform" that conveys a certain cultural significance in the urban landscape, enabling complete strangers to make assumptions about his work environment and job status without ever exchanging words with him.

in that industry or service, is performing the key function. It is like being at the top of the food chain for cities in the region.

The now familiar ringed model of the city by E.W. Burgess (1925) came from this "ecological" approach (Figure 1.1).

As we examine this model, which Burgess applied to Chicago, it is important to remember that this is an ideal type[1] of a city, rather than a specific city like Chicago that prescribes exactly how a city has to develop. The rings labeled in his model don't really extend into Lake Michigan, they are to demonstrate where the Central Business District (Ring 1-Loop) or worker's housing (Zone III) would extend if the city wasn't located next to a lake. The rings around the Central Business District were found in other cities that

---

[1]Ideal type is a concept that Max Weber (1904) created to combine all the essential elements of a social phenomena, without having to represent an exact example of the phenomena. Weber constructed an ideal type of Protestant religion based on the Calvinism that was popular in the United States's early European immigration period for his book *The Protestant Ethic and the Spirit of Capitalism* (1904, 1958). His description of Protestantism was not meant to detail a specific denomination, but was an ideal type of all the Protestant religions in the New World.

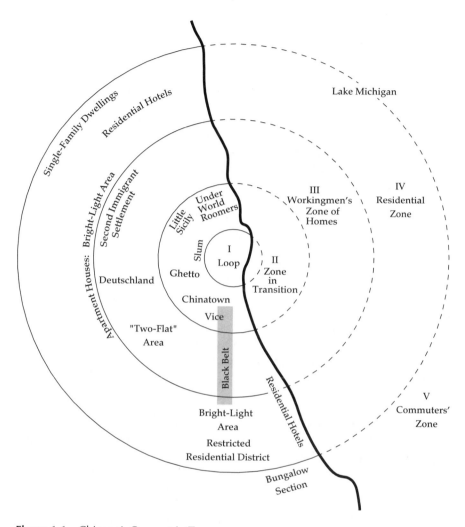

Figure 1.1 Chicago's Concentric Zones
Source: From "The Growth of the City," in Robert E. Park and Ernest W. Burgess, eds., *The City*. Copyright © 1967 University of Chicago Press, p. 55, chart II. Reprinted by permission of the University of Chicago Press.

Burgess examined, but specific neighborhood locations like the Black Belt or Little Italy varied from city to city and by the city's ethnic composition.

The Zone in Transition, an area where deviant culture and the culture of the urban marginal thrive, potently illustrates the city's effect on urban culture. Burgess and Reckless (1925) write that cities ascribe a place for these cultures to exist; in the Zone of Transition abandoned buildings, transient populations, and reduced police presence provide the "resources" and workspace for deviant culture. Let's make no mistake, these are *urban* cultural parameters for deviant culture, because to have massage parlors, nightclubs, or gambling dens there has to be the people and the urban density that only a city can provide. In this zone, the city, through a process of apathy, allows deviant culture to flourish because they are out of sight of the easily offended suburbanite.

Amos Hawley expanded urban ecology's focus in the 1950s by demonstrating quantitatively that urban density *does* increase "creativity," measured by the number of patents awarded to urban versus rural areas. His goal was to show that greater density, and the resulting increased social interactions that this density produces, is a component of urban culture and creativity. Also, that instead of being viewed as a negative fact of urban culture, density could have a positive effect.

Walter Firey (1945) sought to improve on the urban ecology model by challenging one of the most sacred assumptions of the model—that urban land use followed an efficient and predictable course by its function. While attending Harvard, he noticed that the Italian section of Boston's North End wasn't changing according to the invasion and succession model. (See box on pages 12–13.) Italians were staying in the neighborhood and revitalizing the area with cultural elements like specialty restaurants and shops to keep Italian members from migrating out to the suburbs. The Italian community felt that they would lose part of their Italian heritage and culture by moving out to the suburbs and assimilating to the Anglo culture. The neighborhood carried a sentimental attachment, as well as embodying the values and sentiments of the Italian community it came to represent. Families became the "method" by which this cultural attachment to the North End of Boston was maintained; Italians achieved this by buying the apartment buildings they lived in, rather than buying houses in the suburbs. By having their families stay in the buildings that they owned, the ethnic community defied the ecological model of invasion and succession. That model predicted that Italians should assimilate and want to live in the suburbs, yet some urban cultural element kept them in the North End. Sentimental attachment to the neighborhood and a desire to maintain their cultural identity challenged the assumptions of simple efficient land use models of urban ecology.

Firey also found that land could have a symbolic value that can be held across several ethnic or cultural groups. Specifically, he found that the Boston Common and Revolutionary War monuments in the downtown area are so symbolically important to Boston's citizens that these areas have resisted the ecological pressure to use these lands more efficiently. It may seem like historical sacrilege to many Americans, but these Revolutionary War icons are in the way of efficient use of municipal land, roadways, businesses, and housing that would make more urban sense from a rational perspective. But, the urban and national culture has given these areas meaning far beyond their "rational" use. From a cultural development point of view, Firey's improvement on the urban ecology paradigm shows that urban space isn't just a container for culture to be created in, but that space has *meaning* to that cultural production. We will explore this further in a later chapter, but for now, just think of the differences in the Chicago blues sound as opposed to the Memphis blues sound. The Chicago sound emphasized the electric guitar player as vocalist. Because of Chicago's urban history, the most desirable bands to feature at nightclubs had fewer musicians who could produce the same amount of volume on stage as larger ensembles. These smaller groups featured legendary musicians such as B.B. King, Buddy Guy, and Muddy Waters. The Memphis sound featured larger bands with horn sections that drew on Memphis's historical association with jazz music. These cities hold different meanings for the cultural producers that produce blues music there, so the music they produce is *different*. The venues, the musicians, the audience in the urban environment have a sense of history and meaning concerning their city; they look for this meaning to be reproduced in the urban culture.

A peculiar example of this meaning being reproduced in urban culture comes from Austin, Texas, in which a large oak tree in the city center was rumored to be the spot where white land-grabbers and Indians signed a treaty in the 1800s. Named the Treaty Oak, it was the victim of a disgruntled drifter, who poisoned the tree. Most Austinites would not have been able to locate the tree if they had been looking for it, prior to the poisoning, but an outpouring of grief and emotion was directed at the tree and this crime. After first making the local and then the national news, an almost humorous amount of attention was paid to this forgotten landmark by people all over the country, in the forms of cards and donations dedicated to the tree's health. An emotional trial of the perpetrator and heroic efforts by tree surgeons punctuated the end of this saga, in which the drifter received jail time, and the tree was saved from an obscure death by removing half of its limbs and constructing a shade canopy to allow it to heal. Land, buildings, and objects in the urban environment often defy normal explanations and expectations, they become part of the urban culture.

The human ecology or urban ecology school of thought was dominant in the field of sociology until the 1960s when critical theorists began to debate the urban paradigm. These critical theorists from the Marxist school of thought as well as those from the Race/Ethnic fields of study pointed out that the urban ecology method of analysis tended to reinforce the status quo of white dominant power structures in the city by labeling these processes "natural urban processes." But even before the growth of critical Marxist analysis of cities, another kind of perspective, of the Urban Anomie Theory, was attempting to shed more academic light on the city than the urban ecologists were capable of.

Urban Anomie Theory

Louis Wirth (1938) wrote about city population density and social classes, but from a perspective that looked at how the city affected its citizens. Specifically, Wirth noted that urbanites become desensitized and closed off from the people and environment that surrounds them. One would go insane from sensory overload from the city if we tried to process and evaluate all of the stimuli from the hundreds of people we encounter in the city: thousands of sights, sounds, and smells. Urban citizens have to filter more of these stimuli out during a day, leading to a "removed" character and colder disposition, according to Wirth.

Wirth's perspective came from Georg Simmel's paper "The Metropolis and Mental Life" (1905), in which Simmel proposed that the sensory overload of living in the city (sight, sound, and smell) produces stress in the individual. The adaptation this type of stress produces in the individual is to distance themselves from each other in the city and to become more rational and calculating in their lives. Louis Wirth's "Urbanism as a Way of Life" (1938) borrows the concept of anomie from Emile Durkheim, applies it to the urban model, and demonstrates that social differentiation increases with population density and division of labor. Urbanism increases social and personality disorders and ailments, versus those living in rural areas. Literally, living in the city has an effect on the group and individual—and this effect is inevitable. The interesting outcome of culture in the urban environment is that the social distance we get in the Wirthian Theory promotes freedom to explore self-expression and creativity. Because we are removed socially from all of the people we meet in the city, we are not constrained by the many norms that these people would like us to follow. We are separated and isolated in the city, which can lead to anomie, loneliness, and suicide, but which can also provide the freedom for personal expression, creativity, and deviance.

Urban Culturalist Theory

Herbert Gans (1962) also looked at urban dwellers, and he developed a typology of the urbanite. From bag ladies to cosmopolites, Gans maintained, the city appeals to different segments of the population. Some need the social services of downtown government offices, like the homeless, while others desire the theaters, universities, and nightlife a city has to offer; but they are all drawn by the city to live in its boundaries. In effect, Gans was saying that certain people pick the urban way of life and are *predisposed* by their choice to adapt to that way of life. His typologies of urbanites were never to be used as exhaustive scientific "phyla" of city dwellers, but instead were designed to show how some dominant lifestyles are shaped by the city.

Herbert Gans (1962) was influenced by the work of Robert Park and E.W. Burgess of the Chicago School; specifically, he focused on how life in a city took place in the small groups of families, friends, and neighborhoods. That these small groups, particularly enclaves of cultures like Little Italy or Chinatown in the city, actually *intensify* culture, rather than disintegrating culture (as the Wirthian perspective promotes). This cultural perspective maintained by Gans claimed that urban ecological factors have no direct negative effects on groups or individuals (as Wirth mentioned there were). This is not to say that the city has *no effect* on groups or individuals, just that the negative effects are insignificant and the existence of small coherent groups in the city (i.e., Little Italy) intensify culture and creativity. For ecologists, who see the city's size as a fracturing stress on small ethnic communities, and assimilationists, who see the city as the best platform for the dominant group to slowly mold the small groups of minority groups into the majority group culture, the city is not such a benevolent force. Gans fought for his theory's place in the discipline against those who see the city as a dark force that has a negative impact on groups.

Howard Becker developed a term "social world" that came from the Chicago School's work and also from Herbert Gans's work on the compositional nature of the city's many overlapping communities. A social world is the totality of experiences and relationships of an enclave, neighborhood, or work environment. As urbanites, we live in different social worlds simultaneously; moving seamlessly from the neighborhood social world to the work social world to the family social world. An entire social world is created around the world of culture production. For example, an entire social world has developed around the culture production of classical music in almost every city in America. A group of municipal elites organize for tax funding (local, state, or federal) to pay for facilities, musicians, and staff for the orchestra needed for classical music performance. The audience, staff, and musicians create a social world for the production of this specific kind of culture, including specific institutions (a symphony or opera company), specialized communication language (the text of *La Boheme* or *Madame Butterfly*), and a set of norms unique to this social world (wearing tuxedos to performances). The institutions created for this urban culture are the municipal arts council and the orchestra itself (staff and musicians organized bureaucratically for efficiency). The specialized communication of composers, music signatures, instruments, rehearsal times, and gigs[2] are part of the cultural exchange in this social world. Examples of norms unique to the social world of classical music would include the seating hierarchy of instruments within a section of the orchestra, the authority of the conductor to guide and interpret a piece for the orchestra, and the wearing of appropriate formal attire for performance. We will discuss classical music in more detail in Chapter Four, but clearly, as a social world classical music represents a form of urban culture.

These four theories are some of the best suited for understanding urban culture in the context of this textbook. However, there are other urban and music theories that might help us understand urban culture in a more modern sense. Let's begin in the modern exploration of urban sociology with the work begun by the Chicago School or Urban Ecology Theory.

---

[2]A "gig" is a musical performance for which a musician receives payment.

INVASION AND SUCCESSION

Invasion and succession is an urban social theory that states that a new group (usually we are discussing immigrant groups) will first take up residence in the least desirable areas of downtown to take advantage of cheaper rents and employment opportunities in the inner cities. These employment opportunities are usually in the manual labor sector, which is often more forgiving of poor work histories or language skills. The Chicago School's urban ecologists noted that as one immigrant group was moving in to an area—for example, Italian and Jewish immigrants from 1880–1920—another group of immigrants that had come to this inner city area years before was moving out to better housing. The Irish, who started to come to American cities in the 1840s, were moving out of inner cities to the first ring of suburbs, replaced in the inner city by Italians and East Europeans. One group of new, poor immigrants invades, while another group of more affluent immigrants surrenders the area to move to a better neighborhood. Clearly, this takes time and does not happen overnight, but the process of invasion and succession is always proceeding and is almost invisible in our modern cities.

An example might be found in New York City's Mott Street and Little Italy. At first, this area of lower Manhattan was the point of entry for almost every ethnic group seeking housing and employment that came through Ellis Island. For a while the Irish were the dominant group in this area of lower Manhattan, but were quickly invaded by the Italians and Sicilians who made a cultural home of the area in the 1880s. While still having a diverse population (Poles, Czechs, and Germans) it was the Italians that became quickly associated with this section of Manhattan, even to this day. Other groups have come to this area, but have encountered the cultural dominance that the Italian community has on the area. However, the invasion-succession process is a constant force to be reckoned with, and today the Italian restaurants, shops, and residents are feeling the invasion process from the growing number of Chinese immigrants, just a few streets over in Chinatown.

The theory of invasion and succession introduces two important ideas into the paradigm of urban ecology: race and ethnic relations and the process of assimilation. Urban ecologists had made note that African Americans lived in different parts of the city and that immigrant groups also lived in segregated areas, but there was no real theoretical basis for the continued segregation of blacks in urban ecology. With the exploration of the invasion and succession urban phenomena, disparities in the rate of housing segregation between ethnic immigrant groups became apparent, as well as disturbing rates of isolation and segregation for African Americans. These disparities were not connected with the length of time a group had spent in the United States becoming assimilated, but with the color of their skin. African Americans should have been able to invade and then move to better housing long before immigrant groups of the 1880s, but persistent racism has thwarted their efforts, along with African mixed populations such as Puerto Ricans, Haitians, Dominicans, and Afro-Cubans. Racial and ethnic social theorists have better explanations for this persistent racism than the simple invasion and succession model. These theorists feel that the race of the group is an important reason why they suffer continued segregation, in particular African Americans and Hispanic Americans.

Assimilation is another idea introduced to urban ecology through the exploration of the invasion and succession model. Assimilation is the process by which a minority group becomes assimilated into the dominant group, as the Irish have become assimilated into the dominant English (Anglo) society of America by work relationships and intermarriage. From their past of being a hated minority group, the Irish gained work—then personal and finally marital relations with the dominant group. The process of assimilation, which all of the European immigrant groups endured, means giving up part of one's old culture and adapting to the new dominant culture. Cities are the places where this process of assimilation took control of immigrant groups and was part of the urban culture that broke these new groups down to conform to Anglo culture. We will explore this concept further in the text.

MODERN ADAPTATION OF THE CHICAGO SCHOOL

Two modern theorists in the urban ecology tradition that might help us understand the city as a site for cultural creativity are John Kasarda and Douglas Massey. As one of the principal developers of Skills Mismatch Theory, Kasarda (1993) explains the condition of modern cities in the United States by examining the problems of the inner city. Cities are still manufacturing important goods for sale, but today these are high-tech goods made in the suburbs of the city. The skills mismatch is here in the suburbs, where high-tech jobs require education and employment skills well beyond the abilities of the inner city resident. There is a class and race mismatch that becomes apparent in Kasarda's analysis, as well as the skills mismatch. White middle-class workers are in the suburbs, where the high-tech jobs are, and these are the workers with the requisite skills to do these jobs. Thus, the inner city becomes the location for unemployment, lack of education, minority families—in effect, doubling the burden on the services of the city, while the tax dollars for better jobs remain in the suburbs. Culturally, our cities become divided, with the growth of suburban culture at odds with inner city culture. We will see how this effects long-term culture production from the inner city to the suburbs in later chapters.

Methodologically speaking, the Chicago School's use of labor and job data, as in Kasarda's work, or the Census data, which Massey uses in his model, has been one of its strongest elements. Marrying the theory to hard data, like using census numbers, is very attractive to researchers who want to be certain that the theory they are using is valid. Using data and numbers allows urban social science some measure of the confidence that hard science enjoys in predicting future events. Urban ecology is able to efficiently use data and can explain most urban developments in the Western world. On the weak side of urban ecology, the theory reifies the status quo and is only really good at predicting the future the moment it becomes the past. Also, numbers only give us part of the equation for understanding something as complex as urban culture; we need to know more about the human actors beyond numbers and demographics.

Douglas Massey and Nancy Denton (1989) employed U.S. Census information to examine the residential segregation and disparity between the races in America's large cities. He discovered that far from following the old Chicago School's model of assimilation and invasion/succession, the modern city kept certain racial groups in crippling poverty more than other racial groups, in what they term "hypersegregation." African Americans are hypersegregated in 125 U.S. cities, which means that the poor census tract that an urban African American lives in is more likely to border another census tract that is poor and African American. This is different than white poverty, where the next census tract over might be middle class or Hispanic. The effect of this is to concentrate and isolate urban African American poverty in the inner city. Hispanics also suffered from hypersegregation, but not to the same degree as African Americans. Again, this is counter to the assimilationist model that postulates that over time in the host country immigrants will achieve acceptance by the majority group. What Massey has uncovered is the fingerprint of racism in our nation's cities. This isolation makes poverty for those in hypersegregation much more difficult to escape, and the inner city environment actually impedes their progress out of poverty. Urban culture in this state of segregation and poverty takes on some of the message and pathology of the urban experience.

Hawley, still of the Urban Ecology Theory (1950), stated that this phenomenon of urban density actually sparked creativity and fanned the flames of innovation. Living around other humans in close proximity must either provoke the element of learning or perhaps the wide diversity of peoples in the city creates a wide range of learning environments. Hawley even attempted to prove this theory by comparing the number of patents applied and awarded to urbanites compared to rural Americans. He found many more patents applied for by urbanites versus their rural counterparts. The critique of this study is similar to the theory previously mentioned that the diversity of a city creates its own culture. Hawley doesn't present any evidence that it is the urbanites in the dense areas that are applying for the patents. He also doesn't address that cities have more education and financial institutions than rural areas, and it is the presence of these institutions that make patents and cultural innovations more prevalent in cities. Yet, beginning with the theories that make use of quantitative, empirical data has some methodological attraction for a first research step.

URBAN CONFLICT THEORY IN THE MODERN AGE

We haven't discussed Marx's Conflict Theory for a few pages, which might lead us to believe that in the modern era of cities, Marxism has gone the way of the former Soviet Union. This is not true. Modern innovative theories that are in the Marxist tradition are extremely important to urban sociology and our examination of urban culture. An excellent example of this is John Logan and Harvey Molotch's 1987 use of Marxian analysis to look at land use in the city. Referred to as "political economy theory," which means that political power is constantly being traded as in an economy, these authors find that land is not being used in an efficient, logical manner as the human ecology perspective would have us believe. Land is used for elite interests because in the city's "political economy," the rich elite of the city have more political power to use than other groups of citizens. Land is traded and its price manipulated by a combination of rich developers and power-hungry government officials, not for the rational or best use of the land, but strictly for economic gain.

Logan and Molotch discovered two kinds of land use, one based on the exchange value of land and the other based on the use value of the land in a city. Exchange value is when elites and the city utilize land, or decide not to use land, based on its economic exchange value. Use value is what land could be or should be used for. An example of this process would be holding a piece of downtown-area land and refusing to develop the land or build anything on the land in hopes the property around it might increase in value, and then selling it for its exchange value. Use value would be to use the land for housing, infrastructure, or education. The impact on urban culture comes from the manipulation of city land. Not enough schools lead to a lack of education and literacy, not enough hospitals and the city's population is too sick for cultural exchange, and lack of affordable housing leads to slums and class division in the city's culture. Culture production in the city, like other kinds of production, also needs a space for its production, and if space is unavailable for culture production because of exchange value then culture will be restricted.

Other prominent authors in the Marxist tradition have written about the state of the urban inner cities, comparing them to colonized nations. This neo-colonial argument states that the inner city is colonized by middle-class and wealthy citizens as a center for business and government interactions, but these same citizens flee to the suburbs to live. The result is a shrinking tax base in the city limits, because these citizens take their income and residential money to the suburbs, out of the hands of city taxation. Yet, these same citizens want top-notch fire, police, water, roads, and power in the city when they come to work. They just don't want to live in the city, where they will have to pay for these expensive services. They also, as a group, tend to demand high tax abatements for their businesses and highways to the suburbs. Who is left to pay the city taxes? The inner city poor, who these theorists point out are disproportionately minority—much like traditional, historical colonists, the minority citizens (conceptualized here as the "indigenous" urban population) are left to shoulder the tax burden after the jobs have been appropriated from them and moved to the suburbs by the colonizers.

An alternative Marxist explanation of the plight of inner city African Americans is offered by William Julius Wilson (1978) in his controversial book *The Declining Significance of Race*. With a title like that, Dr. Wilson's book quickly became a lightning rod of opinion on both sides of the racial debate, with conservatives fixating on the title (and little else) and proclaiming that the African American Dr. Wilson had said that race didn't matter in society anymore. Liberals, in turn, claimed that Wilson was abandoning the cause of civil rights by focusing exclusively on class, rather than the political struggle for equal rights.

It turned out that both of their assumptions were incorrect; Dr. Wilson's work did address racism, but in a very unexpected way. In the United States, the racism of slavery continued well past the Civil War and infected all the institutions of the country. A principal institution of racism is a two-tiered wage system developed in the North during the 1900s industrialization period. As former slaves came to Northern cities out of the oppressive Southern sharecropping economy during the Industrial Revolution, they were paid less than white workers in the industrial factories. Because of their value as possible strikebreakers and the dominant racist attitudes of the time, white workers in the North feared and hated black workers. As we roll the history clock forward to the late 1960s and early 1970s (after landmark Civil Rights legislation had been passed), Wilson states that the condition of African Americans has more to do with the results of this racist two-tiered wage system of the 1900–1920 period than of premeditated, current racism in our society. How could this be? The initial period of racism left blacks in economically depressed neighborhoods, because of the two-tiered wage system. Over time, this disparity in wages depressed land values, produced poor schools, and left deteriorating neighborhoods for African Americans. Their communities left them without the education or job skills necessary for the postindustrial city economy. This process (racism and classism) produces the pathologies of inner city culture by robbing one group of the resources to help themselves at the same time concentrating their poverty.

Manuel Castells employed Marxist analysis to discover the effects of local organizing on city development in *The City and the Grassroots Movement* (1983). Rather than these local grassroots movements organizing their activities around neighborhood production (as a neighborhood of factory workers might organize), Castells found that successful grassroots movements were in fact organized around neighborhood consumption of services (water, education, housing). These neighborhoods demanded services and organized to force those in power (usually the government) to deliver these services. Castells historical perspective demonstrates that these grassroots movements have delivered the range of city services that we expect to be available: schools for our children, running water, sewage treatment, police protection, flood control, and roads were all luxuries, until urban citizens took action. The impact on our modern city's organization is immeasurable; all of these services are how we evaluate whether a city is functioning today, and at one time, less than a hundred years ago, these services were considered extravagances.

The Informational City (1989) is another important work from Castells that describes the city, only this book focuses on the postindustrial age and how our cities fit into this worldwide informational society. Labeling this new mode of social, economic, and technical organization The Informational Mode of Development, Castells is actually describing a new revolution in production, as in the agricultural revolution or the industrial revolution. Society, and the cities and regions within our society, will be transformed by this new mode of development, such that capitalism itself will be restructured around informational advances. Cities have changed already because of the informational mode of development. Not just simply a skills mismatch of people in the city to the location of potential jobs, but a substantial change in how the city fits into this new kind of production has occurred and will continue. Historically, the city was the "place" production took place and the cultural, social identity, and issues of the city had to be taken into account when evaluating production from a business standpoint. For example, if a city had a poorly educated population, then education would have to increase or business would leave the area because of the lack of skills. Now, space is more fluid and business can locate tasks to different "spaces" around the globe through the use of technology, because information doesn't have the space constraints of an automobile plant or agricultural processing industry. One can locate the physical manufacture of a product in Malaysia for the cheap labor, but keep the information-intensive design in Los Angeles and the administration of the company in Denver as one desires. No longer does a company or a government have to physically locate themselves near the production. This gives business tremendous mobility, but no urban loyalty. The space-intensive industries of previous decades are being moved to urban areas outside of the Western world's dominant cities to take advantage of cheap labor and the fluid nature of informational space.

Finally, another of the Marxist-influenced scholars that must be mentioned is Peter Ward, in his multilevel analysis, Mexico City (1998). It is important because in many ways this book was one of the first texts to show the link between the urban environment and culture. In his detailed examination of Mexico City's politics, urban structure, community life, and economic stratification, it was the culture of Mexico City that became a recurrent theme to the reader. Specifically, Ward examined the architecture of the city to illustrate the cultural remnants of its colonial past in the older sections of downtown, the wrenching poverty of shantytowns that organize and demand city services like power and water, to the ultramodern high rises for residential and commercial use that have become an advertisement for Mexico's entrance into the First World of industry and finance. Architectural culture even has an impact on the social worlds of Mexico City's residents, as the older, colonial influenced buildings have become sites of popular resistance to the commercial dislocation of residents for commercial or industrial space. The buildings themselves with their own patio and atrium design have fostered a solidarity of residents that would be unheard of in a U.S. city, where apartment buildings breed reclusive lifestyles and privacy. The city's architecture of gated neighborhoods also underscores the class division in Mexico City. Lacking a coherent middle class, the city is in a visible state of turmoil as the rich, modern architecture of Mexico City's elite attempts to displace the colonial buildings of its past.

URBAN CULTURALIST THEORY AS A MODERN APPLICATION

To demonstrate the importance of other disciplines in illustrating the breadth of the urban experience we can turn to political science and the work of John Mollenkompf (1983). He qualifies as an urban culturalist, because he believes that federal policy and funding through programs, like urban renewal, fundamentally change the city. The city's design and its social workings are able to be manipulated by federal "culture." According to his work and that of others who study the importance of various layers of government on city structure, HUD, the federal government's Department of Housing and Urban Development, has been changing the city's design and structure for the past fifty years. Urban renewal was the response to the urban decay noticed by city leaders in the 1950s. The New Deal's involvement in providing much needed housing could be said to be the beginning of Washington's influence on our cities, as city governments built the first government housing projects in the 1940s and 1950s designed to help the homeless of the post-Depression era. The federal money devoted to urban renewal and housing in the 1960s for low-income Americans shaped many large cities by demolishing some decaying downtown areas and creating the large housing towers that have become synonymous with the word "projects." Sadly, rampant corruption at the municipal level has meant that wealthy land developers in the 1960s and 1970s were able to rehabilitate downtown properties for profitable resale at taxpayer expense, while substandard construction and lax building deadlines for homes for the poor have resulted in the long-term decline in the numbers of low-income housing units.

Borrowing methodologies from anthropology, Elijah Anderson in *Streetwise: Race, Class, and Change in the Urban Community* (1990) describes how life and culture are different in the inner city ghetto from the suburbs, due to the structural and historical problems described by some of the theorists mentioned earlier. Anderson describes two kinds of life and family structure, *decent* and *street*. Families that are "decent" have the same value and cultural structures as middle-class families in any segment of society. They are just located by class in impoverished areas. Street families' culture comes from abandonment of middle-class values, because of the harsh realities of inner city life and by embracing the short-term goals of the street economy.

As an example—being able to "take care" of oneself becomes a primary objective in street culture; thus, any minor slight or apparent slight to one's reputation is considered a "diss" or sign of disrespect. With so much riding on one's reputation, even staring at someone in the eyes too long, in this culture, can necessitate violence. Some have argued that there is an entire "culture of poverty" (Lewis 1966) that is different than the rest of American culture. This theory contends that a dysfunctional culture has arisen, centered around men abandoning their families, and that this abandonment creates continued poverty. Rather than structural imperatives like the economy or education, it is the culture of poverty keeping the poor disadvantaged. Anderson (1990) seems to view the culture of the street more as a reaction to poverty than a creator of poverty. This reaction to inner city poverty still creates culture; in fact, much of what we associate with Hip Hop or Rap music culture is the repackaging of street culture. Included in this repackaging and reiteration of street culture is the linguistic norms (words like "dissin" for disrespect), normative structure (violence and guns solve any problem), and fashion culture (bandannas representing gang colors and low-riding automobiles demonstrating street identity).

ROOTS OF CULTURE

Human beings are somewhat unique in the animal kingdom, we have specialized feet to walk upright as our principal means of locomotion, a spinal cord that enters at the base of our skull for remaining upright, opposable thumbs as neat accessories for picking up objects and manipulating them, and the ability to vocalize in a peculiar range, which has led to our linguistic structure. The truly impressive piece of biology that we possess, however, is our oversized brain, which we use to coordinate all of the other special features. In many ways, we are some of the weakest animals on the Serengeti, and it is amazing that we weren't turned into human "McNuggets" in the first thousand years of evolution. We are slow, weak, with no fangs, claws, fur, or even a tail. So, how did we get to the top of the food chain?

Some feel that it is our ability to produce and consume culture that has propelled us up the food chain. Our ability to use tree limbs as clubs and spears created a cultural artifact that supercedes fangs or claws, especially as we band together as gregarious clans. We have been able to adapt to the environment through cultural innovations of fire, clothes, and shelter to render growing fur obsolete. Our success was so impressive as a species that we were able to keep ever-larger-growing groups alive and fed through agriculture and eventually city building. Today, we organize ourselves into groups based on kinship and culture (Irish, Italian, Japanese, and so forth) which has enormous impact on the urban environment. As for the tail . . . while many of us might like to have the extra appendage and there is a humorous aspect to performing tricks with one, we've lost little ground in the animal kingdom by losing ours.

The question becomes whether culture is a learned or biological behavior. From the perspective of learned behavior, our ability to produce and consume culture is behavior that we learn from the group that raises us, most often our clan or family. We transmit the knowledge of culture production and its meaning from one generation to another through the learning process; this is why culture evolves and its meaning changes over time. Oddly, most of the theorists that favor biological explanations of culture would agree with the same description of culture transmission as those that favor learned behavior explanations. Even biology proponents concede that human beings are instinct-poor creatures that must *learn* from our parents all the skills necessary to survive. A biological explanation of culture, however, is rooted in our biological design, rather than proposing that we have instinctual learning like other animals. So, while accepting some parts of the cultural learning thesis, the biological argument becomes a question of how we learned culture to begin with. The biological side's response would be that we are biologically programmed to do culture.

THE DEVELOPMENT OF URBAN CULTURE

For our discussion of urban culture, these arguments of biology or learning are purely academic. By the time human beings settle in even the earliest cities, systems of language, writing, and education are in place to pass on knowledge. The experience of living in larger, stationary groups that grow more heterogeneous as time goes by is critical to the development of what we will call "urban culture." Let's begin simply enough with the growth of differentiation that cities promote. When humans were living in small wandering kinship bands, developing new forms of culture was infrequent, and only the limited contact with outside group members would allow for any new cultural exposure. So, there was little cultural differentiation, experimentation, or exposure.

Cities allow for contact with people from different cultural and kinship groups, and some theorists believe that this process of contact with different groups has increased our creativity and advanced our culture. It is certainly true that most major cultural innovations in the past two thousand years have either been invented or developed in the city, but conflict theorists would point out that these innovations rarely were allowed to come from or benefit minority group members or lower-class members in the society.

SOCIOBIOLOGY AND THE DEBATE
OF NATURE VERSUS NURTURE

A division of sociology preoccupied with this debate of nature versus nurture is sociobiology. Often maligned for its association with the Eugenics movement,[3] the more scientific-minded adherents of sociobiology today argue for a genetic-based development of culture founded on what they term "cultural universals." Sociobiologists argue that these cultural universals could *not* have been transmitted by learning across continents and time, so they must be based in the biology of the human species. For example, language is a cultural universal because, while there are hundreds of different known languages, all human societies speak *some* language. It is found in every civilization on earth, thus it is a cultural universal.

Another example favoring some "natural" explanation for social phenomenon is the universal cultural taboo against incest. This taboo is present in all societies, across time, and on all continents inhabited by humans. Yet, conflict theorists have noted that this prohibition against incest did not extend to all strata of society: most notably, the aristocracy from ancient Egypt (where the most extreme examples of brother–sister intermarriage was practiced), ancient Rome, the Middle Ages, and the French and modern English aristocracy, where royal bloodlines are heavily favored in marriages. Thus, cousin-to-cousin intermarriage is possible to this day amongst noble families. If the cultural prohibition against incest is somehow a component of our genetic heritage, then why doesn't it apply to these privileged groups? To conflict theorists, this is a serious issue for the sociobiological argument.

On the other hand, proponents of learning theory are hard pressed to account for these "cultural universals" brought up by the sociobiologists. Many elaborate theories of seafaring Egyptian explorers having an influence on Mayan temples or Celtic invaders traversing the globe spreading culture like Johnny Appleseed have been offered to explain cultural similarities across the globe. The problem is that a completely learned-based theory of cultural transmission is methodologically challenged, since no consistent agent can be uncovered to account for all "cultural universals." In the end, we must look at either set of theories (biology or learning) as being incomplete and offering only partial explanations as to why humans are such culture producing fiends.

---

[3]A movement of intellectuals and ideologues who advocated that there were substantial differences in IQ and ability between the races, and that the races should be kept separate (with whites occupying a superior position).

Urban culture tended to benefit the elite classes of any urban society. If it is true that minority and lower-class group members don't get to make contributions to societal innovations, then how is a diverse population a benefit to creativity? It could be argued that just the presence of a diverse element in the city sparks creativity and innovation.

It isn't necessary for us to decide on one or more of these urban or cultural theories now. We will be referring to them often, so it is important now just to understand the various theories and how they are different from each other. But the most important idea that we must take with us from this chapter is that there is something special about the city and the culture produced in the city. Social norms and cultural innovations are affected by the different social groups, social classes, ethnicities, social density, and institutions of the city, making both the city and its culture unique.

References

ANDERSON, ELIJAH. 1990. *Streetwise: Race, Class and Change in the Urban Community.* University of Chicago Press: Chicago, IL.

BECKER, HOWARD. 1963. *Outsiders: Studies in the Sociology of Deviance.* Free Press: New York, NY.

BURGESS, ERNEST W. 1925. "The Growth of the City: An Introduction to a Research Project," from *The City.* R.E. Park, E.W. Burgess, and R.D. McKoware, eds. University of Chicago Press: Chicago, IL. Originally published 1916.

CASTELLS, MANUEL. 1983. *The City and the Grassroots Movement.* University of California Press: Berkeley, CA.

CASTELLS, MANUEL. 1989. *The Informational City.* University of California Press: Berkeley, CA.

CHOMSKY, NOAM. 1965. *Aspects of the Theory of Syntax.* MIT Press: Cambridge, MA.

ENGELS, FRIEDRICH. 1958. *The Condition of the Working Class in England.* Trans. W.O. Henderson and W.H. Chaloner. MacMillan: New York, NY.

FIREY, WALTER. 1945. "Sentiment and Symbolism as Ecological Variables." *American Sociological Review.* pp. 140–148.

GANS, HERBERT. 1962. "Urbanism and Suburbanism as Ways of Life: A Reevaluation of Definitions." *Human Behavior and Social Process.* Albert Rose, ed. Houghton Mifflin:; Boston, MA. Pp. 625–648.

HAWLEY, AMOS. 1971. *Urban Society.* Ronald Press: New York, NY.

KASARDA, JOHN. 1993. *The Impact of Skills Mismatches, Spatial Mismatches, and Welfare Disincentives on City Joblessness and Poverty.* Oxford: Cambridge, MA.

LEWIS, OSCAR. 1966. "The Culture of Poverty." *Scientific American.* October. Pp.19–25.

LOGAN, JOHN, AND HARVEY MOLOTCH. 1987. *Urban Fortunes: The Political Economy of Place.* University of California Press: Berkeley, CA.

MARX, KARL, AND FREDERICH ENGELS. 1897. *Capital.* Trans. Eden and Cedar Paul. Vol 1. Dutton Press (1976): New York, NY.

MASSEY, DOUGLAS, AND NANCY DENTON. 1989. "Hypersegregation in U.S. Metropolitan Areas: Black and Hispanic Segregation along Five Dimensions." *Demography.* Vol. 26, pp. 373–391.

MEAD, GEORGE HERBERT. 1934. *Mind, Self, and Society: From the Standpoint of a Social Behaviorist*. C. Morris, ed. University of Chicago Press: Chicago, IL.

MOLLENKOMPF, JOHN. 1983. *The Contested City*. Princeton University Press: Princeton, NJ.

PARK, ROBERT. 1916. *The City*. R.E. Park, E.W. Burgess, and R.D. McKenzie, eds. University of Chicago Press: Chicago, IL.

RECKLESS, WALTER. 1926. "The Distribution of Commercialized Vice in the City: A Sociological Analysis." Publication of *American Sociological Society*, No. 20.

RIIS, JACOB. 1890. *How the Other Half Lives*. Scribner and Sons: New York, NY.

SIMMEL, GEORGE. 1905. "The Metropolis and Mental Life," from *The Sociology of George Simmel*. K. Wolff (ed.) Free Press (1964): New York, NY.

WARD, PETER. 1998. *Mexico City*. Wiley and Sons: New York, NY.

WEBER, MAX. 1904. *The Protestant Ethic and the Spirit of Capitalism*. Scribner and Sons (1958): New York, NY.

WEBER, MAX. 1921. *The City*. Free New York Press (1966): New York, NY.

WILSON, WILLIAM J. 1978. *The Declining Significance of Race*. University of Chicago: Chicago, IL.

WIRTH, LOUIS. 1938. "Urbanism as a Way of Life." *American Journal of Sociology*. Vol. 14, pp. 1–24.

CHAPTER TWO

The Urban Environment

As we studied in Chapter One, urban sociologists feel that the city affects (1) the people and (2) the processes in the city. In this chapter, we are going to discuss the city's impact on the people that live in its boundaries and the impact the city has on the businesses, structures, and services in its boundaries. One of the keys to understanding the city's impact on us is to delve into how the city organizes the places in which we live. Race and class are the two most important factors in how people are organized in the city. We see this type of organization in the predictable structure of our cities, in which the poor and minority groups live in easily identifiable areas. Differing theories abound about the significance of race and class in the city, but it is clear that people are grouped in the urban environment according to these factors.

Work is the third important urban organization factor. Businesses and work do not grow randomly in the urban landscape, but are organized by the city according to the business's function. So, when a factory is constructed in the city, the issues of land, power, water, transportation, and labor define where it will successfully fit on the city's map. Work and business have to fit into the city plan and the city's environment, together with where workers live. As race and class organize people in the city environment, work and business play an important role constructing the urban space as well.

HOUSING IN THE URBAN LANDSCAPE

E.W. Burgess (1925) sketched a model of how a city is put together, which we saw in the last chapter and will examine in detail here. A true model, it was never intended to actually resemble a real city, but instead was meant to be a way to help researchers think about the building blocks of a city.

Its bull's-eye design is undeniably recognizable, at the center area is the central business district (Zone I—Loop), where the city's initial business infrastructure would develop. Railyards, canals, and roads converged around this area for product distribution. Water, waste, and electrical services developed, and government administration (municipal, state, and federal) were all located in this central area of the city for reasons of accessibility. A central business district is the focus of both government and business activity. The next significant area is the industrial zone, where industry and manufacturing businesses, which need horizontal space to perform their business tasks, can congregate to be close to the distribution nodes of the city center. The services and infrastructure being built by the city center will initially benefit the industrial zone. Working-class housing (Zone III) followed by middle-class housing (Zone IV) make up the following rings, and in the farthest reaches of the design were the suburbs of the wealthiest urban dwellers. City services and infrastructure will be extended to these housing rings connecting the value of housing to the city's services. Value of one's house is connected to your class position, and the type of housing and city services an individual is able to obtain has historically been tied to their race. Obviously, the city you live in does not look like a bull's-eye exactly, but you may have noticed this general design and that the poor and minorities are segregated into certain areas of the city, often near the industrial section of the inner city. This is consistent with the Burgess model, and it helps us to see how the city organizes where people live and work.

Housing in the city is organized and built (with the city's permission) according to affordability. In the modern age of subdivisions, houses are constructed with whole neighborhoods of housing stock in the same price range, aimed at similar types of buyers. This effectively groups the people in the city by income, and thereby, class. It makes sense, to a certain degree, as the first large groups that needed housing close to their place of employment were the working classes during the city's industrial period. The housing had to be affordable for this group, close to the factory or other place of employment, and constructed quickly enough to provide for the burgeoning growth of the industrial sector. Thus, little attention was paid to the land these houses were constructed on, or for that matter, the design of the houses themselves. Services (water, waste, power, police, and fire) would be extended by the city to these areas to make them more attractive and habitable for the target market of working-class citizens. Because of their elite position in the city's social hierarchy, the wealthy landowners were able to demand valuable city services for their neighborhoods, though their homes were often outside of the city's boundaries. Money and power elicit an almost instinctive class grouping in the urban environment that impacts city culture and city structure. The housing of the wealthy will be constructed on more scenic land far from the city's industry and working class. With this instinctive class grouping, there is a racial component as well; we all recognize the "minority" areas of our cities as we recognize the working-class areas. Race is a more complex urban issue than class, which we will discuss in depth later in this chapter. For now, we will leave the discussion at the fact that race and class group people in specific parts of the urban areas.

Individuals don't purchase or seek housing to fit an urban theory, but they do purchase housing that they can afford and that they feel comfortable with. What one can afford in a house we quickly associate with class, because earning power determines how much of a house an individual or family can qualify to buy. That would seem to be a straightforward class issue, in which the cost of housing groups people of a certain income bracket together in areas where there is similarly priced housing. The reason this matters to those that live in these neighborhoods can be summed up in a few illustrations. From a city's viewpoint, municipal spending in a given neighborhood will be related to the tax dollars and votes that are generated by that given neighborhood. *Theory Break*: Marx used the word's "political economy" to describe how power is used and traded like a widget in an economy between social classes. The number of votes and tax dollars translate into political "money" or widgets that translate into better services from the local government. So, in effect, where you live in a city can determine the types of services that are delivered to your neighborhood. An example of this would be the state of your roads, the quality of your water, and the quality of schools in your neighborhood. In most towns in the United States, the safety of roads and water don't vary enough from the wealthy to the working class neighborhoods that there is any real danger, unlike in the developing world, where the poor areas in a city might lack roads, water, and sewage services.

However, educational facilities often vary radically from the wealthy and upper-middle-class areas to the poorer districts of a city in the United States. The quality of a citizen's education can have a real and direct impact on the quality of this person's life. A bad school can leave a child ill-prepared for college entrance exams or disillusioned with the learning experience. As a specific example, a difference of 100 points on the SAT exam can mean the difference between acceptance and rejection at a college or university.

Theory Break: Max Weber referred to these life choices like education by another name: "life chances." These life chances are our ability to access the important opportunities in society like education, housing, social networks, financial connections, and even political choices. These are real "chances" that affect our lives and can effect what social class one is in or even one's life expectancy. If one is sick and has health insurance, one's chance of living longer is better. If one has the opportunity to get an education, one's chances of having a more prosperous and rewarding life has improved. We also know that living in a certain place can affect one's ability to access these life chances and that a citizen's social class and race can place one in a specific area of the urban environment, and this in turn can effect the life chances that citizen is presented with in the future.

So, why don't people just move to where the good schools and neighborhoods, and hence the good life chances, exist? Regrettably, it is not that easy, because of the prejudice and systematic barriers that stand in the way of those who wish to access improved life chances, these opportunities can

DISCRIMINATION IN HOUSING

Adding the dimension of race to what we know about class makes the meaning of where we live even more potentially grim. Race can be an even stronger factor than class in its ability to group people in the urban environment. Discrimination and prejudice combine to make racial segregation in U.S. cities a modern-day reality.

Discrimination against racial minorities was the law of the land for many states until the Civil Rights Act dismantled the laws that prevented many black and Hispanic citizens from being able to fairly buy land and housing. Unfortunately, even after this period of official discrimination was over, institutional racism has continued in the home lending and building industry, where minorities have been denied loans or access to housing that they were qualified to receive.

One process of regulating the racial groups that live in a given area is called "redlining," and it occurs in many kinds of businesses, where minority clients are charged more or receive inferior service because of their race and location. This includes not being offered opportunities (work, housing, finances) that white clients are offered. A white home-seeker will be shown all possible properties that they qualify for, while a minority applicant won't be shown homes they qualify for in predominantly white neighborhoods; this is called "racial steering." The house you live in may actually have undergone these urban selection processes. The impact this discrimination has had on the individual can be summed up in the extra money that your family had to pay (or didn't have to pay, as the case may be) or the opportunities that were or were not afforded you, based on your location. Perhaps this seems paranoid to some readers, but consider that in the same way you know where the "good" and "bad" areas of the city are located, so do potential friends and employers. Coming from a "good area" of town means that an individual is perceived as being better, richer, more racially acceptable than someone who lives in a bad area. Consider how many times you have been evaluated based on where you live, and that you may not have been aware of. While our choice of where to live is constrained by many factors, the city can act to affect the decision in many ways.

be difficult to attain (see the box, "Discrimination in Housing"). Minorities are often unable to change their social condition as easily as white citizens. Where a person lives is not just a fact of their life and background, but a driving force that can be used to push them up or down socially and economically. Neighborhoods are socially constructed areas defined by the class, race, architecture, and government services (roads, transportation, education) available, and these neighborhood variables impact the individual by society's assumptions. Education level, for example, is an assumption often made by people based on the type of neighborhood and schools one has attended; bad neighborhood equates with a bad education, and then that label is applied to the individual. Most homebuyers, particularly those of the middle class, are aware of the school districts that they reside in, and that the school district was an important consideration for them when considering a home purchase. The importance of education is essential to the middle class and their status position; this is why education fits so prominently into their housing choices.

If you are not a homeowner, discuss with someone you know who is a homeowner about the elements that went into their choice to buy a home. Good schools, paved roads, and city sewer systems versus septic tanks probably worked into their decision process long before looking at floor patterns or carpet samples. A connection to the city sewer system versus a septic tank, for example, can improve the value of a home by more than $5000. Many homebuyers select the home they live in *primarily* because of the school system or district the subdivision resides within. So, where you live becomes your "base camp" for accessing life chances, and this base camp has already aided or hindered your opportunity for life chances, even before you became aware of it. In this way, and many others, where we live makes a crucial difference in the direction of our life and the chances we are provided. Our urban "place" and the life chances we have also impact the kind of urban culture we experience and participate in.

RACE AND CLASS

We have discussed race and class and how these factors might work against someone finding housing in the city. We should discuss the important theorists that have written about race and class, how they come together in the city and define life chances for the individuals living in the city. The two most important contemporary urban theorists in this field are William Julius Wilson and Douglas Massey. Both of these authors have focused on the condition of blacks living in U.S. cities, and have come up with distinct theories to explain the isolation and deprivation of blacks in the urban environment.

William Julius Wilson's controversial book *The Declining Significance of Race* (1978) postulated a radical new perspective on how the economic conditions of inner city blacks developed in American cities. A blend of Marxian and U.S. labor history, Wilson's book traces the beginning of the black urban underclass to the mass migration North, for industrial jobs, by rural Southern blacks during the teens and twenties. Once in these urban industrial centers, blacks were often pitted against whites by industry management, to drive down wages, resulting in a two-tiered wage system—one for whites and the other for blacks. A long-term result of the wage inequality was the creation of two economic classes in the city, separated by race. This wage disadvantage also resulted in a spatial disadvantage, where black workers were often segregated in the city by their income and by direct housing discrimination.

Inner city neighborhoods of black workers grew around the factories they worked for, depending on them for low-skilled job opportunities, but as the inner city factories closed in the 1960–70s, whites moved from the surrounding neighborhoods. An urban black underclass began to grow in the inner city, disconnected from the white middle class in the suburbs. Wilson clearly identifies prejudice and discrimination as the root causes of black poverty, but it is the prejudice and discrimination of this period of migration and deprivation (the 1920s–1960s) that left blacks in the inner city disadvantaged. The second tier of the pay system led to inferior housing, deteriorating neighborhoods, and substandard schools for blacks, permanently leaving inner city black families behind in skills and education.

When the social and legal changes of the sixties took place, the condition of inner city black life chances had been so subverted by years of discrimination that the inner city minority population was incapable of taking advantage of these new opportunities. Years of this disadvantaged status, rather than modern forms of continuing white discrimination, have placed the large populations of inner city minorities in the desperate position they are in today. Poor housing led to substandard schools, and the same hard work on the part of black families that helped to pull immigrant families out of poverty only went half as far, because they were paid half the wage of whites. Years and years of these conditions leaves a community without the economic, social, or educational resources to attract business or secure employment for their community.

In the urban frame, the significance of this theory is that these inner city areas are so behind in skills, education, and other life chances that there is often little in the way of urban renewal or other rejuvenating social programs that can save them. Wilson points to the advantages of programs, like Affirmative Action, in increasing minority enrollment in college and minority employment in government jobs, which lead to the resurrection of a black middle class (Table 2.1).

Unfortunately, this small African American middle class is not enough to substantially help the depressed inner city. In fact, there is no convincing evidence to suggest that Affirmative Action is helping inner city black populations at all. Apparently, Affirmative Action has helped blacks outside of the inner city, those with better skills, better education, and improved life chances find access to college enrollment and government jobs.

However, the inner city blacks, who cannot raise themselves out of the economic and social "hole" they are still in, cannot take advantage of these Affirmative Action opportunities. One has to be close enough to the SAT entrance score set by a college before the Affirmative Action benefit can help a minority applicant. If you don't get close enough to a score of 1000 on the SAT, for example, then the small increase in your score by the college due to Affirmative Action can't raise you to the 1200 minimum entrance score required by many colleges. Possibly, it is the social isolation and economic

Table 2.1

	National Average	White	Black	Hispanic
Percentage Completing High School~	83.10%	87.90%	78.10%	57.20%
Unemployment^	6.00%	5.20%	10.90%	7.50%
Median Income*	$ 40,136.00	$ 40,790.00	$ 31,921.00	$ 25,271.00
Worth**	$ 40,200.00	$ 49,030.00	$ 7,073.00	$ 7,225.00

~ U.S. Census 2000

^ April 2003 Bureau of Labor Statistics

* Income can be most easily thought of as what one earns from a job. This information is for males working full-time and the whole year. From the 2001 survey of workers. U.S. Census

** Worth is all assets (mainly one's home) from the 1995 Survey. U.S. Census

deprivation that wears down on the inner city dwellers and causes them not to pursue the benefits of college and government employment. *Theory Break*: Wilson's theory is that the long history of discrimination against blacks left them underskilled and undereducated, becoming an underclass in America's cities. Warehoused in the inner cities, they have become so disenfranchised that the programs of Affirmative Action cannot help them; they are too far removed from this world.

Douglas Massey also feels that the racial and class structure of our nation's cities is due to prejudice and discrimination, but in his book *American Apartheid* (1993) he leads us to a more active and sinister picture of the American city. While acknowledging the effect of the prior discrimination against blacks and their life chance deficiencies after the Northern Migration, Massey's work focuses on the current spatial predicament of the races and classes. An active form of current discrimination in personal relationships and housing is at the root of the racial and class distribution, according to Massey. A phenomenon he and writing partner Nancy Denton refer to as "hypersegregation" occurs in inner cities due to rampant discrimination after WWII, in which poverty and isolation combine to produce a unique type of disadvantage.

When comparing impoverished inner city neighborhoods, Massey and Denton used census tracts to measure the number of people living in poverty and the racial makeup of the census tract. This is where they found that white poverty, black poverty, and Hispanic poverty were different from one another and that those in poverty who suffered from hypersegregation were surrounded spatially by a crippling lack of life chances. With the census tract as a good representation of a neighborhood, Massey found that whites in poverty weren't always surrounded by poverty in adjacent census tracts. A white poor census tract might have a middle-class census tract adjacent to it or a minority census tract next to it, leading researchers to conclude that there is no warehousing effect of the white poor in U.S. cities. Black census tracts in poverty are more likely to be surrounded by other minority census tracts that are also impoverished.

Why is that important? It demonstrates that there is warehousing of the minority poor in our inner cities and that it is much more difficult to elevate oneself from poverty when all your surroundings are also poor. This last point might be confusing for many of us. How can my surroundings affect my ability to climb out of poverty? We have already discussed that the address an applicant gives on a resume or the neighborhood he or she comes from might subject them to a certain amount of prejudice. For example, an employer may be aware that the area suffers from a high crime rate, and therefore may make the assumption that the individual with an address in that area was involved in criminal activities or is just part of a "bad crowd." That opinion puts the applicant at a disadvantage in comparison to another applicant, who might not have to overcome this prejudice. If a person is impoverished and surrounded by census tracts in the same kind of situation, opportunities for better jobs and education won't be available in that area. An example of how important a person's social network is to success would be the myriad of scholarship opportunities, job opportunities, college programs, and internships you have heard about from friends and acquaintances, as a college student. It's common for many young people to gain their first job on the basis of a recommendation from a friend or relative. The difference for an inner city youth would be that few of their friends are employed and that the recommendation from a member of their family, or a friend, would not be helpful. Their social network is stuck in the same poverty as themselves, so they don't hear about scholarships, internships, or jobs.

This spatial isolation can produce a myriad of detrimental cultural reactions from both minorities and Caucasians in the city. White Americans who only see the inner city minority resident from the freeway or on the news don't try to empathize with a life circumstance *very* removed from their own. It is easier to blame the victim of this poverty than try to understand the complex urban-economic-social relationships that created the inner city slums. Whites also fail to acknowledge the legitimate concerns and fears of the entire minority community because of the spatial segregation and racism (Feagin and Sikes 1994). Even the experiences of middle-class black Americans being mistreated by law enforcement wasn't validated until the videotaped beating of a black man in Los Angeles gripped America in 1991. And then the jurors from the ultra-elite community of Simi Valley *still* acquitted the police officers of any criminal wrongdoing despite the video evidence. For inner city minorities, the cultural reaction of nonparticipation in the dominant society's norms, laws, and education leaves this group stigmatized and unable to escape. Not being concerned with education leaves the inner city resident unprepared for jobs skills, use of Ebonics and slang terminology brands the individual as a suspect member of a suspect group, and ignoring the laws of dominant society has left the judiciary prejudiced against inner city youth. Today, an African American juvenile is seven times more likely to do jail time for the same offense as a Caucasian youth, who will receive probation. The isolation of the inner city has affected all of these levels of society and continues to leave this group disadvantaged. Hispanics and blacks are suffering from a kind of poverty that is more severe and isolating than the types of poverty that whites are exposed to in the city. Many recent Asian immigrants to the United States, possessing few language and cultural skills, found themselves in poverty when they arrived here, but they did not seem to suffer the isolating poverty of blacks and Hispanics. This runs counter to most assimilation theories and even class-based theories that would have to assume that Hispanic and African American groups who have been here longer should be doing better than Asians, spatially and economically.

Massey and Denton's study of the hypersegregation of the urban minority poor leads the reader past poverty and class issues, since class and poverty do not seem to affect racial populations in the same way, to a more complex and troubling explanation of urban poverty—racism. It is the one social factor that can explain all of the disparate features of the city, and it fits the historical context of blacks in America. The reason that blacks had a different experience in our cities, and that they represented an underclass in those cities, was racial prejudice. According to Massey's work, prejudice and discrimination did not dissipate after the 1960s, but is still alive and very much well in America. This discrimination keeps blacks segregated, their neighborhoods inferiorly funded for education, business reluctant to invest in their communities, and crime an ever-present reality. Were it not for existing forms of racial discrimination, blacks would have utilized the many years of cultural assimilation (knowing the American culture and language), education (the national average for years of schooling is a difference of less than one year; whites have 11.3 years, blacks have 10.5 years), and work history to purchase housing away from the inner city and in more affluent areas. This has not occurred for blacks and some Hispanics, despite recent immigrant populations who have successfully made these spatial adjustments.

Massey and Denton studied America's largest 125 cities in their examination of hypersegregation and found that where there were large groups of blacks and Hispanics in the inner city, there was also hypersegregation. Spatially isolated, unemployed, low in job skills, and dependent on social service, those that are hypersegregated are not just poor but suffer a myriad of debilitating effects of poverty.

Massey (1987) applied this same kind of study to Europe's largest cities and found that race, more than class, determined the spatial grouping of populations in these cities as well. An even more disturbing aspect of these studies that was surfacing wasn't just that there was racial segregation, but that the *kind* of race determined how segregated this group would be in the city. Specifically, the darker immigrant groups from the Middle East and Africa were more isolated in European cities than lighter races, despite members of the darker races having been in the city for a greater length of time.

An example would be the difference between Jamaican immigrants and Pakistani immigrants to London, England. Jamaican immigrants, who were encouraged to come to England in the late 1950s and early 1960s to fill skilled and semiskilled labor positions, continue to live in predominantly poor and black neighborhoods of London, despite being in the city for several decades. Pakistani immigration to the London area occurred in the 1970s and early 1980s, yet they are not as spatially isolated or disadvantaged economically. Arriving later and often with language barriers, one would assume that Pakistani immigrants would have a more difficult time acclimating to their new environment. Yet, it is the darker Jamaican immigrants and their children (often born in London) that suffer more pronounced spatial isolation. Again, one would expect that more recent immigration that possessed fewer language skills would be more segregated.

Now, one might wonder if Pakistani immigrants were more affluent and educated when they arrived in London than the Jamaican immigrants, and that might explain their less segregated status in London. While that is an excellent challenge to work of this kind, most urban researchers would agree that the extra years of schooling in London by the Jamaican immigrants, and their children having been born in London, would counter most economic differences between the two groups, especially when considering the language barrier of the Pakistani group. While perhaps not reaching parity with a new, affluent immigrant group, the Jamaicans should have at least been able to alleviate some of their poverty and isolation through their many years in England. Sadly, this type of segregation, based on skin color, is present in all of the cities that Massey examined in Europe. If we trust Massey and his methods, then race matters a great deal in the urban environment, and it is being used to group people in certain areas of the city.

BUSINESS AND JOBS IN THE URBAN LANDSCAPE

In the explanation of urban theorists (see Chapter One) there was a discussion of urban ecologists, who thought of the city's growth and operations like a living organism. This urban organism reacts and acts upon its physical environment, processes goods to maintain is survival, performs services and tasks to achieve efficiency (as well as waste management), and if successful, the city will grow. The internal organization of this "city-cell" follows some regular patterns for housing and business development. For example, many businesses initially locate their operations downtown to be near power, water, and transportation hubs, as well as being close to government entities (municipal offices for permits, tax assessor, politics; state agencies or their outlet offices; federal offices for the post office, government contracts, federal taxes). As a city grows, however, the need for horizontal space, like that needed for manufacturing and industry, becomes difficult to maintain or purchase downtown.

In recent times, many high-tech and light manufacturing businesses have purposely located in the suburbs to avoid downtown and to be near their more suburban, middle-class workforce. Of course what they were avoiding were the impoverished minorities in an inner city with a crumbling infrastructure. This often leads to another section of industrial building (often referred to as light industry, like hi-tech firms) farther from downtown. But, this area needs services too, and the city is often provoked to providing roads, water, sewer, and electricity to accommodate these suburban businesses. One can see how the "organism" analogy for city growth and operation caught on. Some might question why the city could be provoked or encouraged to provide these expensive services to businesses in the suburbs instead of the inner city.

The key difference between the inner city and the suburbs is tax dollars and influence in the local political process. Cities constantly need to raise revenue and a new business coming to town will provide employment, products, and tax revenue. Cities will serve businesses that can create revenue and employment where the businesses want to locate most of the time. Businesses are also positioned in the urban environment by municipal government interests, as well as the functionality of the space they occupy. For example, businesses or industries that take up a lot of space or are noisy (i.e., an airport) will more than likely be located away from residential areas. So, the function of an airport positions an airport in the urban environment due to its needs and impact on the city, i.e., traffic and noise. In the case of an airport, the cost of the land needed and the municipal authority combine to place an airport in a specific location in the city.

Most of the time, the needs of business supercede the needs of residential dwellers and, because of their access to municipal leaders, a tension among business, residence, and municipal governments develops over key issues. This is an example of how space in the city is politically dynamic.

Sometimes communities can band together and fight businesses in the way they use urban space. An example of this might be the location of a factory that pollutes the local environment. The community would organize itself into a political force of voters and contributors to oppose the location of the factory to municipal leaders. Often, municipal leaders are resistant to such organizations, because of the cozy relationship politicians have with business leaders, but a community can break this cozy relationship by using the media and voting pressure. This can be difficult to sustain and organize within a neighborhood, and this kind of organization of community members is almost impossible across neighborhood lines in the city. Neighborhoods are often in competition with one another, because if a polluting factory isn't located in your neighborhood, they may try to put it in mine. We will discuss in Chapter Nine how urban geography is a distinct kind of urban culture.

Where an individual works in a city matters to their lifestyle, because certain areas of the city pay better for the same kind of employment or are cheaper to live in or commute to. The location of your workplace matters because impediments like traffic, taxes, and pollution are not spread equally in an urban environment. Downtown is often the most difficult and costly location to reach due to traffic. Wages for certain job categories like retail or low-skill service jobs are often less, due to higher taxes and higher rent in a downtown location, but there are often many businesses and government agencies downtown to lure employees. Pollution is also more pronounced downtown, due to manufacturing and automobile congestion in this area of the city. Yet, many of the people that work downtown live in the suburbs and are beyond the taxing authority of the city.

Theory Break: Many Marxists feel that this is a way that the wealthy upper class dominates the urban environment. Suburban workers and their employers want the expensive services of a downtown area (power, water, roads, police, and fire), but ultimately they take their paychecks home to the reduced taxes of the suburbs. This forces the city to raise taxes within the city limits to cover these services, while suburban districts can pay a nominal fee to extend existing city services to their area. The suburbs then can pour the money they saved on taxes into attractive showcase school districts that are the main lure of suburban communities. So, the downtown area has a double burden: all the taxes, traffic, and pollution that business can produce, but none of the skilled people or taxes to make the situation better. Culturally, this can put a strain on inner city or downtown residents, and perhaps that is why inner city culture can be so rough.

The abandonment of the inner city by businesses that are tired of high taxes and a desire of businesses to relocate nearer their suburban employees has caused the inner cities to economically implode on themselves. There are few jobs and few opportunities left for inner city citizens. In a sad twist of fate, the only available semiskilled or unskilled labor positions (often the best form of employment for inner city minorities) have been moved to the suburban ring of the city. Jobs at the malls and in food or retail service businesses are often the match for low-skilled workers stuck in the inner city. Far from their neighborhoods, these service jobs rarely offer benefits or incentives to make the long bus rides to work worth it, if the bus route goes from the inner city to the suburbs at all. *Theory Break*: A competing explanation of the condition of the inner city is that there is a skills mismatch between what businesses need in the way of skilled labor and the lack of those skills in the inner city. Businesses aren't intentionally hurting a group or area of the city, it is just that this area doesn't have the resources (job skills) that businesses need.

Cities not only influence business development within their boundaries, but the interaction *between* cities also affects business development. Specifically, a large city will perform what is called a "key function" dominating the production and distribution of goods and services in a region. Smaller cities often respond to this domination by the larger cities and are given auxiliary business functions to service the key function. For example, smaller cities around the Detroit, Michigan, area perform smaller, specialized service tasks for the large automobile industry in Detroit itself. The businesses in Detroit, due to their size, can force the smaller urban areas to perform auxiliary functions for the automobile industry.

Sheer size can also direct these auxiliary functions for a smaller city to serve a larger city. For example, there are many small cities around New York City and Los Angeles that exist only as bedroom communities for the major city's workforce. These bedroom communities have little in the way of their own business development and can really be thought of as suburban extensions of the larger city. Another example of key or dominant function is monopolizing transportation services. Maintaining a railroad hub or airport is an example of a city's size being able to direct businesses that need the service to locate in their urban environment. Many businesses might want to relocate beyond the city limits, but they cannot be away from these transportation services. The city, in effect, directs them to locate near these important and expensive services. Business cannot afford to create these transportation services themselves, but are dependent on the city to develop and manage them. So, the city and business combine to create and maintain employment opportunities and services, which then "choose" how neighborhoods or city districts will be integrated in the urban environment.

CULTURE PRODUCTION

Cities don't just happen, they are *made*. The relationships of people within the city are shaped by the places they live, the schools they attend, the businesses they work in, and the communities they identify with in the city. These relationships will form the basis of urban culture production and will mark the differences between urban culture production and other forms of culture production. With over 80 percent of Americans living in the urban environment, some might wonder what *isn't* urban culture production. For our purpose, urban culture *needs* the groups, services, and businesses of the city to function. Urban culture is influenced by the city that it is made in, to the point of distinction from other cities, i.e., Chicago blues being different than Memphis blues.

Elites and businesses in the city are not just bystanders, who are patiently waiting for cities to sort out their dominance in a region. Real estate developers, bankers, builders, and other individual elites in the city push for pro-growth and business friendly governmental policies for land use and zoning (Feagin 1998). Their close relationship with local political leaders allows these elite and business interests to define the direction for most cities. This direction includes how space in the city will be used and how resources will be allocated. The only counter to this pro-growth coalition are grassroots voters' movements, like environmentalist and housing reformers, and unions. These groups push for a vision of the urban environment that is people centered rather than profit centered. Yet, without revenue from business and taxes, how do these groups hope to pay for their people-centered city? Inherent in any large city is a culture of conflict between these interest groups and the urban classes they represent. Types of urban culture grow out of these conflicts, pro-growth and pro-business cultures that might stress the city's economic function or people-centered cultures that might value community issues more than economics. Both cultures can be beneficial to urban art production: pro-business cultures usually result in revenue for the city and the opportunity to fund large, high-art projects like symphonies and operas, while people-centered cultures might produce less revenue, they often support the arts through attendance of popular, indigenous art like blues or folk music.

An example of a type of culture *needing* the city is its art scene, which needs artists, galleries, and patrons that only an urban landscape can provide on a consistent basis. An area or group of galleries becomes known as an art scene in a city, and the patrons and other artists follow to locate in this area. The art scene becomes part of the unique urban culture of that city. Culture that gains an urban distinction might be exemplified by the paintings and other works of experimental artists in New York's Soho district before it became gentrified. Andy Warhol to Jean-Michael Basquiat created works and personas that could only be a part of the underground New York artist culture. No other city would have been as receptive to this experimental artwork as New York's art community. Many of us would have trouble identifying their work as art, but art patrons definitely know this experimental artwork as New York art.

The urban neighborhood of artists and galleries in Soho made painting and sculpting in this abstract and experimental fashion acceptable, and because of the established personalities and burgeoning galleries, Soho made being an artist profitable. Abstract and experimental art had found a home and a community in Soho that it had never before had. As many developing artists can attest, starting a career in a new medium can largely be an unrecognized labor of love, and there are only a few places where the kind of artistic experimentation that the Soho community engaged in can be rewarding. These welcoming art communities are located in large, metropolitan areas that have other, more established, art centers of production and consumption. The more established art centers allow for experimental art communities to grow around them, because the institutions (art galleries, museums, art stores, media coverage) that service the more established art community can also aid the experimental community.

Being large and metropolitan is not enough, however, for art communities to flourish, as in the case of Dallas, Texas, or Phoenix, Arizona. Both of these cities are large, metropolitan areas, but neither are renowned for their experimental art communities. New York has a large community of artists as well as art dealers and, probably most important, art consumers. To some degree, this is a function of size, but that is not the only requirement. After a large population has reached a critical mass, when there are enough people to allow the creation and maintenance of a phenomenon, the city's businesses, demographics,[1] place, and function in the regional hierarchy,[2] consumption patterns,[3] and urban "taste" direct what kind of culture will be successful in their city.

---

[1]The kind of people that live in a city define its needs from outside its boundaries, and what it can produce.

[2]Cities are placed in a regional hierarchy by what function they perform in their region.

[3]A city has a consumption pattern based on its population.

CRITICAL MASS

A *critical mass* might be thought of as the minimum number of individuals it takes to make something happen. For example, it takes a minimum number of people to field a baseball team, and then more people to field two teams to play a game. That would be the critical mass. It is possible to play with fewer individuals, but then there would be aspects lacking in the game, like whether there are holes in the outfield or not enough batters. People that you had assembled to play the game would also probably get bored with a game that didn't operate or feel like a real baseball game. The cultural product, a baseball game, doesn't really function correctly until you have the correct critical mass.

Unlike baseball, critical mass in the study of cultural phenomena is *not* an exact number of required participants to have culture, but is more of a *minimum number* of people to sustain a cultural activity. The minimum number for cultural activity consists of a minimum number of artists, consumers, venues, audiences, distributors, and auxiliary businesses to sustain the activity. In general, it becomes an exercise in deduction; where researchers find the smallest urban population that a cultural phenomenon exists—that is its critical mass. We deduce the critical mass of people that sustain a phenomenon from the smallest area that currently sustains it. Being able to regularly *sustain* the activity becomes part of the definition for our purpose. Being able to have a music concert once during a Christmas fair does not imply regular, sustained activity, nor does it accurately reflect the minimum number (critical mass) to accomplish this task.

Howard Becker (1971) and Samuel Gilmore (1990) worked on this idea of cities influencing culture and the effect the urban environment has on culture production. Becker developed the concept of "art worlds," in which a social world would develop around the production of artistic products. Relationships in the art world were built upon urban art production, and these relationships expressed the norms and values of art production, and later art consumption, in this urban community. A specialized communication based on the norms and language of art would develop in the art world. Specialized communication (an insider's use of specific terminology) reinforces these relationships into stable, if not formalized, networks. An example of a specialized norm and linguistic device in the area of experimental art might be to refer to another artist's work as being "worthy of Deck the Walls." The chain store Deck the Walls is a successful print and framing chain located in many suburban malls, but that is where the linguistic insult is buried. Referring to an experimental artist's work as if it is so banal that it belongs in a suburban strip mall is a grave insult. Only an insider would be aware of the low opinion experimental artists have of this suburban store and would catch the significance of the statement.

The art world takes over an identifiable space in the city that becomes associated with the production and consumption of art, and this area spawns auxiliary businesses and associated culture as well. Returning to Soho in Manhattan, the number of art supply stores, small to medium art galleries, art restoration services, and art pieces being displayed in Soho easily differentiates this area from other neighborhoods. Many of these businesses, like art supply and art restoration services, are auxiliary in nature; without the art world in Soho they would not be successful. This distinction of the Soho community is based on its artistic consumption and production.

Gilmore (1990) emphasizes the collective nature of art production and offered his term "social world" to describe classical music production in Manhattan. The social world of uptown is dominated by the university musicians and community that surround Columbia University, while midtown classical music is centered around the opera and symphonies of Lincoln Center. These communities or social worlds influence the kind of music they produce. The midtown community performs a very traditional style of classical music for their audience, while the uptown classical musicians have more freedom to experiment, because they are protected from the commercial expectations of the Lincoln Center audience, because of the uptown community's association with Columbia University. True experimentation in classical music occurs in Manhattan's downtown community, where all the conventions of classical music have been abandoned. Because of the tightly knit group of experimental musicians and alternative venues in the area, the downtown community is able to push the boundaries of classical music. The urban environment provided the "natural resources" of audiences, musicians, money, and venues, but each community or "social world" in the urban environment adapted to the production of classical music culture from these resources in a different way.

Uptown's musicians and classical music could thrive and experiment within the academy of the university setting, and these musicians only have to conform to the rules of the university's vision of classical music. Musicians in the midtown area experience far less creative experimentation and freedom, due to the overwhelmingly restrictive expectations of the opera and symphony audience, but they are able to reap greater monetary rewards from their affluent patrons. Downtown's innovative approach to classical music, including its presence in less common venues and uncommon events (gallery openings and performance art) has increased experimentation for small ensembles (Gilmore 1990). The economic rewards of these smaller venues, however, are not great, and many of the artists in the downtown social world do not earn enough money to survive on their own musicianship.

The key to understanding this landscape of culture production and consumption is to understand how the city affects these communities differently. Race and class are obviously at work in this landscape, because classical music tends to attract a predominantly white, middle-class to wealthy audience. The institutions that are built to be the venues and training grounds for classical music are in the city, and the venues are built to accommodate white, middle- to upper-class taste. Cities don't just house culture, as many of us might assume, but cities *influence* the culture in their borders and filter the tastes of the classes, races, and communities in the city. To understand how the city affects this cultural influence on its art producers and how the city filters its communities' tastes, we have to analyze the intersection of where the city's structure and the city's art worlds come together. We should also find a great deal of urban and social theory when we examine these intersections in the following chapters.

References

BECKER, HOWARD. 1971. *Culture and Civility in San Francisco*. Transaction Press: San Francisco, CA.

BURGESS, E.W. 1925. *The City: A Research Proposal*. University of Chicago Press: Chicago, IL.

FEAGIN, JOE, AND MELVIN SIKES. 1994. *Living with Racisim: The Black Middle Class Experience*. Beacon Press: Boston, MA.

FEAGIN, JOE. 1998. *The New Urban Paradigm: Critical Perspectives on the City*. Rowman and Littlefield Publishers: Laghern, MD.

GILMORE, SAMUEL. 1990. *Art Worlds: Developing the Interactionist Approach*. University of Chicago Press: Chicago, IL.

MARX, KARL, AND FREDERICH ENGELS. 1864. *Pre-Capitalistic Formation*. Transl. Jack Cohen. International Press: New York, NY.

MASSEY, DOUGLAS. 1987. "Ethnic Residential Segregator: A Theoretical Synthesis and Empowered Review." *Social Science Review*. Volume 69, No. 3.

MASSEY, DOUGLAS. 1993. *American Apartheid*. Harvard University Press: Cambridge, MA.

MASSEY, DOUGLAS, AND NANCY DENTON. 1989. "Hypersegrgation in U.S. Metropolitan Areas: Black and Hispanic Segregation along Five Dimensions." *Demography*. Volume 26, pp. 373–391.

WEBER, MAX. 1921. *Economy and Society*. G. Roth and C. Wittich (eds.). University of California Press (1978): Berkeley, CA.

WILSON, WILLIAM J. 1978. *The Declining Significance of Race*. University of Chicago Press: Chicago, IL.

CHAPTER THREE

Evolution of Culture in the City

Gideon Sjoberg was one of the first sociologists to examine, in-depth, the ancient city and its structures in his book *The Pre-Industrial City* (1965). Those of us who have never given the city much thought might feel that cities are the same everywhere, and we might be surprised to learn that the function, structure, and culture of ancient cities were much different than modern cities. The look, feel, and even smell of these ancient places would baffle the modern urbanite attempting to navigate its streets.

To give us a quick historical reminder, much of human history has been spent as wandering nomads in small kinship groups. Anthropology has shown us that these small bands of humans traveled, at times, great distances as *Homo sapiens* spread from Africa to Europe and Asia. Rarely occupying an area for too long, these early hunter-gatherers followed the game that sustained them. When an area was occupied, either seasonally or continually, the small band would defend it from others, thus no multigroup civilizations grew in these very early associations. It wasn't until the invention of agriculture that human groups were able to progress past this early nomad culture. This is not to insinuate that culture wasn't a product of this preliterate period, the cave art and tools of these societies are present for us to study today; it is only that this culture took longer to diffuse to the whole population of humans and was less dynamic because of the separated and isolated way these humans lived.

The next phase of human cultural evolution was the agricultural revolution. Some might be confused by the term "agricultural revolution," because we are accustomed to using the term "revolution" with a quick, violent, and decisive event that we see on the media. This kind of revolution, however, spanned hundreds of years across many continents. Yet, it was no less dramatic or decisive than any modern street demonstration or political coup d'etat. Dropping seeds into plowed earth and then waiting for the plants to grow may not seem very revolutionary to us today, but it actually made the first step to urbanization and urban culture possible. In order for crops to grow consistently and in sufficient amounts to sustain a group of humans, the group must stay in the area to tend them. That is common sense, but the way in which that changed human society is more complex. Because this group of humans was staying in one area for an extended period of time, they would begin to build more elaborate shelters, as opposed to using what was already available, as was the case with "cavemen." A group staying in one area will alter the space to fit the group's needs, including creating new social meanings to the area, for example, living areas, agricultural areas, waste areas, sacred spaces, and profane spaces. Caves, for example, are damp and uncomfortable with little protection from the elements. If a group intended to stay in an area for a long period of time, a cave would not suffice, and a more permanent, man-made dwelling was necessary. Also, the dampness of caves made the storing of grain and seed nearly impossible. So, primitive settlements began because of the growth of agriculture and were able to grow beyond simple kinship groups because of the stability that agriculture provided (i.e., food resources, man-made dwellings, a permanent cultural place).

After a period of agricultural settlements spreading from area to area, the division of labor in human groups began to grow as well. *Theory Break:* "Division of labor" is simply the manner in which a society organizes the tasks that must be done in order for the society to function. Who completes these tasks and the relative importance of the task assigned will play a part in the class divisions in society that occur shortly after a complex division of labor is instituted. In tribal societies, Emile Durkheim (1895) pointed out that there is very little in the division of labor; few people have a specialized job, because the tribe members each do their own necessary labor. They build their own shelters, fashion their own clothing, make their own spears, and while the whole group may go hunting, there are no specialized tasks for the tribe members.

As the division of labor increases in the agrarian-based settlements, the first specialized tasks appear—kings and priests. In a tribe, there may have been a chief and shaman, but there was very little difference between the rest of the tribe members and these other jobs. In fact, in the beginning a chief or shaman still had to contribute to the hunt or tribal activity just like other tribe members. The lack of division of labor in the tribe couldn't support a full-time member that did not contribute. When humans settle in agrarian communities, the agrarian farmer begins to produce a surplus of goods at the same time that different members of the agrarian society are becoming more specialized at their tasks. First, kings and priests develop their specialized tasks, often in concert by having a religion deify and legitimatize a ruler. Then the ruler needs a group of specialized warriors to collect taxes, enforce the peace, and protect the fledgling empire; thus an army is born. Generally, at the same time, a group of farmers begin to accumulate more wealth and land than others, a group who trade the farming surplus and form an elite class of landowners and merchants. This elite class is where the nobility will be drawn from to further coalesce power around the king.

At this time, four important cultural inventions occur that were impossible before these proto-urban settlements develop.

1. Institutionalized Religion
2. Hierarchy and Class Division
3. Currency
4. Cultural Artifacts that Denote Class and Conspicuous Consumption

INSTITUTIONALIZED RELIGION

The first, institutionalized religion, needed permanent settlements, because before then religion existed only in a localized fashion. A shaman may have held a position of power in the tribe and may have performed formal ceremonies and functions for the tribe, but most of his power lay in the traditional authority of his office and his own personal charismatic authority. Max Weber (1921) differentiated between that type of authority and the institutional or rational authority that we accept in societies today.

To have rational or institutionalized religion and expect a group to accept the authority of this religion, the group must be in a permanent settlement and the religious practice and institution must be larger than the abilities of the individual priest. A group or class of priests must exist, and the institution of religion (services, festivals, and buildings) must seem much larger and awe inspiring to the individual citizen for this urban culture to survive in the ancient city.

Why is all this necessary? Aside from attempting to answer some of life's more intricate questions,[1] religion is also a cultural invention that

---

Traditional Authority—Kings or chiefs enjoy this kind of authority, where the traditional role of the king is accepted by the society and is usually passed on to their children unquestioningly.

Charismatic Authority—This style of authority resides in the special talents and charisma of a leader, rather than the lineage of a king. (Examples: Gandhi or Hitler)

Rational or Institutionalized Authority—The authority in this type of society comes from the society's members accepting the rationality of laws and legal structure.

Max Weber 1921

---

[1]Why am I here? What is my purpose? Is there an afterlife? It is religion's role to answer these types of questions for its followers.

promotes social cohesion and direction. When human groups were in tribes, the whole group believed in the same folk religion of the tribe and this solidified tribal identity and cohesion. As our permanent settlement grows in population, different peoples will begin to settle the area that won't possess that same kind of religious belief. The settlement must achieve with a cultural tool what it could not achieve through the simple homogenous identity of the tribe. The settlement creates an institutionalized religion that lends credibility to the leadership and cohesion to the rest of the society. A key tool of religion for maintaining this legitimacy was the building of ziggurats, pyramids, and cathedrals, which could only make sense in a permanent settlement. These structures solidify the religion's place in the social and political structure of the settlement by impressing the population with the sheer magnitude of their size, thus bringing order and focus to the underclass during the often lengthy building period of the structures. These buildings also lend permanence to the settlement by the obvious permanence of these religious buildings. Institutionalized religion is part of the city and is crucial to maintaining the social solidarity of the city.

The Great Pyramid of Giza, Egypt illustrates the tendency of permanent human settlements to erect great monuments such as this to unify the population under a coherent and omnipresent institutionalized religion. Political leaders often rely on organized religion to establish order among those they are governing. This became particularly important as these permanent settlements began evolving into large urban centers.

HIERARCHY AND CLASS

When we see the organization and permanence of the settlement, one of the things we also see is the cultural evidence of a hierarchy of class. The clearest evidence of this class division in ancient cities is how the land was used in the ancient city—a class hierarchy pattern rapidly emerges. Unlike the modern city, the ancient city did not have a great deal of land specialization. Very little of the land within the city had a specific use; it was used haphazardly as business, residence, or storage in an unplanned fashion. Most ancient city residents lived and worked in the same structure, due to the limited space within the city walls. The only specific area in the ancient city that was devoted to special usage was the aristocratic palace, the religious cathedral, and the police or guard barracks (Sjoberg 1965).

Thus, the first class division in the ancient city was about societal power and the control of urban space. Soon after this first division of space and society in the ancient city, an elite group of landowners and wealthy merchants would position themselves in the housing nearest the main city plaza (palace, cathedral, barracks), where the "power" in the city existed. This is different than our modern-day urban culture, where the powerful rich move to the suburbs, away from the downtown area of the city. In an ancient city, a culture of "centrality equals power" developed for this small elite as they struggled for housing near the palace. In addition, it was also very important to have space inside the city walls for protection, not only power. Hierarchy and class were expressed through control of urban space, and it could mean the difference between life (inside the walls) or death.

CURRENCY

Another innovation of the urban empire was the standardization of currency that again could not have occurred without permanent settlements and the beginnings of ancient cities. Many ancient cultures had some type of currency, though these cultures might have been nomadic. The element that a growing urban community brings to the advent of currency is *standardization*. A currency is standardized when it is used consistently in a given area and its value is accepted by all participants, which also makes it more versatile than other types of currency. The first types of currency were coins stamped out of a precious metal, and these coins were intrinsically valuable.[2]

---

[2]Today, our currency has symbolic value. A dollar bill is merely a piece of paper, and is only worth more than other pieces of paper because, as a society, we've all agreed that it has value. However, none of that value relates to the piece of paper on which the dollar bill was printed. Metal coins were valuable due to the actual weight of the metal they were stamped from.

The need for currency came out of our ancient cities' desire for taxes. Before standardized currency, when a ruler wanted to collect taxes, he would send troops out to collect goods, including grain, produce, and livestock. At first, this was a workable system, because often the ruler did not produce his own food stores, so livestock were valuable. The priests that the king closely worked with didn't produce any food either. Thus, these ruling classes were able to sustain themselves off the surplus production of those they taxed. Later, after some years of maintaining this system, the inefficiency of troops acting as herders and laborers and managing the "taxes" collected became apparent. If this burgeoning empire circulated coins to the population, taxes and all other financial transactions could occur more efficiently. The average farmer at this time had little use for currency in his daily life, because if he needed a good or service, he bartered with other farmers for it. Currency becomes handy for getting things from traders and merchants who may not be willing to trade silk and salt for chickens and eggs, but for most early urban dwellers, currency was rarely a requirement beyond taxes and foreign exchange. It takes a city to provide the permanence and stability needed for the standardization of currency.

CULTURAL ARTIFACTS THAT DENOTE CLASS AND CONSPICUOUS CONSUMPTION

The sign of conspicuous consumption for the city's new elite class was the purchase of exotic new clothes to denote their high status. Currency was used to bring new fabrics and dyes to the cities and the elite eagerly devoured them. An enforced certification of the classes and their apparel soon followed, including rules regarding the type and color of the fabrics worn by each class. For example, the elite Roman citizens were entitled to wear white togas, which were denied to other, lower classes.

Also, in the Middle Ages, the color purple was designated exclusively for the nobility, while during the American colonial period, only men of status wore wigs. It is easy to find numerous examples of how rules about clothing have been used to designate class and income level in social situations. This is merely one way that culture production in these new cities was used to separate the new classes. The everyday display of wealth is only important if there is an audience to witness it and understand its implications, which was provided by the lower classes in the cities. That is an important aspect of this kind of consumption-production of culture—that a part of what the urban environment supplies is the creative material (people divided by class) to create the new kind of culture (clothing) in the city. The other part of urban culture consumption and production is the audience for culture, which is also vital. Often forgotten, the audience that witnesses a new urban culture process is the second part of "conspicuous consumption," which the urban environment supplies through its population density and organization. This is necessary for the new culture production to be relevant.

For our discussion of the urban environment's effect on culture, let us examine some of the fashion and architectural patterns of the ancient urban area. As we have already discussed, one of the important innovations of the ancient settlement is the hierarchy of class into several divisions (nobility, priest, soldier, merchant, artisan, and farmer) by occupation and wealth. This social hierarchy begins the cultural idea that certain groups of people in the settlement are superior to other members of the urban society. With the multitudes of people in the city, a system that displayed the social hierarchy to the multitudes was needed.

To display this rank and division, another cultural invention occurred—fashion that denoted status. Clothing and housing are the two primary categories of this fashion trend for our growing settlement. Trade and currency bring new fabrics and dyes to the different classes of the urban settlement, but actual laws develop to enforce the possession and display of certain cultural fashions. From ancient China's Peking came the roles regarding architecture and coloring. In the Forbidden City, actual areas of the city were reserved for the emperor and nobility exclusively, as well as an enforced code that stipulated that no home in the city could be over one story tall. The higher-level buildings were reserved for the emperor alone, so it is obvious that this policy was used as a cultural tool to demonstrate the emperor's superior position to all others in the city. Color for buildings had also been regulated, and only those of noble or wealthy birth were permitted to paint their homes, which is also a clear, cultural, delineation of class. Peasants were prevented from adorning and painting their homes, while the nobility and upper classes painted their houses red, purple, and green. The color gold, of course, was restricted for the emperor's use alone (MacFarquhar 1972, in Macionis and Parrillo 2001).

These distinctions between classes were vitally important for the easy functioning of society, as in the Roman Empire. Remember that one of the cultural tools that the Romans used to separate their citizens from others was the white toga, used to symbolize the rights and privileges that Roman citizens enjoyed, which other city dwellers were excluded from. Another freedom extended to Roman citizens in the appropriate dress was the freedom to travel from province or region without fear of official harassment, which also extended to freedom from local incarceration or prosecution when away from Rome (Sjoberg 1965). So, obviously, when backed up by cultural norms and the power of a large empire, even a large white sheet can be a powerful cultural tool.

A more recent example from America's colonial history is the significance of the wig, not for well-to-do ladies, but as a status symbol for men. Wealthy men of status in the colonies brought the wig tradition from Europe, where the wig was often a symbol for nobility. In the colonies, the wig was worn most often as an urban status symbol for men of "position" and "breeding," who owned land and property. The rustic and rural regions of the colonies, though, disdained the useless and increasingly "urban" custom of wig adornment for men. After the Revolutionary War, during which many colonists did not support a rebellion against the crown and wore wigs as a sign of their support of British culture, the wig increasingly became associated with the aristocratic era of Europe that many in the Americas wished to leave behind. So, the changing consumption pattern of wig wearing, due to the Revolutionary War, made the fashion of wig wearing from the cities obsolete.

The Automobile as a Cultural Artifact of Class and Conspicuous Consumption

As the United States turned the century from the 1800s to the 1900s, the growing population was moving west and building new cities as they expanded. Yet despite this period of urban growth, the majority of American citizens still lived in rural areas. In the Roaring Twenties, America was still a rural nation as it struggled with Prohibition and the illegal speakeasies (often linked to organized crime, which we'll discuss later) that cropped up

---

SETTLEMENT OR CITY?

Notice that we haven't used the words "urban" or "city" very much in our discussion. There is a healthy debate centered around when a settlement becomes a city. What are the criteria for being a city? The number of people in the settlement, the number of years at its current location, population density, and the number of permanent structures are all useful measurements of urbanization. Unfortunately, sometimes a settlement possesses some of the necessary numbers, but not all of them. The ancient city of Dublin, Ireland, is an example of this.

Dublin has been settled in some capacity for 8000 years. The first settlements of the Stone Age tribes date back to 6000 B.C.E. Known as a center for Ireland's Celtic population, the city was home to the Celts from 600 B.C.E. when they brought the first iron weapons and the Gaelic language to Ireland (Poole 1996). The city's modern name comes from the Norse words "dark water," as the Vikings invaded and settled the area in 840 C.E. bringing their culture to the growing urban settlement. While displacing some of the current inhabitants, the Vikings settled, traded, and intermarried with the local population of Dublin as they had with most of Ireland's southern sea towns. Incidentally, this is where the red hair of the Irish comes from, since the Viking population had a prevalence of the recessive gene that causes red hair, while the Celtic population had dark hair. Dublin became a true city, as opposed to an oft-invaded sea town, sometime during this period of Viking domination. While it has been inhabited for over 8000 years, it cannot really be called an 8000-year-old city. It is an 8,000-year-old settlement that became a city between 1,500 to 500 years ago, depending on the criteria one uses for a definition of a city. Some would say it finally became a city only after successive English invasions brought the British urban planning model to Dublin's streets and neighborhoods.

Some anthropologists and sociologists would give the Dublin settlement urban status when it had as few as 500 inhabitants, as they have argued for other ancient cities like Jericho and Baghdad (Macionis and Parrillo 2001). Other researchers prefer to wait until there is some measure of self-sufficiency by the urban area to distinguish it from the mere random gathering of families in a rural settlement. This self-sufficiency is difficult to gauge, because no one is around to describe the city or settlement, and our only evidence of this time is often buried several feet under existing settlements and cities. A measure of self-sufficiency would be some evidence of planned farms to feed the city and planned roads to carry goods from the city. It may seem that there *would* be no way to determine that an ancient city had planned roads or farms, but modern archaeological techniques (like satellite imaging) are able to determine ancient farmland from fallow, and satellite images are able to locate the geometric pattern of planned roads from long-abandoned settlements.

during this period in rural roadhouses and urban clubs. However, despite the nation's rural roots, a new technology emerged in the twenties as the new status symbol for America. It also fundamentally changed the shape of cities across the nation and around the world. Discussing the invention of the automobile may seem odd in a chapter devoted to ancient cities and culture, but we can now see the similarities between ancient and modern cities and culture. Many U.S. cities make the same progression from rural to urban in the 1920s as did ancient cities. In modern times, the automobile is a key piece of technology and culture that provokes the change. The automobile becomes an important urban status symbol for the wealthy and middle classes to possess at the same time it is changing a rural population into an urban population. It also actually remakes most North American cities, road by road and neighborhood by neighborhood, to fit its demands.

We should start with how America in the 1910–1920s was a rural nation with only 20 percent of its population living in cities. The automobile at this time was a rich man's toy, and only the internal combustion tractor would have appealed to most rural Americans to own. But as the Twenties roared, the automobile was becoming more common in the big city, making horse travel passé. Rural areas were now more accessible to the city because of the automobile and new roadways.

The automobile made travel into the city more common as suburban and semirural homeowners could now go into the city in the morning and come home at night. The price of an automobile in the 1920s was actually becoming more affordable to a growing segment of workers, who were earning a steady wage, though for most Americans it was still out of reach. The Stock Market Crash of 1929 and the dust bowl disasters of the 1930s saw great migrations of Americans westward to the new cities of the West looking for better lives. This mobile migration was unprecedented in its size and scope; millions of America packed up and left their homes.

America made this migration in automobiles. Whole families climbed into trucks and autos of the time with everything they could carry; sometimes an entire clan would combine resources to buy a rickety truck to head west. The economy did improve in the late 1930s to the early 1940s, but by then a plot had been hatched to change cities based on the automobile.

The appearance of the automobile as a cultural icon is an important reflection of the city's mood and the driver's status. Few theorists have tried to link the design and look of the automobile to urban ideology, but a quick look at the photos of the Model T Ford and the 1950 Cadillac clearly demonstrates that something is going on in car design.

So what is the urban connection? In the first picture, the early-twentieth-century Ford is one of the first production cars in the world, referred to as a Model T and nicknamed the "Tin Lizzie" (1913–1927). We see what is effectively a motorized carriage with little difference in design from a horse-drawn carriage except for the absence of horses. What makes this urban?

Two women ride in a Model T Ford. This car was produced between 1913 and 1927 and represented a major advantage for cities: Essentially a horseless carriage, it required far less space to maintain than horse-drawn carriages—perfect for the urban environment, in which space is always at a premium.

MOVIES TELL THE STORY

Most film fans remember *Who Framed Roger Rabbit?* (1988) as an innovative combination of live-action and animation filmmaking, set in the 1940s. It told the story of a washed-up private detective and his unlikely client, an animated rabbit. One of the subplots of the movie was the fictitious evil corporation "Cloverleaf Industry" and their attempt to close down Los Angeles's Red Car electric car line by building a highway through the fantasy district of Toon Town. The movie's subplot was fiction, but a real conspiracy did shut down the Red Car in Los Angeles and every other city streetcar line in America.

The "Big Three" automakers were the principle conspirators of the removal of the electric car, but other conspirators ranged from oil, steel, and concrete companies to city leaders who were looking for the "city of the future" in highways of concrete. The first order of business for this conspiracy to change the city was to eliminate the efficient and effective electric trolley lines that were central features of almost every mid-sized city in America. It wasn't easy to accomplish this at first, but the ideology of progress that gripped the nation at this time, combined with corporate pressure to eliminate trolley and tram lines, won out under pressure to build highways to the suburbs. Automobiles were seen as progress, and the automakers were able to characterize the trolley lines as passé technology to civic leaders.

The second part of the plan was to actually build the highways, and the destruction of one part of urban culture led to the whole redesign of the American city. Highways for cars and off-ramps that break up neighborhoods have reshaped how we think about cities and how we traverse them. Most mid-sized to large cities have not just one highway loop, but two or three that encircle the city, and these loops have the city dweller focused on travel time and traffic jams, more so than getting to know their neighbors. The impact on cities that these highway loops have had can be seen in the movement of people and jobs to the suburbs. Cars and highways have made it easy, first for white, wealthy and then middle-class urbanites, to move to the suburbs, but these urban cultural artifacts have also made it easy for the new generation of jobs (hi-tech and service jobs) to move to the suburbs. Cars and highways have also helped to leave the city's poor, low-skilled, and minority citizens in the decaying inner city. In the movie, Toon Town is saved from the Cloverleaf plot, but in the real world the construction of the megahighway system of Los Angeles and the destruction of the Red Car line did lead to the isolation of the inner city.

Horse-drawn carriages took up too much space for the horses, hay, feed, and so forth in the urban housing district of small towns. Old homes in some of our cities still have the barns and carriage houses of the horse-drawn era, and one can see how maintaining horses in an urban home could be trying. The size and convenience of the car for wealthier urbanites became a sign of status versus the peasant-like status of walking or the outdated style of riding a horse. This clearly shows a link between the new automobile and the influence of the city.

By the time the 1930s arrived, cars were significantly more prevalent in American life and a design change had occurred. After enduring the Stock Market Crash and the Great Depression, the car buyer wanted a larger car with the feeling of security, evident in the curved and hulking form of the 1930s-model Chevy. The urban influence is evident in its tire and chassis design that was made for paved roads—unlike the "Tin Lizzie's" design, which was for rural and unpaved roads—and greater speeds than previous engine designs could achieve. More space in this car reflects the desire to transport more people in greater luxury than the Model T could provide, as the car became necessary for the urban family.

The 1950 Cadillac Coupe de Ville embodies the optimism and modernism of the decade with futuristic fins and chrome, and the urban importance of this car as a status symbol. The U.S. population was definitely beginning to be an urban one and the automobile is the most visible status symbol of this change. Ostentatious, gaudy, and futuristic for its time, the

The luxurious 1950 Cadillac Coupe d Ville, with its futuristic fins and chrome, reflected the modernistic, materialistic spirit of the 1950s. By this time, the car had become more than just a means of transportation; it had become an important status symbol reflecting the economic achievements of its owner.

Coupe de Ville reflected the need for the new suburban family to display its wealth and status. Cars were more important as urban status symbols than as transportation and we can see the car's symbolic value in its extreme design. As both a symbol and a means of transportation, the automobile continued to exert pressure on the city's design by encouraging ever-increasing larger highways and neighborhood arteries.

By 1999, the Ford Explorer sport utility vehicle (SUV) and its slightly larger counterpart, the Ford Expedition, reflected the changing city and the urbanite of the twenty-first century. A city of large highways leading to suburban neighborhoods that are increasingly separated from the center city is the environment of the SUV, not the great outdoors. Part status symbol (most SUVs rarely leave the pavement) and part reflection of the prosperous times of the 1990s, the SUV reflects the desires of the new "urbanite" who is wealthy, suburban, and holds a service-oriented job. The SUV design is large, and its image as outdoor assault vehicle tempers its real use as suburban bus. Suburbanites wanted a vehicle that served their urban needs, but one that possessed a design that could transcend their suburban lives.

Cars are a reflection of our culture. They no longer just serve the transportation needs of the population, but now reflect the urban culture of their drivers. These drivers, in turn, exert pressure on cities to accommodate their vehicles. What is it that the urban driver wants for his or her car? Bigger, faster roads and highways with fewer traffic jams and shorter commuting times from the front door to work or school. As we have discussed, this has changed the design of the city into a collection of sprawling suburbs with loops, thruways, and beltways of roads for the automobile culture we have created. Pollution from all these new, bigger cars has also changed and altered the urban environment. Despite the common knowledge that automobile emissions cause pollution, there have been few movements by urbanites toward mass transit to reduce pollution from automobiles.

The power of our urban automobile culture is significantly more potent and meaningful than any rational person would think. The fact is that cars have been given the power by our culture to define who we are by what we drive. The classic image of a midlife crisis is the slightly balding fifty-year-old man driving a brand new . . . sports car. No rational explanation for this behavior exists, but to many men entrenched in middle age, those fast cars represent powerful sex appeal and a connection to their rapidly fading youth. And, of course, where will he want to take this marvel of internal combustion painted the stereotypical fire engine red? Cruising on the streets of the city, so that he and his car can be seen. Anyone who sees the car will intuitively understand his message: "I am powerful, because I have a powerful car. Admire me and my conspicuous symbol of wealth and youth." *Theory Break:* Urban culture regarding automobiles has a gender component. Men typically have this kind of relationship with their car and self-image; women facing a midlife crisis rarely buy a sports car to compensate. Yet, this may be changing, as the fastest growing truck and SUV-buying demographic are women. Perhaps women wish to participate in the urban tradition of having their automobiles be advertisements of their self-image and want to change the assumptions of "soccer moms" made when driving minivans or station wagons.

For other urban drivers, a minivan may represent safety, a large truck may show rugged character, and a luxury car represents status. All of these cultural meanings of the automobile are found and reinforced in the city. *Theory Break:* Our culture gives us a way to feel about cars and ourselves in the city. The way people feel about their cars, the meaning we attach to one car over another, has come from our urban experience that personalizes and values a car, as much as the cowboy valued his horse. The city is more likely to produce cars that equal driver's personality judgments, because of the rapid assumptions urbanites must make about the large numbers of strangers they meet everyday.

THE INDUSTRIAL REVOLUTION AND URBAN PLANNING

One of the things that sociologists focus on more than other disciplines is the Industrial Revolution, and in America, the Industrial Revolution shaped and built our cities like no other event. E.W. Burgess's (1925) examination of Chicago shows a city built around a central business district with an industrial ring that clearly is designed to make goods for a broader public beyond the city's borders. Our need to have cities make things (things we call "culture") in an industrial manner changes the city's design from a colonial grid design that served an urban elite with marketplaces to trade goods into a city design of rings or zones for industry and homes for industrial workers. First, let's briefly discuss the colonial design and then we will explore the changes the Industrial Revolution brought to our cities and the culture that they produced.

The idea to design a city in the new world (as opposed to letting a settlement grow around a fort or harbor, like many early Eastern cities developed in the American colonies) seems to have been most successfully realized by William Penn in his grid design of Philadelphia (Figure 3.1).

This style of urban planning became very popular, and as many of the Eastern harbor cities were growing larger, their city leaders forced Penn's grid design on their city's growth. New York City's grid design can be seen as one travels north of Battery Park and the city becomes more ordered. The city couldn't be completely retrofitted into a grid design because of existing homes, streets, and businesses that had evolved from the first settlement at the far end of the island, so the grid design begins north of Battery Park. Many Western cities grew with a new revision of the grid plan from their first inception, the most dramatic example of this being Phoenix, Arizona. An entire city is laid out in a perfect grid, which is most dramatically apparent when viewed at night from a plane.

The grid design fit perfectly with the planned and "ordered" philosophy of the new industrializing, yet colonial nation. This became part of the

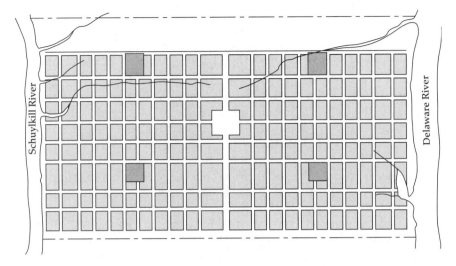

Figure 3.1   The Gridiron City: William Penn's Philadelphia Plan, 1682.

new urban culture: planned cities, planned businesses, and planned lives. "If we can study it, plan it, and build it, *anything* is possible." This was the planners' philosophy, at the end of the nineteenth century and the beginning of the twentieth century. Science and technology were newfound "religions" and new city planners rushed to embrace these philosophies. Cities wanted industry within their borders in the 1900s, because it brought jobs, votes, payrolls, housing construction, and tax dollars. It also brought overcrowding, pollution, and sprawl, but cities would have seventy-five years or more to recognize these problems.

Inconveniently, the best place for the new urban industrial businesses was right next to the power, water, and transportation hubs of the downtown districts. *Theory Break:* The tremendous amount of *horizontal space*[3] required for large industries prevented the location of factories in the central business district itself, but in the next ring or zone, outside of the central business district, industry was able to find adequate space and utility accommodation— called the Industrial Ring. Early power plants, which did not have the technology to generate wattage across long distances, were also located nearby. Water was also a necessary building block of business as it was used to generate power, cool and clean factory operations, and then any industrial waste could be dumped in a convenient creek or river nearby.

Transportation resources were also a requirement for these factories: rail, truck, ship, or canal barge. Industry needed some way to transport their

---

[3]To understand this idea, you can think of an automobile construction line with a conveyor belt moving cars to the assembly plant, which requires a lot of horizontal plant space.

heavy raw materials in, and their finished products out. The location of industrial businesses produced design changes in the city by locating housing for workers and the middle class in the rings just beyond the industrial ring. Highways and roads to service the growing legion of cars, together with bus routes and streetcars that linked these rings, changed the colonial city into the industrial city design we are familiar with. While the grid pattern had given way to the industrial urban culture of the ring design, the city was still being "planned" by important elite groups; only this time their goal was industry instead of the colonial trade of America's early cities.

Industrial rings and the automobile have changed the design of the city and the relationships of the people in it. Thus, the culture and cultural products of the industrial city were changed too, because of these industrial land and automobile changes. To serve the needs of growing cities, culture had to be marketed and shipped in new ways to make them more accessible to automobiles and suburban dwellers. From this change in city structure came the development of strip malls and supermarkets. These two suburban cultural innovations of strip malls and supermarkets changed urban cultural products forever. Before suburban rings and the industrial mode of protection, everyday activities were more difficult and time consuming. One could not get all of their food, clothing, and merchandise in just one place prior to the strip mall and supermarket.

Circa 1900, preparing a meal for your family was a difficult and lengthy exercise in the city. First, you would have to visit a dry goods store, bakery, greengrocer, and then the butcher, after which one would have to hurry home (by foot or streetcar) to prepare the meal, because refrigeration consisted of a box with a block of ice in it, if you could afford an icebox at all. The only reprieve from these errands was the home delivery systems provided for milk, eggs, and butter. These tedious tasks often took the majority of a woman's day, since it was customary for the wives to do the cooking at this time in the middle and working classes. This set of tasks would also need to be repeated every day. If clothes, shoes, or professional goods or services were needed, then a trip downtown was also necessary in addition to food preparation. All of this changed during the suburban period with the growth of the supermarket for all food-related items and with the strip mall and the megamall, which were all located in the suburbs near their clientele. *Theory Break:* Functionalist urban planners would point to these technological innovations as evidence of the rational and efficient nature of the suburban design.

THE GROWTH OF THE SUBURBS

The new suburban consumer was reached with new forms of advertising and new ways of doing old advertising to attract them. Principal among these new cultural marketing tools was television. Targeted at primarily suburban dwellers, the entertainment audience of the first twenty years of television was white, middle class, and living outside the inner city. Often the first commercial message of television was an attempt to get consumers to return to the retail business centers of downtown. It was soon clear that businesses that were closer to their suburban customers were having the most success reaching their customers through television. Suburbanites were unwilling to drive to the center city to shop, they wanted easier access to their consumer goods. Urban retail culture bent over backward to accommodate their desires.

Strip malls and large megamall complexes grew to fill the needs of the suburban consumer. Shopping close to home for all your needs becomes a suburban obsession. This obsession was aided by television programming and marketing for a suburban audience growing increasingly separated from the city itself. The suburban consumer now becomes an engine of commerce to American business. A literal rush to the suburbs of businesses to serve suburbanites blossomed through the 1960s and 1970s.

As supermarkets and strip malls grow to serve the suburbs, we see the first symptoms of how the city will change in the near future. Only thirty

---

INDUSTRIALIZATION IN ROCHESTER, NEW YORK—INDUSTRY VERSUS ENVIRONMENT

George Eastman founded the Kodak Company in Rochester, New York, as one of the first companies to provide portable cameras and photo processing to consumers via mail. This was an innovative approach to personal photography; a small box camera would take photos, the customer would mail them into the factory to be processed, and then the photos would be returned to them through the mail. While there were other camera companies at the time, the Eastman camera and mail-in process created a multibillion-dollar industry. The urban impact of Kodak on Rochester is multidimensional. In one way, Kodak makes Rochester the modern industrial city it is with tens of thousands of jobs, service expansion in the city, and philanthropic gifts of libraries, parks, and colleges from Eastman himself. The other reality that Kodak has provided for Rochester is the largest single polluting entity in the entire state of New York, pumping 28 million pounds of wastewater annually into the local Genesee River and burning several million pounds of chemicals in incinerators that release carbon monoxide, sulfur dioxide, and dioxin into the air (Robinson 2000).

Businesses like Kodak present tremendous contradictions for the urban population: jobs and tax dollars that Kodak provides to Rochester versus air and water pollution that destroy the environment. The city produces all kinds of culture—jobs, taxes, and pollution; it also produces the government regulators that we turn to to protect us from our cultural choices and the urban social movements that organize to protest businesses like Kodak.

years after the suburban boom of the 1950s, the United States' central cities were making fewer industrial items (like cars, stereos, and televisions). There is an abandonment of the inner city by factories and retail businesses, depleting the area of jobs and commerce. Employment and money are moving permanently to the suburbs, as are television and advertising. The inner city was turning into a service center for its inhabitants, administering its police, roads, water, schools, and telephone hookups, while the good-paying jobs moved closer to their workforce in the suburbs. A postindustrial city has its own contradictions as it moves from a place that employs urban citizens to make cultural products for foreign markets into a place where suburban citizens are consumers of services that the city provides (airports to Internet connections). Yet, the city has fewer resources to fix its problems and provide these resources, due to a shrinking tax base because the suburbanites, who drive in for employment, are most often in incorporated "cities" that are designed to evade municipal taxation; so, the city loses money and people who would normally help fix the city's problem. In addition, the suburbanization of the city creates sprawl and extra traffic burdens at the same time demanding that the city maintain the same level of police, road, and water services when they come into the city to work, without contributing any tax dollars. Compounding this problem is the final shift of voting power from the city's center to the population in the suburbs. The outcome for the city and its cultural future is that the suburbs will be controlling what services cities will be providing by applying their political voting muscle. These new political suburbanites will tend to favor the suburbs' cultural needs (new highways, more soccer fields, tax abatements for suburban businesses) over extending social services and developmental assistance to the central city.

Homes changed in architecture and design due to the changes in the city's culture and the growth of the suburbs. For early homes in the city's center, choosing either the bungalow or a multistory design was unimportant. Whatever the home design in the 1880s–1920s, it was close to the street, and homes were as close together as possible. No large lawns or backyards, and no space between the housing units was the way neighborhoods grew at that time. Planning and designing suburban neighborhoods was a skill many years in the future. Neighborhoods in the central city were managed by "planning and zoning" committee edicts, and their shape, appearance, and housing rules were often afterthoughts, rather than plans. Some benefits of this loose structure for housing were the lack of restrictions on one's house and property by the city, developer, or local residence associations. The city wasn't involved in setting rules for painting, ornamentation, or even the kind of structures one could have on their property. The central city is where we find houses with "mother-in-law" apartments in the back of the property to provide additional streams of income from one's property. In modern subdivisions, single houses aren't allowed to have rental property on the same lot, yet these apartments in downtown subdivisions allowed large families to stay together or gave them the ability to have a renter's monthly check to aid in mortgage payments. The culture of downtown housing was able to allow as much latitude in property use by the citizens as possible. Often the lack of restrictions also allowed for home businesses in these neighborhoods, which closed the gap between work and housing. Modern subdivisions won't allow home businesses in an area zoned as residential. Another difference in these downtown subdivisions is their placement on their neighborhood lots; specifically, downtown homes are often placed right on the sidewalk or within feet of the curb. The architectural effect of inner-city architecture is to shrink the distance between one's neighbors, who would be visible from the stoop or porch, and the public on the sidewalk. Critics say that what these neighborhoods lose is often individuality and privacy, as well as a front lawn that suburbanites expect from their housing. Some theorists feel this is the way we should revitalize suburban architecture to return to this more open use and architectural closeness in design.

Interestingly enough, this older style of neighborhood design is making a comeback called "The New Urbanism," in which new subdivisions are being constructed with these important older-style design specifications of houses being put close together, closer to the sidewalks, with large avenues and neighborhood parks. The idea of the New Urbanism is to make subdivisions more pedestrian and people friendly, as opposed to modern suburbs that are more car friendly. Older neighborhoods have this more human and organic design that favors people's needs in their housing environment, while new suburbs are more responsive to the needs of the automobile. Some critics have objected to the New Urbanism as being too idealistic, since we do now live in a world that is dominated by our cars and we can't really go back to a nostalgic yesteryear. They feel that taking away our cars represents an infringement on a pragmatic way to live our lives. Architects maintain that New Urban neighborhoods make your car obsolete for going to the store, school, or park, because these things are walking distance from home. Some of these planned neighborhoods have work locations within walking distance of the homes to have a total community experience, where one never has to leave. Unfortunately, that is another criticism of this cultural return to yesteryear, that this kind of total community cuts off the rich, middle-class white population from the rest of the city. In Chapter 2, we discussed how culture in the city could create division and separation between groups, and we will cover this in more detail later in the book.

Architecture in the suburbs can be urban culture that creates separation between classes and races. In our efforts to have a "home and a yard of our own," we have unintentionally, or as Merton put it, "latently" created a culture of division in our urban environment. There are divisions between the inner city and the remaining portion of the city, between the city and the suburbs, between our houses and our neighbor's houses, and most importantly between our fellow citizens and ourselves. Class is immediately obvious in suburban architecture, as newer homes create divisions between income groups and what size and location of home they can afford. This separation is not only between city and suburbs, but also between stratified neighborhoods within suburbia. Those suburbanites that can afford a

$500,000 home don't want to share any more in common with those in a $200,000 subdivision than they do with an inner city neighborhood. With one possible exception . . . race. Suburbanites that can afford over $150,000[4] for a home are most often going to be white, and that racial element has traditionally kept suburbia relatively homogeneous. However, the future may hold a new set of possibilities for the suburbs since there has been a growing percentage of minorities in traditionally white suburbs in the past fifteen years (U.S. Census 1990 and 2000).

URBAN PRESSURE AND THE DEBATE ON WELFARE

Another example of urban culture creating division in our city is welfare policy, where the manifest function of welfare is to help poor people in a troubled economy or through a personal setback. *Theory Break:* A latent function of one welfare policy rule was to actually discourage welfare recipients from working. Known as the 100 Hour Rule, in the 1960–1980 welfare program Aid to Families with Dependent Children, or AFDC, if a welfare client worked more than one hundred hours in a month, then their benefits would be curtailed or discontinued with the rationale being that anyone working 100 hours or more did not need welfare. This policy actually discouraged welfare clients from working more than 100 hours, not because they would lose some of their welfare dollars, but because the *entire* family's medical benefits would end. Those reading this passage who have children will understand all too well how this would be a latent disincentive to finding permanent work if your entire family lost its health insurance because you worked more hours. The low-skilled jobs that many welfare clients find do not offer health benefits for their children, and the few jobs that do offer benefits won't start their health coverage for three months. Again, those readers with children know that a responsible parent doesn't gamble the health of their children for three months on a new job. It makes more sense either to not find full-time employment, or to lie to AFDC caseworkers and tell them you could only work 100 hours. The urban impact of this welfare policy took years to be seen. The urban poor developed an entire cooperative, informal culture to get around welfare rules (i.e., employers that know to say employees only worked 100 hours, trading of food stamps for money or other goods, having fathers maintain a fraudulent separate address to maintain welfare eligibility for their children).

The urban impact of these last two examples has been dramatic since 1995. For welfare policy, both conservatives and liberals felt the impact on the city and the poor on public assistance was bad enough to change the welfare system. Conservatives felt that welfare "trapped" the poor in a cycle of

---

[4]For those in urban areas with exorbitant home prices, translate these numbers into appropriate home prices for your area.

government dependence (the actual number of welfare recipients with multiple consecutive years on assistance and/or multiple generations on assistance is quite small, but the public accepted this argument) and that there was a great deal of fraud in the program. The last part of the conservative argument was crystallized by former President Reagan creating the urban myth of the "Welfare Queen" who was cheating the system and getting rich. This *is* a myth; welfare is the most heavily policed government program and the percentage of fraud as compared to white collar crime, IRS filings, or the Medicare program is small. Welfare fraud that did occur was most visible in the city, where groups of inner city minority poor created resentment among middle- and working-class citizens that felt they were getting off without working (although 60 percent of adult recipients work).

Liberals also felt the welfare system was broken because of all the "hoops" the poor were made to jump through to get the benefits. A different office visit for welfare, food stamps, childcare, Medicaid, and job training was necessary, leaving the recipient with little time for anything else besides attending to their benefits. Being on public assistance could actually turn into a full-time job for many clients. So welfare policy changed in the mid-1990s with stiffer penalties (including penalizing a child's benefits for a parent's failure in the program), harsher work requirements, workfare (having to work for their welfare money, either for local government or local business), absolute time limits on receiving benefits, limits on federal expenditures, and the creation of "One Stop Centers" to avoid duplication within service agencies.

These changes have altered one latent function in welfare's design (i.e., the 100 Hour Rule) but have inadvertently put pressure on other urban institutions. Principal among these new latent problems is the lack of available urban childcare for welfare recipients who are trying to work or increase their education and can't find adequate or available childcare. This has put a strain on urban childcare centers, which often can't fulfill the demand of yuppie couples who are willing to pay premium prices, let alone the underclass and urban poor on fixed payments from welfare's childcare system. Housing has also been strained in all urban areas, as the number of low-income housing units has declined since 1980, while demand has increased. The cost of obtaining housing in most cities is well beyond the paltry government subsidy for housing, causing the demand for existing public housing projects to increase. More people living in fewer low-income units at a time when many of these units are deteriorating has led to a predictable cultural reaction: anger and violence. In New Orleans's decaying housing projects, the city has set street lights to blink yellow after dark in front of some of the most dilapidated and violent projects, due to the increased number of carjackings, a disturbing cultural response to the terrible housing options imposed on those receiving public assistance.

Many feel that the new policies have worked because we have seen a drop in the number of welfare clients, but closer inspection in our cities find an increase in demand from private charities and food banks. Aside from the type of inner city culture that welfare creates, the bigger picture is that a cultural division has been created separating and stigmatizing the inner city minority poor on assistance from the rest of the city. *Theory Break:* C. Wright Mills challenged us to use what he called the "sociological imagination." Briefly stated, if something is happening to an entire group, like a disproportionate number of African Americans in poverty, then individual-level explanations, like "they must just be lazy," are an inadequate explanation for a widespread phenomenon. Since that explanation will not suffice, we are left with a structural explanation. For minorities in poverty and on public assistance in the city, society's racism is that structural explanation.

References

Burgess, Ernest W. 1925. "The Growth of the City: An Introduction to a Research Project," from *The City*. R.E. Park, E.W. Burgess, and R.D. McKoware, eds. University of Chicago Press: Chicago, IL. Originally published 1916.

Durkheim, Emile. 1895. *The Division of Labor in Society*. MacMillan (1933): New York, NY.

MacFarquhar, Roderick. 1972. *The Forbidden City*. Newsweek: New York, NY.

Macionis, John, and Vincent Parrillo. 2001. *Cities and Urban Life*. Prentice Hall: Upper Saddle River: NJ.

Merton, Robert. 1957. *Social Theory and Social Structure*. Free Press: New York, NY.

Mills, C. Wright. 1959. *The Sociological Imagination*. Oxford Press: New York, NY.

Poole, Susan. 1996. *Ireland: Frommer's Guide*. MacMillan Travel: New York, NY.

Robinson, Judy. 2000. "The Kandid Coalition Takes on Eastman Kodak." *Grand Score*. Vol. 3, No. 2, Winter. Page 1.

Sjoberg, Gideon. 1965. *The Pre-Industrial City*. Free Press: New York, NY.

Weber, Max. 1921. *Economy and Society*. G. Roth and C. Wittich (eds.). University of California Press (1978): Berkeley, CA.

U.S. Census. 1990. *Census of the Population*. U.S. Government Printing Office: Washington, DC.

U.S. Census. 2000. *Census of the Population*. U.S. Government Printing Office: Washington, DC.

CHAPTER FOUR

Music in the City

What came first, music or musicians? Did we as human beings have some innate conception of music or making music, or have we come to classify the noise making of certain individuals (let's call them musicians) as "music," because that is our socially defined category for what they do?

Innate or biological perspectives favor an explanation of music in our physiology and genetic background. *Theory Break*: The sociobiology paradigm believes that if a concept exists in all societies throughout time, then the concept must be biological in nature, rather than social, because social learning cannot successfully transmit all such concepts everywhere. These researchers feel that the presence of music in all known cultures, including preliterate culture, demonstrates a biological predisposition to making music. In other words, since African societies who had music could not have transferred music to Incan societies in the Americas through trade or contact there must be some common element between the societies, i.e., a biological link.

THE FIRST ORGANIZED MUSIC MAKERS

We began to make music with the first instrument we possessed, our voice. The rhythms, lyrics, and music we made with this instrument, and the instruments we invented to accompany our voice, are all a component of our capacity to hear and our capacity to speak. For example, we don't make music above our hearing range (i.e., versus marine mammals, whose songs extend far above and below our hearing range) or in a way that is incompatible with our vocal range, because of the need for our music to have a vocal quality (again, despite the wide range of tonality our musical instruments could make).

From a more anthropological perspective, music becomes a method of "ornamentation," like special masks, clothes, or feathered objects that give our cultural events their unique or special quality. Music becomes a way to ornament a ceremony to make it special. This is not just a concept for primitive tribal societies, because our modern societies do the same thing with music as ornamentation. The ability of music to make events special and unique becomes valuable in every early society. Ceremonies create a group response, and these responses help to create group cohesion and solidarity because of the shared experience of the ceremony. Often controlled by religious leaders for religious events, this need for artistic ornamentation leads to a specialized category of laborers called musicians.

For sociologists like Emile Durkheim, it is music's relevance to defining space as sacred or profane and music's creation of a specialized labor category that is very intriguing. *Theory Break*: Durkheim's theory (1915) states that one of the first things that human societies did that clearly separates them from other animals was to define space and objects into sacred (special or holy) and profane (not special or unique, but everyday). This delineation of sacred and profane is obviously one of the initial steps to the creation of a religion and religious group. Music becomes a powerful tool in the creation of special and sacred events. Durkheim predicts the rise of a priest or shaman as one of the first specialized members of a tribe of previously equal members. Priests, and the category of chief or king, are the first rungs on the division of labor scale above the ordinary tribe members. The special place in the village or protocity that the kings and priests occupy illustrates how the concept of sacred and profane can be applied to a city.

Then, it is the priest or shaman that will also be one of the first musicians in the tribe. Why? Because the priest will at first have to make his own music (rattles, drums, chants, singing, and the creation of flutes and wind instruments) before he can convince other tribe members to specialize in music production for him. Durkheim (1895) classified societies as to how many labor categories or how much *division of labor* was present to illustrate how advanced the society had become (the more division of labor, the more advanced). The glue that holds societies together, from primitive societies to advanced societies, is social "solidarity." Primitive societies have mechanical solidarity, in which members believe in the same religion and rules, and have very little social differentiation (only a few different categories of members—chief, shaman, warrior, women, children, roughly in that order). Modern urban societies have hundreds of job categories and are held together by the interconnected nature of our jobs, not our shared belief system. Durkheim called this "organic solidarity."

Music's function in our society has changed as we have become increasingly held together by organic solidarity. While still helping to make ceremonies and events "special," if not completely sacred, music has also become commerce and business. In the West, music is part of the capitalist system of production and exchange and has become *very* big business. Culture products, including music, are the United States's second largest export category behind weapons exports. Now, there are many different categories of music to fit the consumer's taste (rock, jazz, religious, classical) and many different categories of musicians as well (guitarist, violinist, singers, pianist, and conductor). There is also an entire retail industry designed to supply specialized music to specific audiences of music consumers. Within these retail businesses are specialized occupation categories—radio and TV personalities for music; music critics in print, radio, and TV; record executives; recording engineers; TV and video music show personnel; down to the lowest-paid music store clerks. Sociology is particularly fascinated with human society from the Industrial Revolution to the present, because the human groupings in our society (race, class, gender, education, occupation) took on new and more significant meanings after the Industrial Revolution. For sociology's examination of music, it is the commodification (i.e., the social process by which an element of culture, such as a song, that might not have an immediate value becomes an economic commodity that benefits an industry, such as music publishers and record labels) and specialization of the music that occurs while it is produced in the racial, class, and gendered communities of the Industrial Revolution that is important. The individuals that make up these communities of different races, classes, genders, and so forth are important to understand as audiences and musicians.

PRODUCING MUSICAL CULTURE

Music is made by musicians. That seems simple enough, yet many researchers have forgotten that the group identities and urban influences of these musicians are key to understanding modern musical production. Music, itself, has been a forgotten field of study until recently in sociology, despite the undeniable social component of making music. Anthropologists and ethnomusicologists have been left to study music, but recently some key sociologists (Blau, Frith, Finnegan, Wicke, Martin) have produced research that reminds us all of the social dynamics in music. Except for the lone piano or guitar singer-songwriters, music is *made in groups of musicians* called ensembles or bands *for* other groups of people, called audiences. That is sociology! These groups, musicians and audiences, are shaped, molded, and placed spatially together by urban factors. For our discussion, it is not the internal angst or tortured soul of the artist that is important to making music, since this will vary widely from musician to musician, but it is the group and urban influences that shape modern music making.

While the internal mechanisms of *why* a musician makes music (in an often unforgiving and inhospitable environment) may vary, the social group identities and urban factors of music making *are* able to be understood by sociologists. Audiences and musicians are products of their social and urban environments, which are best understood by sociologists. Musicians make music first in the ethnic community that they are raised in; whatever ethnic group that may be, it is that group that matters initially. From this community, the individual will first learn what is defined by the group as music and musicianship, i.e., white musicians growing up in a white community would learn classical music, Sousa-like band music, or perhaps country music. But, it would be unlikely that a young white musician would be steeped in African American blues music or in the full discourse of rap music. The music of the community affects the musicians and potential musicians at a subconscious level, before they are even able to make a choice about the music that they want to make. These community identities of race and culture occur because of numerous social factors. The social history of a group can influence a group's cultural identity. For instance, a history of racial segregation and oppression, urban histories, like neighborhood in and out migration, employment dynamics, poverty, or even zoning changes can change the identity. Musicians grow up and are raised in these urban histories and identities, and these cultural factors are evident in their music production.

The racial communities that form part of our social identities are spatially located in our cities due to the historical pattern of immigration and segregation of the city. We should remind ourselves that up until 1965, our nation's cities were segregated by official mechanisms of the state which came about through a social process of white oppression and discrimination. This segregation would affect musicians in that city and all of the people they associate with (or would not associate with). Social division in the city, particularly official state-sponsored (now illegal) segregation, group some people together because of their racial classification and divide others for the same reason. Musicians come from these segregated communities, both white and black musicians, and initially reproduce the music and culture they have learned in these communities.

Many black musicians were raised in urban communities of Gospel, blues, jazz, rhythm and blues (R&B), and later rap music in these segregated areas. Many white musicians were educated in the classical music tradition or grew up in the country music tradition. Many Hispanic musicians were raised in urban neighborhoods with Tejano, Ranchero, Salsa, Samba, Tango, Brazilian, Cuban, and various forms of Latin pop music, while at the same time their ethnic community acted as a bridge between the white and black communities. This "bridge" function in the urban environment often meant that Hispanic musicians also had to learn the traditions of the white, Hispanic, and black communities. *Theory Break*: Hubert Blalock (1967) called this the "middleman minority function," a social function below the dominant group, but occupying a position superior to the lowest group. Often, this group performed tasks that the dominant group did not want to do, but they did not want contact with the lowest social group, so the middleman minority was employed. Culturally, the middleman had to be able to deal with both groups.

Few white musicians would attempt to cross the racial boundaries of the city to learn about the other communities' culture during this time. But the power of the racial pyramid allowed whites to go to minority communities without severe social sanction, because they were at the *top* of that pyramid. Black or Hispanic musicians would find it more difficult to cross the racial boundary into white-only establishments, because they would be facing the official legal, sometimes violent, barriers enforced by the white communities. Until the 1960s, very little racial boundary crossing occurred in America's race conscious society, because of these significant barriers.

Today's cities don't have the official segregation of the Jim Crow laws of the South. As we discussed in Chapter 3, America's cities are still segregated by the informal means of indirect institutional racism. These informal social means still keep the neighborhoods, clubs, audiences, and musicians separated from each other. This separation of ethnic and racial communities is a function of the segregation in the urban environment; the degree and extent of the segregation has to do with urban factors like the length of the period of official segregation, employment dynamics, wage histories, and so forth.

Aside from influencing musicians as they grow up, the racial communities in the city also affect the actual music production process. First, we must understand a little about music to understand how music is produced. Bands are composed of several musicians who may not have known each other previously but who have come together to make music. If the urban environment is divided racially and economically, like most U.S. cities, then at the beginning, music will follow the city's divisions with white, middle-class musicians finding each other because of proximity, and black musicians finding each other the same way. It will take an alternative way of associating in the city to break this powerful set of social barriers and produce music that transcends these racial class divisions. That is where the city's zoning and regulation of venues becomes important to the urban musician. If the venues can begin to break the racial divide, then musicians will begin to associate beyond the city's social boundaries. If there is no alternative way to socialize, then musicians of different races and classes will have few opportunities to meet and play music together. The city designates entertainment areas in the city by planning and zoning regulations. These are the areas that musicians meet in to make music and form the "nuts and bolts" of music production.

Even before they get to a venue, musicians must accomplish a plethora of social tasks: meet each other, decide on fellow musicians and a musical style that all of the musicians agree on, pick music and appropriate songs for the available audience (for example, a gothic cover band of Marilyn Manson's hits probably wouldn't be popular in Lubbock, Texas's country bars), and last but not least, decide on a rehearsal space. Let's examine that social process more closely, because all of these musical decisions have an urban component. For instance, an aspiring musician must choose from the available local players that would be interested in their style of band. The reader may assume this local reality, but this decision is part of an essential urban dynamic in music making. Unlike a corporate firm in Atlanta that might start a nationwide or large regional search for an employee, a band needs a player that is local, because a band cannot pay moving expenses or salaries to an out-of-town musician. So, how the city is divided by race and class becomes part of a preselection process of what musicians are available to produce music, and the zoning of city businesses will determine what clubs will be available to transcend these divides. A local government that is racist or that is against nightclubs and bars might limit the number of business permits that it issues or restrict them to a specific part of town.

Once local players are assembled into a band, music must be picked that will please a local crowd—not a choice of music that might please a record executive or radio programmer, but one that will first please a local urban crowd and a local club owner. A band must first have success in their local urban environment if they are to have a chance at landing a record contract. That is an *urban factor* of musical production, not regional, national, or international, but urban. Again, that may seem obvious, yet this is a crucial component of modern music making that is urban. A novelist hoping to sell his or her novel to a major publisher in New York City doesn't have to change the style of writing to appease the local audience or newspaper critic in their home town. But before a band makes it nationally, they have to make local audiences happy, and often local and national tastes don't mix.

Even finding a place to rehearse has an urban component to it, because if your fellow band members don't have a garage to rehearse in, you have to find a place that will let you make a lot of noise. Apartments and condos won't let you have a band rehearsal because of the noise, and many neighborhoods won't even allow a band to rehearse in your garage without calling the police. Many cities have small auxiliary businesses, which have evolved to specialize in providing rehearsal space for musicians. Again, it is the city that will determine the viability of this auxiliary business. There has to be sufficient demand. If a city doesn't make room for auxiliary businesses for music, yet another urban barrier is constructed, the municipal planning and zoning board. If a city doesn't want to allow music businesses, because they think it may lead to a culture of noise, alcohol, sex, and related violence, then the planning and zoning board can refuse the necessary permits for a rehearsal business or any related music business. Essentially, the city can pull the plug on music culture easier than on almost any other type of urban culture production by denying the zoning for music-related businesses.

THE SOCIOLOGY OF MUSICIANSHIP

Notice that we have not discussed *why* musicians make music. The reason for this is simply that why a musician makes music is an internal issue. Individuals will vary as to their motivations for producing culture and ultimately this is sociopsychological. There are some common threads in creating music that have a social component. Musicians playing popular music styles (rock, country, jazz) often have said that attracting women and fame were the reasons that they started making music (most of these musicians were male and between 18 and 30 years old) (Turley 2000). On the other hand, most classical musicians in this age group don't have any illusions about early fame or groupie attention. They have different goals: playing in an orchestra and perhaps conducting or having a solo career. To be fair to the popular musicians in your city, most of them have realized that the rock star life of sex, fame, and riches is available for an extremely small percentage of musicians, but that is still the goal of many local musicians. They produce much of their music culture without the possibility of immediate rewards, yet they do it anyway.

So, a better question is why they would continue, despite the meager rewards, to try and be musicians. Part of the answer is that they still dream of being a big rock star, but most musicians make music in their everyday life because of the importance of music in their life and the personal expression that music allows them. Many musicians could not imagine doing anything else, despite the meager real world "rewards" of being a musician—usually long nights, long tours, no health care, no retirement package, and little net profit. The inherent social and personal value of making music outweighs the lack of reward and the social value and social reward varies by urban location.

Ruth Finnegan's (1989) *Hidden Musicians* examined urban musicians in England to find who makes music and how they make music in the city. Her findings challenge the assumptions of musicians as born rock stars and working-class heroes. Most musicians playing pop music were working-class males who barely made beer money with their music, but even more surprising was *where* most of the city's music was made. Schools and churches are not what we usually consider music venues, but if we think about the total amount of choir, band, orchestra, and recital events that schools and churches sponsor in the city, we can see that they are the most prevalent music venues. For musicians trying to "make it" playing popular music in the city, the same issues of rehearsing, playing, and gigging were similar to those that we have already discussed. Urban musicians will face these same issues in almost any urban environment, but another sociologist educated in England's cultural production found a unique aspect of England's education system that made the English bands of the 1960s and 1970s the innovative chart toppers that they were.

Art into Pop (1987) details Simon Frith's analysis of the art colleges that England provided for its nonuniversity-bound teenagers and that inadvertently created its national and urban music scenes. Almost as an antidote to the urban constraints of the real-world drudgery of music making, Frith finds that England's art colleges were miniculture communities that allowed young, urban art school students to experiment with identity, fashion, and music in a safe environment. The Beatles, Pink Floyd, David Bowie, and the Sex Pistols all started playing gigs at art schools, and these bands changed not only music, but also entire fashions and generational identities for England. The art schools became insulated communities where a band not only could play music for their fellow students (a built-in audience), but also could wear different clothes, hairstyles, and identities that became wedded to the new music. They made music at art schools because the educational system, through its art schools, made music making safe and attractive, free from serious economic constraints (the student received tuition and other support for attending art school) and guaranteed a built-in audience. The art schools were the perfect experimental laboratory for pop music to incubate before hitting the London club scene.

From these art schools, bands reinfiltrated their urban haunts with new sounds and styles that made them unique, eventually making it to London, where all English pop music is evaluated. At art schools, new generations of musicians and audiences were being trained to accept and demand new things from popular musicians including fashion, identity, and social meaning. All of these changes from the art school bands culminated in the club scene of London, because that was where the major media and broadcasting companies were located, and that is where bands had to be noticed. Drawing the bands, audiences, and media companies together elevated the previous stuffy image of London in the 1950s to the now infamous swinging London image of the 1960s and 1970s. Frith feels that it was this art school movement that accounts for the successive British bands that took over America. Only San Francisco's hippie community from 1967–1971 could really rival the new waves of British bands from 1960–1985. Successive British invasions brought the mop top Beatles in the early 1960s, the mod look of The Who in the late 1960s, the glam androgyny of David Bowie in the early 1970s, the rebellious

The punk movement in general and the Sex Pistols in particular reflected the pessimism and aggression of London during the mid 1970s, a time of extremely high unemployment and very little hope for the future among English youths. Not only the music but the fashion accessories associated with this movement—safety pins used to mend gaping holes in clothing, hand-painted messages on T-shirts and jackets— revealed much about this particular urban subculture at this point and place in history.

punk image of the Sex Pistols in the late 1970s, and a revival of the mod look for New Wave bands in the early 1980s.

MUSIC CONSUMPTION

Music is consumed in some way in every small town and every large mega-lopolis in America, either by buying CDs or going to see live music shows. Let's examine some specific urban areas to see how they handle music production in their environment. Since making culture has become an important function of every urban area, how a city goes about producing culture should be unique in each instance. To try to show the diversity in the world's music production and the cities that sponsor that production, we shall begin our examination by looking at specific styles that predate Western music. Music is made throughout the world, but in this chapter we will be concentrating mainly on Western musical styles to try and make this information relevant to Western college students.

As we examine history, we find that China began a bureau of popular music in the Han dynasty in 120 B.C.E. to monitor and collect popular songs of the day, because the dynasty understood the power music had over the masses to transmit ideas and sentiments about society and government. Cities and provinces were the collection points for the Chinese Bureau of Popular Music, because these were the natural centers of musical activity in China. There was also an interest in the social control of music, and the cities in China were the most important arenas to control music. If some objectionable musical content or style would cause trouble, it would be felt first in the cities. This tradition of monitoring urban music consumption is still practiced in Communist China, where threatening ideas in popular music are censored.

India's ancient indigenous music was also made in the provincial territories, with the major cities acting as collection points for musical styles and musical masters to practice their arts. Less bureaucratic than Chinese music, India's musical masters honed their art in rural areas but performed their important musical works in urban areas in front of royal courts and large crowds. A more formalized system of music making than in China eventually developed among India's master musicians. These masters transmitted the regional ragas (specific song forms) to the varied societies within the Indian subcontinent (Punjab, Sinalese, Madras) which valued the music for entertainment. Cities had what the music creators needed to sustain their art—paying students and paying audiences. So, as we work through Western examples we should keep in mind the long and significant histories of other music traditions in non-Western societies (Turley 2000).

For Western music, let's begin with European classical music and the urban influence on classical music at two different time periods. From the seventeenth to the eighteenth century, Vienna, Austria, was the center for innovative composers and musicians.

One of these composers, Wolfgang Amadeus Mozart (1756–1791), was the son of a demanding father, who was a musician and composer that had traveled around the courts of Europe with his son, a young musical virtuoso and performing oddity. This training and exposure to the royal courts was invaluable for the young Mozart, but it was his life in Vienna that made him the memorable historical figure he is today. Competition for the royal court's patronage and access to Vienna's famed Opera House was fierce, and no other city had the depth of talented composers as Vienna. Mozart's exposure to court norms and tastes made him a popular choice for court composer.

Theory Break: Again, this is an example of "key function," where Vienna's dominance of the musical art culture in the region draws the talented artists from other areas to that city. More opportunities are generated in these dominant cities for artists and creativity, because a dominant or key function city draws patrons and venues as well as artists to the city. Production becomes more centralized, with the dominant city taking resources from a less dominant city's production into auxiliary cultural production. This happens for a couple of reasons. In a city dominant in music production, the less dominant surrounding cities in the region may begin to specialize auxiliary areas of music production, like instrument construction, to supply the need of the dominant city (which may be so expensive to live in that mere instrument craftsmen couldn't afford to live there). While no memo from the dominant city was issued to the less dominant city saying "make instruments—not symphonies," the economics of the urban hierarchy was surely plain enough for artists to know that they should travel to the dominant city for composing and performance, while auxiliary producers of instruments had to spot the niche that they should fill in a smaller nearby city.

Returning to Mozart, no one would deny the genius of his compositions, but it is equally true if Mozart had been a small-town choir director in the far reaches of Finland, rather than in Vienna, his genius would be unrecognized. The urban environment allowed Mozart to explore fanciful themes in his operas (a magic flute, a sultan's harem) that would have been taboo in more conservative and provincial areas. Vienna's community of composers and musicians also provided Mozart a rich heritage of the previous Viennese masters like Franz Joseph Haydn to draw from (Grout and Palisca 1996). At the same time, this dominant music city brought other musical traditions to Vienna that went well beyond the great masters. Vienna in the eighteenth century was a very diverse urban art community. Francis Steven of Lorraine, a Frenchman, was the emperor; Pietro Metastasio, an Italian, was Vienna's imperial poet; Johann Hasse, a German, was its opera master; and Giuseppe Bonno, born in Vienna but educated in Italy, was the Imperial Kapellmeister (Grout and Palisca 1996). Combining these other musical heritages with Vienna's illustrious past brought about challenging new forms of music and made them acceptable to musically educated patrons and audiences.

Creative composers and musicians fascinated Vienna's royal court and bishop, and this fascination became the conspicuous consumption of the ruling elite in Vienna, which supported a growing number of composers and musicians that eventually became an urban community of musicians. For this time period, the rich already possessed palaces and fancy clothes, so they chose to conspicuously or visibly consume music to display their wealth and taste. This was done through the commission of specific music for weddings, funerals, and celebrations, as well as having the great composers give the family private music lessons or performances. The ultimate expression of conspicuous consumption by the elite was to have one's own orchestra.

A "Vienna sound" was created by this urban community of musicians that was different from Rome's religious-influenced operas or France's musical theater. The music direction that Vienna took was *not* because of one patron (like the bishop or king) or due to one musician, but of the *entire* community of musicians. Ludwig van Beethoven (1770–1827) was part of this community of musicians and is painted by history to be a difficult and recalcitrant recluse who dealt with his growing deafness by shutting out the world. The city of Vienna played a bigger role in Beethoven's life and music than most biographies have illustrated for music fans. For classical music fans of our time, Beethoven has achieved mythical stature due to his musical genius and haunting symphonies, but there was an entire urban music community that recognized the temperamental genius of Beethoven. One of the key figures to recognize Beethoven was Mozart, who allowed the young Beethoven an opportunity to give him a private recital. This community of musicians and patrons supplied him with court commissions, students to give lessons to, and fellow musicians that also believed in his music enough to perform it. The last element of the social urban influence on music is the chance for performing in front of an audience. Performance is what has separated Beethoven's compositions from those of dozens of fellow composers at this same time that we *don't* remember because their works have not been continually performed. Musicians that performed Beethoven's music, patrons that supported him, and the crucial audience that received his compositions are urban elements contributing to Beethoven's success in Vienna.

RACE AND CLASS IN URBAN MUSIC PRODUCTION

The two sociological relationships that haven't been dealt with in our discussion of music so far are race and class. Overwhelmingly, it is affluent white people that support, perform, and consume classical music in the United States and Europe.[1] White music patrons may place the opera house or cultural and performing arts center in the downtown of a city, but the music featured at such venues is for a white middle- to upper-class consumer. As a further illustration of the impact that class has on the culture in your own hometown, think of your local symphony hall or orchestral venue. If it is not at the local university, then the city probably built the hall for rich, white

---

[1]Not to diminish the contributions of Asian and African American classical musicians, but classical music is still the music of the upper class, which is predominantly white.

people to listen to music composed by Bach and Mozart and performed by the local symphony. The symphony orchestra is paid by city tax dollars with state and federal grants and some private contributions.

Theory Break: This is important from a Marxist perspective. Marxists who study the city and culture would say that the importance lies in the working-class money being used to fund the entertainment of the wealthy. The cost of the purchase of land downtown for such symphony halls and opera houses could have been used for hospitals, schools, or libraries. Without asking the working class (who are rarely elected municipal officials), the local government usurped the tax dollars of all city residents and spent it on the musical tastes of the wealthy.

To think about it from another angle, most Americans prefer country, rap, pop, or rock music and have probably attended few or no classical music events in the past five years. Yet, the local city council hasn't devoted land, funds, staff, and budget for the local musicians to play any of these types of music for the public, despite the preference of most urbanites. These tax abatements and government subsidies for music performances would be helpful to any venue owner, including the clubs that play the music most people prefer, but the funds are devoted only to the support of classical music. Clearly, class and race are important components of the position of classical music in our modern city.

New Orleans, Louisiana

The development of jazz in New Orleans is an example of the intersection of history, race, class, and urban design. Having a unique history of French influences (along with some Spanish) in the early 1800s,[2] New Orleans's society was stratified with white French landholders on top, slaves on the bottom, and a middle class of mixed-race free men. The urban history of this group of mixed-race free men and women becomes crucial in understanding the city and for understanding jazz. In the East Coast colonies of the Americas, the "religious" colonists abused their female slaves and continued to enslave the offspring of these unions. In New Orleans, the offspring of French and African unions[3] were granted a special middleman minority[4] status (Blalock 1967). Over a period of time, this middleman group grew and took up residence in the French Quarter of New Orleans, with white French fathers often providing money, housing, and education—if not their name to their children. The niche these middleman groups filled were the merchant and skilled service jobs that New Orleans rich whites didn't want to do, and the African slave class couldn't do.

---

[2]Rather than a Puritan colony of English settlers.

[3]Another example of middleman groups are Japanese laundry owners or gardeners in the 1920s.

[4]A middleman minority is a racial or ethnic group that performs service-sector functions between the most subordinate and the dominant group.

A middleman minority and the area of New Orleans that this group dominated created a unique space in the city for culture to develop; this space was the French Quarter. But, it wasn't until after the Civil War and the imposition of Jim Crow laws (which served to reduce the Creole society to the same social level as former African slaves) that the urban space in New Orleans was able to incubate a new type of culture. Prior to the Emancipation Proclamation, slaves in French New Orleans were granted more freedom than in the Eastern colonies under British or U.S. rule. These freedoms included a free assembly of slaves on Sundays, where Africans kept many of their musical and cultural folkways alive (Turley 1995). French colonies were mandated to maintain brass bands for morale, a mandate that put Africans in possession of brass instruments in an unstructured environment.

The outcome of these freedoms was a protojazz movement of African American musicians with exceptional talents but little formal music training (Turley 1995). Creoles, displaced from the New Orleans social order by Jim Crow laws, were educated and did have musical training, often concentrating their careers on music lessons, church music, and ragtime piano music. Black musicians lived in Uptown New Orleans, several miles from the Creole French Quarter at the turn of the twentieth century, but both groups of musicians were drawn to the Storyville red-light district (just above the French Quarter and the docks on the Mississippi). Brothels, bars, and clubs were common in Storyville, and the patrons were not limited to sailors and river men, but to others in New Orleans as well. Music was the element that kept patrons entertained in the bars and in the nightclubs while waiting for rooms at the brothels. For black musicians, it was an opportunity to play music and get paid, but for Creole musicians, brothels and clubs were a social step down from the churches, conservatories, and concert halls that they were accustomed to.

The urban connection for this mixture of history, race, and music was the appropriation of urban space for nightclubs and music to grow in Storyville and the French Quarter. To these areas, black musicians brought a rich heritage of improvised protojazz music and talent. Creole musicians brought musical literacy and the orchestration of the European-style music. When combined, these two musical heritages made Dixieland jazz. While the beginnings of jazz bands were in many places in the South at the turn of the twentieth century, it was the urban areas of New Orleans, in the French Quarter, that brought Creole and black musicians together in a musical laboratory to refine New Orleans jazz, and even more importantly, *write the music down on paper.*

New Orleans's commanding presence at the mouth of the Mississippi River meant that all trade and culture on the river either leaves or enters through New Orleans. Dixieland Jazz, which is a mixture of jazz and ragtime, quickly moved up the river from 1905 to 1915 making important stops in Memphis, Kansas City, and Chicago. In each of these cities, black musicians raised on the rural blues responded to jazz by creating bands of their own local, urban flavoring. Memphis managed to maintain a rhythm and blues flavor in its music to this day, due mainly to its stronger than average African American community. This community, the center of many "Negro Only" banks, insurance companies, and business groups that Jim Crow laws demanded in the South, was prosperous before the Great Depression. Unlike Chicago jazz, which kept its performance focus on white audiences, the jazz in Memphis was directed at the African American community.

A correlation has been drawn by sociologists between the new Italian and Sicilian immigrant communities of 1880–1920, the clubs they operated for organized crime, and the African American jazz music that they needed for their clubs. This group of new immigrants changed "male only" saloons into entertainment clubs for dates, drinks, and deviance; first in New Orleans, then in Chicago. This was a new cultural invention, the urban nightclub (Morris 1980). Before this invention, bars were awful places that only the worst social elements would frequent. Race, crime, and music eventually made the Chicago jazz scene of the 1920s what we think of as the "Roaring Twenties." The mobster's upscale nightclub, the black musician of jazz, and illegal alcohol were combined and pitted against the unpopular Volstead Act outlawing alcoholic beverages.

Sadly, this odd partnership ended when Prohibition ended, because jazz was no longer necessary to entertain in illegal speakeasies. In contrast, Kansas City maintained an illegal presence of untaxed booze, dirty politics, and mobster nightclubs throughout the Depression and World War II, with the jazz scene playing an important role. Therefore, in an industrializing urban environment where crime, racial separation, and music were present, early jazz music thrived. Jazz grew in many urban centers and absorbed the cultural characteristics of the urban environment around it. So, by the 1940s, jazz music sounded different when it was produced in Kansas City or Chicago than in New Orleans or New York. Each unique urban environment influenced the music that was created there.

MUSIC AS A CULTURAL ARTIFACT

Location of a city matters to the city's inhabitants and to the type of production that the city can engage in. A port city needs accessible waterways as an example, and the layout of roads, bridges, and train tracks can be crucial to any city's survival. An extreme example might be that Denver, Colorado, isn't going to be a major player in the ocean tanker construction market, because it isn't on an ocean port and is in fact a mile above sea level. In this section, we are going to examine the impact of location on East Coast and West Coast rap music.

While there is some spirited debate as to the true origins of rap, one clearly identifiable root of rap is the spoken and sung poetry and music of New York's Gil Scott-Heron. In Scott-Heron's work we hear the rapid rhythmic speech that will come to identify modern rap music as well as a bitter, sarcastic, and Afrocentric view of America that will also define much of early rap music from New York City. Grandmaster Flash, Fab 5 Freddy, and the Sugarhill Gang were New York City's innovators in the early 1980s, where rap music was a party music for the African American and Puerto Rican communities. Few other urban communities were aware of rap music, but the uniqueness of this urban art form was soon going to be exploited by the pop music industry.

The rap world might have stayed in the five boroughs as an indigenous music form if it wasn't for two songs: The Sugarhill Gang's "Rapper's Delight" and New Wave star group Blondie's number one hit, "Rapture." The party anthem "Rapper's Delight" was an excellent example of New York City's ethnic community rap music. Boastful and witty, the Sugarhill Gang's song became a party standard in New York. In the midsection rap of "Rapture," a song that in other respects resembles other New Wave hits of the 1980s, Blondie references Fab 5 Freddy, who helped to construct the rap section and appeared in the video. Blondie's song was the first mainstream song to feature rap in any way. As an interesting sidebar, New York avant-garde artist Jean Michel Basquiat also appeared in the video as a DJ.

While created as primarily party music, the African American community in New York soon found that rap music was a very effective way of communicating to their urban community. Like the political imagery employed by Gil Scott-Heron, New York City's Public Enemy began to use rap music as a way to render social commentary. At this same time, less political bands like Run-D.M.C. and other New York rap musicians were being offered major label record contracts as rap music's popularity was growing. Rap grew first in the African American community and then in Hispanic and white communities outside of New York State. Popular rap forms in the 1980s were still the party music format of New York City aimed at black audiences in the United States, but Public Enemy's underground popularity and an angrier style of rap music began to grow. On the West Coast, in Los Angeles, angry, real-life rap music was mirroring the bleak existence that was disintegrating African American neighborhoods in that city.

Gangsta rap wasn't formalized political discontent or an example of the leadership in the urban community (unlike Public Enemy, whose lyrics mirrored many civic and religious leaders' positions, including Reverend Al Sharpton and Louis Farrakhan). The anger and animosity of gangsta rap reflected the economic condition of urban black males, particularly in Los Angeles, who were turning to gangs and crime "to get paid." Music demonstrates the different urban feeling of America's two largest urban African American communities. New York's community was initially searching for entertainment from rap music and then political direction, and that was reflected in New York's rap acts.

For the Los Angeles community, rap music was a new form of expression that initially imitated the New York party music, but quickly changed to reflect the brutal lives of young people who were listening to the music. Rather than being escapist entertainment or political message, gangsta rap is the angry, dispossessed voice of young black men whose urban experience was one of drugs, violence, gangs, police abuse, weapons, and unemployment. Audiences responded immediately to the emotion of gangsta rap; the angrier the music, the more popular.

Other dispossessed communities in Los Angeles also used the powerful music form of rap to voice their discontent. Mexican Americans in particular blended the Spanish language and the rap form to create yet another new urban cultural form—Latino rap. Again, this community voiced its own angst about losing its Hispanic identity in an Anglo city, the threat of encroachment from guns, drugs, and gangs. Finally, Latino rap was an expression of macho identity through the voice of male Latin rappers, a common component to Hispanic culture. Puerto Rican rappers were crucial to New York's early rap community, but never found a national voice on a major label. Mexican American rappers had better luck when the music industry's attention shifted to Los Angeles to spotlight Latino rap.

In this instance, rap music is a cultural artifact urban researchers use to learn what a specific community thinks of their urban environment. From this artifact, we learn that the forces of poverty, unemployment, drugs, crime, and racism have produced two different musical responses in the two largest U.S. metropolitan areas. The reaction in New York City might be characterized as initially escapist, then turning political in its character. Los Angeles's rap music is more violent, angry, and unfocused on solutions for the urban community. Its message is a fatalism wrapped in the "gangsta" language of its violent streets. We can postulate too, that New York's more densely populated African American neighborhoods might produce music with a more specific message, either to forget about the urban conditions through partying or to organize and fight, politically, against a common enemy.[5] Los Angeles's neighborhoods are less densely populated, the rap music imported from New York becomes less fun and political, more a forum for anger, violence, crime, gang affiliation, misogyny, and drugs that are the realities of many distressed inner city neighborhoods.

URBAN MUSIC CONSUMPTION

People listen to music on the radio, computer, or CD player, in clubs, on elevators, and at concerts, to name a few of the most familiar places and methods of music consumption. The music industry highly regulates this consumption of music. The music we listen to on the radio, in elevators, and in dance clubs has been paid for in royalties to authors of the music through two large companies: ASCAP and BMI, who license the music for performance. At large touring concert halls, the bands you are listening to are most often the authors of many of their songs, but a license must be paid for any music that is not their own. When a CD is purchased, *you* have paid the record company, store, distributor, marketers, publisher, author, and finally the artist or performer for the right to listen to that music. The one place defying this juggernaut of corporate and legal control of music is the Internet,

---

[5]The "enemy" is much less well defined in rap music, but usually consists of some white power figure—police, government, and so forth.

where music is being traded and listened to without the royalties, fees, or licenses being paid. This unregulated music trade is an urban question of "place," since in all of the previous examples of music consumption there was a place of performance, a place of transmission, or a place of transaction or purchase. But, before we delve into a theory of place and a countertheory of capitalist domination, we need to understand the basics of music making.

They are still called "record" companies, these large multinational corporations, even though their business is the sale of CDs. Perhaps mislabeling them record companies has allowed the public to become blind to one of the most powerful economic oligarchies in the world. Despite a multitude of local and independent record labels across the United States and the world, the music industry is dominated by a few huge multinational companies, which sociologists refer to as transnational corporations (TNCs). These companies have offices all over the world, so much like the old British Empire that the sun never sets on these TNCs.

Of the music consumed by the world, these six companies control 80 percent of the artists and music. This means that whether it is rap, country, or even foreign bands like Ladysmith Black Mambazo, a South African vocal group, it is licensed and/or distributed through these companies. These TNCs work together to squelch competition from below by buying musical acts from smaller, local labels. This ensures the continued domination of pop music by these few companies. It also means that the cities that are the corporate headquarters of the TNCs are the dominant urban areas for popular music production.

We ascribe social meaning to places; they do not naturally have meaning. A sense of place is gained from what is most often experienced at that location. For instance, reverence at church or excitement at a football stadium gives these locations a social sense of place. We must remember that these experiences are learned from others and our reactions to these places are also learned from others (Pred 1983). This can be such a powerful social experience that our own sense of identity can be tied to a place, like our hometown or neighborhood, and extracting ourselves from this place can be difficult. A sense of place also includes people, objects, time periods, and culture that we associate with that place. These elements give place a sense of *agency*, so place isn't just where something happened, it had a role in the activity (Casey 1993).

To return to the Internet and our discussion of place, one of the ways that the music industry can control sales and licensing through the clubs, music stores, and radio stations is that all of these businesses take up physical

Parent Company	Subsidiaries
BMG	Arista, RCA Records
British Thorn/EMI	Polygram
Warner Entertainment Assoc.	Warner Brothers, Elektra, Atlantic
Universal	MCA, Motown, Geffen
Sony	Columbia, Epic
CEMA	Capital, Virgin Records

space in some urban location. The physical place can be found by the music industry and legal action can be taken against it, unlike the Internet, which is more difficult to stop because it exists in cyberspace.

LOS ANGELES, NEW YORK, AND NASHVILLE—
THE TRIUMVIRATE

These three cities rule the American musical landscape and, de facto, rule the world's musical landscape. New York was the first musical city giant. As the nation's largest city at the turn of the twentieth century, New York enjoyed the musical pull of Vaudeville, Broadway, and an emerging cultural powerhouse—

NAPSTER AND WHO OWNS DIGITAL MUSIC

Accusing Napster of copyright infringement violations, Metallica and their record label sued the Internet start-up company. Napster responded to the suit by claiming that their company just operated a Web site that offered free software to those online to make the music on their computer into MP3 files to listen to or share. No fees were charged to those online, thus the company made no money from the artists or their music. Napster claimed that individuals were sharing their music files, much like making a cassette recording, and that because Napster wasn't actually sharing or holding files they could not be held liable. The judge ruled that Napster did in fact facilitate the copyright violation of those that used the service, thus denying the record company, publisher, artist, and songwriters their fair compensation. Napster has now become a subscriber service, where users can pay a fee to download music from each other. However, the very week the decision was handed down, several new music-sharing sites were formed offering identical services. These new sites seem content to operate until sued by the music industry, and at this point, there may be too many different services to make that possible. A disturbing new tactic by the music industry is to sue individuals directly for sharing music files. To muddy the waters further, a Dutch court ruled that another music sharing site wasn't in violation of copyright laws, dealing the record industry its first major defeat on March 27, 2002.

The lesson for urban culture is that Napster was untouchable until it became so successful that it opened identifiable office space in a city. Many new companies similar to Napster plan to locate their service and offices outside of the United States, making them effectively immune from American courts and their decisions. If a business becomes too challenging to the music industry, that industry will try to find the offender's place of business to serve legal notice and threaten monetary damages. Urban place has an economic reality.

radio. The first major radio networks were based out of New York, and these chains of radio stations would broadcast the same programs that would originate from New York to its subsidiary stations across the nation. The original radio soap operas (brought to listeners by soap manufacturers), comedy programs, and adventure serials were begun in the Golden Age of Radio in New York City. Orson Welles was able to frighten a large section of the east coast with his radio network broadcast of "War of the Worlds," about an alien invasion, so scary and real to listeners that some thought the show was an actual news broadcast. In the Jazz age (1920–1940), most major recording was done in New York because of the proximity to the radio networks. The huge urban population, along with the recording studios, record labels,[6] and urban radio stations, contributed to the beginnings of swing, bop, and cool jazz.

Only one type of music eluded New York's hegemonic control of the radio waves in the 1930s and 1940s—Country and Western music. The Grand Ole Opry, a historic concert hall in Nashville, Tennessee, broadcasted its own radio programming that was an authentic mix of country, bluegrass, folk, and western trail music. This one program lent a voice to the millions of Americans who preferred Ernest Tubb and Hank Williams to the jazz and pop standards of New York City. This style of programming began to erode the fierce grip New York had on American radio. The elements that make Nashville special at this time were its central geography to the Appalachian Mountains and the Southeast, where country music found its first audience, and the large number of musicians living in the Nashville area. These musicians started their own record labels that were distributed from Nashville, and eventually the city became the seat of country music power and remains that way today. The Dixie Chicks are one of the most successful acts in country music today, but to get a record contract and become famous they had to leave their hometown of Dallas, Texas, and move to Nashville to make it. Lyle Lovett, George Strait, and Clint Black all have similar Texan backgrounds, but they had to move their careers from Texas to Nashville to become famous. That's where the labels, studios, distributors, and promotional machinery for country music is located and to make it in the business, you must be near those elements. *Theory Break*: Performing the key function in country and western music, Nashville drew musicians away from other urban areas.

Los Angeles fits into this diagram of urban music cities as the most dominant city in modern America. Originally, the music industry in Los Angeles grew around the movie industry, serving it with personnel and technicians to make the grand musicals of Warner Brothers and MGM in the 1940s and 1950s. Quickly, however, the big singing stars of the movies wanted to make records in Los Angeles, rather than back in New York, and a new group of major record labels grew out of the California desert. With a growing population of its own and the distribution channels of the film industry to take advantage of, the L.A. record business flourished, taking advantage of the stars and advertising that Hollywood had to offer.

---

[6]A resource that *very* few cities had at the time.

Soon, rock and roll music filled the recording studios of Los Angeles, and to a slightly lesser degree in the late 1960s, the recording studios of San Francisco. Records and the live music industry changed the music habits of the nation. As the people of the nation went West, the culture of America shifted as well. Emphasis on change, mobility, and youth culture took over America with a generation raised on television and rock and roll—the baby boomers. These changes also reflect a new feeling in the nation toward the West and the South as the urban areas of new cultural innovation.

THE SUN BELT MIGRATION

The Sun Belt migration (1967–1977) was precipitated by many events in the nation, not the least of which was the growing dissatisfaction with the urban realties of the Northeast. Large northeastern cities like New York, Boston, Detroit, Chicago, and Philadelphia (in cooperation with midsized cities like Pittsburgh, Cleveland, and Buffalo) were the industrial might of the nation for a hundred years. But, these cities had become dense and unmanageable, and suburbanization had failed to alleviate these symptoms for the cities' residents and businesses. Lured by the lack of major urbanization, the hostile environment to unions in the right-to-work states, and tax abatements promised by Sun Belt cities, the jobs of the Northeast were moved to the Sun Belt. The people followed and the Sun Belt began to boom with prosperity and sprawl. New electric power plants and highways, and the affordability of air conditioning, made the South and West very attractive to business and job-seekers. Not only did power, water, and roads look attractive, but also large houses with larger lots, no state income taxes, no snow, and new schools made the Sun Belt seem like the urban promised land. Through the 1970s and 1980s, the South and West (the Sun Belt) was the promised land. Talk about city growth—cities exploded in these states with jobs and new immigration enjoying all the amenities of the Sun Belt.

Unfortunately, all of the new immigrants to the Sun Belt overloaded the region's cities with suburban sprawl, highway gridlock, and eventually soaring taxation. Southern and western cities began to have the same cultural problems as the big northeastern cities with crime and congestion, but the real sin of the Sun Belt enlargement was the increase in taxation. Culturally, the immigrants to the Sun Belt thought they could have the prosperity of the area without the taxes, but new demands on a city necessitate new taxes. With the complicity of the federal government, trade tariff agreements like GATT and NAFTA (and the proposed FTAA), made the jobs in the Sun Belt only last a short twenty-five years before they moved farther south to Mexico or to Asia.

STYLE, SOUND, AND CITIES

Though the music industry is controlled from the three-city triumvirate of Los Angeles, New York, and Nashville, other cities in America are often "mined" for unique sounds and styles. The music industry is constantly trying to anticipate the next urban trend, and that trend is often found in smaller cities. So, the music industry sends representatives out to these smaller urban environments to capitalize on the musical innovations found there and bring them to the triumvirate for recording and production.

Seattle, Washington

The biggest event of the 1990s from an urban music scene[7] perspective was the explosion of "grunge" music from Seattle, Washington. A reaction to the hair bands and image bands of the packaged "pop" music world, Seattle's flannel-clad "anti-image" bands were the dose of reality rock music fans had been longing for. Some might argue that the flannel and anti-image of Seattle's Nirvana, Soundgarden, and Temple of the Dog was in fact a manufactured image as well, but music fans didn't seem to care. Grunge music was loud, but not as loud or angry as heavy metal. It was anti-image conscious, but not as reactionary as punk music, and grunge was commercially clever without being as polished as the pop rock groups on major record labels. Being removed geographically from Los Angeles didn't save Seattle from eventually being consumed by the major labels, because that is what a dominant industry does—looks for other urban cultures to appropriate. *Theory Break*: Appropriate is a concept borrowed from Marxist theorists in which a dominant culture seizes pieces of a subordinate culture to use for its own goals.

Before the record labels came, Seattle had an urban music scene that was one of the most dynamic in the country, and which gave birth to an entirely new kind of music. Seattle is a shipyard and industrial city. With a working-class history of unionization and labor independence that is behind its uniquely avant-garde sound, the musicians created a more thoughtful and introspective, yet aggressive music. Musicians in Seattle that were free of pop constraints from Los Angeles created a Seattle sound that was just like their city: brooding, intense, and antiestablishment. The urban environment of Seattle created the clubs, musicians, independent record labels, and audiences that are critically important to any music scene. Seattle's dark atmosphere and nonflashy, working-class population helped to make this city's music institutions reflect the city's character. As the major labels invaded

---

[7]A music scene exists when there is present a large enough group of musicians and audience members to sustain a diverse group of venues and musical styles, while encouraging the growth of auxiliary businesses like recording studios, poster shops, record stores, and eventually independent record labels.

Seattle in the 1990s to gobble up every band and record label they could expropriate from Seattle, these major record labels were in effect taking Seattle's urban culture and selling it to a national market. Grunge or alternative music changed America's listening habits in rock music and pop music, as the Seattle urban sound influenced all other urban music scenes in America.

Miami, Florida

Another urban area's music scene that has a growing international importance is Miami, Florida. The city's demographic history has made it the center for Latin pop music. Brazilian samba music, Puerto Rican salsa, Afro-Cuban pop, and Latin pop have all found a home in Miami's diverse music scene, and the world's record labels have set up offices in Miami to try to reach the Spanish-speaking market. Known for its Cuban community, Miami also has a large Mexican, Dominican, Central American, and South American population as well. The demographic makeup and size of Miami have made it the Hispanic culture connection point for the United States to the rest of the world's Spanish speaking countries.

Beginning with the many years of Miami-Havana connectivity during colonial Spanish rule, Miami and Havana enjoyed a special relationship as the shining urban jewels in the Caribbean. Spanish settlers in the United States found Havana to be a welcoming destination, while it was under an American puppet dictatorship until Castro's revolution. After that, the dynamic was mainly of Cubans trying to get to the United States and Miami (a stronghold of anti-Castro sentiment). The rest of the Latin American world has found Miami to be the city that connects Western markets to Latin American markets. Spanish-speaking business and cultural communities have often sought out Miami as the way to connect the Latin American world to the United States. So, as the Latin invasion of Gloria Estefan, Marc Anthony, and Ricky Martin has gripped the U.S. pop music scene, it has been Miami that has been the city to make the "buzz" about their careers.

Both Marc Anthony and Ricky Martin have strong ties to Puerto Rico. Ricky Martin toured Latin America with the teen group Menudo and Marc Anthony has had a distinguished career as a celebrated salsa composer in New York City. However, it was Miami and its throngs of adoring fans that fueled their crossover success. One might be tempted to attribute Miami's urban position strictly to demographics—that a large Hispanic population has led to its unique position. That would be missing the dozens of other cities in America that have large Hispanic populations but do not enjoy Miami's special U.S.–Latin American connection. *Theory Break*: Wilson and Portes (1980) developed their enclave theory to explain Miami's urban population's success. In this immigrant enclave theory, the new urban immigrant seeks out his own ethnic and cultural group (in this case, Cubans seek out fellow Cubans in Miami's Little Havana area), and in this new area they can work with fellow immigrants that own businesses in the city. Being a newcomer isn't a serious impediment because their fellow immigrants will take care of them. This is why Cubans have succeeded, according to Wilson and Portes.

Austin, Texas

The small capital city of Austin, Texas, had typical southern demographics, a dominant elite white population that dictated the urban landscape to the rest of the city's races and classes. A segregated African American community was forced to occupy the city's east side and a Hispanic community was relegated to the city's south side. Each community consumed music and made music within the urban boundaries assigned to it, whites controlling the large concert halls for classical music and touring country music acts, while local country performers played in honky tonks at the city limits. The African American community had juke joints, barbeque and rib houses, and roadhouses for the traditional blues men and rhythm and blues acts to perform in, as well as black radio stations devoted to black musical tastes. Hispanics had clubs and outdoor venues for Tejano and Spanish-language music, which was tolerated because they were deep in the Hispanic neighborhoods, virtually unknown to whites (Turley 2000).

Musicians did not cross these ethnic lines; white musicians played for white audiences and in white clubs and the other ethnicities knew to do the same. This was the urban picture for most of America's culture, not just the South's formal apartheid laws, but also the North and the West, with informal sanctions[8] by club owners and audiences that did not think highly of "mixing the races" and would use these informal sanctions to keep the races apart. The young, white musicians that were coming to the University of Texas in the early 1960s were interested in the folk music movement and rock music of their day, not in the traditional country or blues of their parent's generation. Because no rock clubs existed, and the only country folk music bar was on the outskirts of town, white college students approached the Tejano and black bars in town to let them have a college "rock–folk night" that would bring in college listeners, yet would be on a night that wouldn't offend their regular customers (Turley 2000). At the same time, young college musicians began to start their own clubs in abandoned warehouses and old homes to serve the college crowd, a relatively gutsy move for young kids with little money.

Whether it is Austin's naturally open-minded urban character or just plain luck, the nightclubs in the city eventually began to feature many types of music on the same stage, on the same night. This cultural innovation came

---

[8]Informal sanctions are those measures taken by ordinary citizens rather than formal social institutions; these include ignoring the offenders and shunning them, but may also include threats, intimidation, and physical violence.

from the Austin college rock tradition, where college kids in black and Hispanic clubs often played rock and folk music, followed on the same stage by black and Hispanic musicians. A cross-pollination of cultures took place on Austin's stages. This cross-pollination affected country music in Austin first, as rock musicians like Janis Joplin left Austin in the late 1960s to follow the larger urban rock culture of San Francisco, leaving country musicians with a host of new influences from the blues, rock, and Tejano communities.

However, even when record executives ventured to Austin from Nashville to experience the local talent, they found a sometimes hostile group of musicians, who lacked the desire to mold themselves into the successful musician image of Nashville. These musicians had found a place in Austin, a city that appreciated and admired them for their odd influences and daring music, and they weren't interested in leaving. Willie Nelson and Michael Martin Murphey had escaped Nashville and Los Angeles, respectively, to come to Austin to participate in the raw and untainted urban culture of Austin. In this way, Austin's more free and accepting urban culture brought specific country musicians to the city, away from the more dominant music industry cities because of the unique music culture.

By the early 1980s, the musical styles had changed and white musicians began to flock to the historically black blues clubs of the east side to see the "real thing." It was here that guitarists like Jimmie and Stevie Ray Vaughan received their tutelage from blues masters like T.D. Bell and Long John Hunter. It was Stevie Ray Vaughan who attracted the eye of impresario John Hammond, who had discovered Billie Holiday and Bob Dylan, as a blues guitar talent worth recording and promotion. After releasing an album and making a cameo on a David Bowie album, Stevie Ray Vaughan's guitar playing became the signature sound of Austin. Despite Vaughan's untimely death in 1989, he has become a blues legend and the blues guitar sound he created is inextricably linked to the Austin, Texas, music scene.

So what is a music scene? A music scene differs from a music community (a small, unorganized group of musicians that might be found in any city) in four important ways. First, there is racial crossover, where musicians of one race feel comfortable and welcome making music in a club dominated by another race. Clubs are stratified, in which there are venues that bands start out at and then succeed to better venues. In the city and at the clubs, there are several different kinds of music being performed on a regular basis. And finally, a music scene gives rise to auxiliary businesses that service the music scene (recording studios, music instrument shops, poster artists, and so forth).

Music has a social component to its creation and production. For modern musical production, the social component (race, class, industrialization, social networking) is organized within the urban environment. Musicians create and work in cities long before they become national entertainers, the dynamics of the city influence musical production and the music itself. Once music becomes a national or international product, the dominant music industry cities (New York, Los Angeles, and Nashville) control the creation, recording, publication, distribution, and payment of American music and the world's music.

References

BLALOCK, HUBERT. 1967. *Toward a Theory of Diversity Group Relations*. Wiley: New York, NY.

CASEY, EDWARD. 1993. *Getting Back Into Place*. Indiana University Press: Bloomington, IN.

DURKHEIM, EMILE. 1895. *The Division of Labor in Society*. MacMillan (1933): New York, NY.

DURKHEIM, EMILE. 1915. *The Elementary Forms of the Religious Life*. Free Press (1965): New York, NY.

FINNEGAN, RUTH. 1989. *Hidden Musicians*. Cambridge University Press: Cambridge, England.

FRITH, SIMON. 1987. *Art into Pop*. Methoen and Company: New York, NY.

GROUT, DAVID, AND CLAUDE PALISCA. 1996. *A History of Western Music, Fifth Ed.* Norton: New York, NY.

HARVEY, DAVID. 1996. *Justice, Nature and the Geography of Difference*. Blackwell: Cambridge, MA.

PRED, ALLEN. 1983. "Structuration and Place: On the Beginning of Sense of Place and Structure of Feeling." *Journal of Theory of Social Behavior*. Vol. 13, pp. 45–68.

MORRIS, ROBERT. 1980. *Wait Until Dark: Jazz in the Underworld 1880–1940*. Bowling Green University Press: Bowling Green, OH.

TURLEY, ALAN. 1995. "The Ecological and Social Determinants of the Production of Jazz in New Orleans, c. 1900." *The International Review of Aesthetics and Sociology of Music*. Spring Edition.

TURLEY, ALAN. 2000. *Music in the City*. Duckling Publishing: Austin, TX.

WILSON, KENNETH, AND ALEJANDRO PORTES. 1980. "Immigration Enclaves: An Analysis of the Labor Experiences of Cubans in Miami" *American Journal of Sociology*. pp. 295–316.

CHAPTER FIVE

Art and Sculpture

Often referred to as the "Golden Age of Civilization" (500–400 B.C.E.), ancient Greece was a unique period of urban growth. Cities were minination states, and the nationalistic identities that modern humans think of (American, Chinese, Mexican, and so forth) were at this time urban identities—Athenian, Theban, or Spartan. Called city-states, these small urban empires were the cradle of Western civilization, and their unique organizational philosophies have come to form many of our modern opinions about how our governments and societies should operate. The ideal of Athenian participatory democracy and the severe militarism of the efficient Spartan state came from the city-state period of Greek history. Some of these ideals would return in the political ideas of Rousseau and in the Constitution of the United States, but others would recur in the military horror of fascist states of the 1940s and military dictatorships up to the present day. At the time of the Greek city-states, art and sculpture came to embody and represent the political and social ideals of the city-state. Athenian urban sculpture embodies such ideals; for instance, the achievements of man toward the goal of being near the gods. So, gods were represented in human form in Athenian urban sculpture, with figures of men trying to please and ascend to the level of gods. The Parthenon and Athena's temple on the Acropolis occupy the best space on the highest ground in Athens, because these sculpted buildings represented the ideals of the gods, particularly ideals like beauty and learning. For theorists like Durkheim, urban sculpture would be an attempt to hold on to ideals of mechanical solidarity, in which the entire society was organized around commonly held beliefs.

ANCIENT GREECE

The most famous single example of Greek urban sculpture would be the statue of Zeus in the city of Olympia around 438 B.C.E. Only written accounts of the statue's beauty exist, but clearly a 40-plus-foot statue of the god Zeus certainly made an impression on quite a few ancient authors and is considered one of the Seven Wonders of the Ancient World. Beautiful and awe inspiring, the statue of Zeus was made by Phidias (490–430 B.C.E.), the sculptor of the ivory statue of Athena that graced the Acropolis in Athens and the designer of the Parthenon, as well as several other temples at the Acropolis. Zeus's image was also a point of pride for the new Athenian empire that Pericles (495–429 B.C.E.) had fashioned from the chaotic city-state he inherited. In the same way that the Parthenon celebrates the military victory of the Greeks over the Persians to unify the Greek citizens in support of this victory, the urban sculpture of Zeus was designed to stir the growing feelings of nationalism in the Athenian city-state by exhibiting this huge piece of Greek artwork.

Civic pride regarding these large statues was a part of the growing Athenian identity. Nationalistic pride in the Athenian city-state or Spartan city-state was part of the city-state identity. Did sculpture accomplish all this alone? No, of course not, but urban art and sculpture were tools the new power structure used to celebrate all things Athenian and Greek. They had learned this lesson from their Egyptian predecessors; art, particularly big visual statements like sculpture, have a unifying effect on the population. It was unifying because the urban citizens had participated in its construction and appreciation. The large urban sculpture of the Greek period have a sociopsychological effect of inspiring city-state or nation-state identity in its urban viewer. Just as Herbert Gans (1962) discussed the importance of social networks, neighborhood identity, and the sociopsychological value of place in his Italian-American community, the art of sculpture was a way of instilling these values in the Athenian urban population. Sculpture was put on display for the citizen to admire and share in the sense of community that the figure embodied.

We also see in Athens a specialized group of urban laborers coming together for what would have previously been a pointless task—constructing art. Artists now have a full-time project, and because of the organization of the city,[1] they can make a living producing art. The artists joined another group of people that lacked a pragmatic function—those that took care of the temples and religious functions (priests). But, as we have learned, culture has an odd effect on human beings and these seemingly meaningless tasks actually form the basis of *all* important culture and social solidarity in

---

[1]Specifically, the city organizes and commissions art to be important in the city's landscape; it also has inadvertently organized a large potential population of art buyers in one area, making art sales easier.

URBAN SCULPTURE

Urban sculpture's first meaningful period would have to be attributed to the Egyptian Dynasties, which began in 3100 B.C.E. in the city of Memphis with the uniting of Upper and Lower Egypt. Forcing the city-states of Upper and Lower Egypt together into one kingdom made Memphis a natural location, being on the border of the two. Egyptian pharaohs that followed often built *entire* new cities to be their capitals, so they wouldn't have to share the urban space of the preceding pharaoh. Part of the architecture of an Egyptian capital were obelisks, statues, monoliths, pyramids, and buildings that were in fact supported by sculptured columns designed to honor the Egyptian gods in tandem with the pharaoh that had them constructed. These sculptural adornments served two cultural functions; one function was to glorify the pharaoh through pictographs and hieroglyphics, while the second function of the urban artwork was to strike awe and intimidation in the hearts of lesser citizens.

Whole bureaucracies of artists, scribes, and sculptors were part of the pharaoh's royal court and their job was to construct a larger than life set of sculpture and artwork to honor the pharaoh. These statues and sculptures would also act as the actual structure of the city by holding up buildings and temples. Art was not sheer adornment to these cities, but was in fact *the reason* the cities were constructed, so statues and obelisks were feature points of the city and sculptured columns with detailed art and hieroglyphics held up the roof of the important city buildings. Marxist theorists might point to this domination of urban landscape as an example of how the dominant class (Pharaoh, nobility, priests) uses art to represent their ideals and beliefs (what they called "superstructure"). Pharaohs wished to guarantee their immortality and the ideal that they were gods by constructing these lasting sculptures and the urban arenas to showcase them. Without the urban areas and urban sculptures they constructed, we wouldn't know of the pharaohs of the past. Our conception of major and minor figures of ancient Egypt are built on what we have discovered in the cities and the art that the pharaoh commissioned. The art and urban sculpture serves as cultural artifact, as well as part of urban design, by telling the story of battles, births, weddings, and funerals of elite figures in Egyptian history. So, in many ways the pharaohs' preoccupation with building cities and artworks to guarantee their immortality, ideals, and history seems to have paid off.

The most famous of Egyptian art and sculpture was devoted to the pharaoh's journey into the afterlife. Pyramids, wall paintings, sarcophagi, and death masks were all elements of the tombs that populated the cities of the dead that were built for the pharaohs and nobility.

Specialized job categories of workers lived in and worked in the cities of the dead, either as laborers or artisans, because for the Egyptian pharaoh death was just the next stage of his journey to the gods. The cities of the dead were devoted to guaranteeing his journey and guarding the tombs or pyramids of departed pharaohs. Egyptians had two specialized urban sculpture arenas, one was the pharaoh's new urban capital and the other is the one most familiar to Western eyes, his tomb. It is composed of art and sculpture for the pharaoh's journey from his tomb among the city of the dead to the heavens and the gods. In the tomb, the art and sculptured pieces represented important items, servants, and daily necessities the pharaoh would require in the afterlife, thus making artistry in the city of the dead a valuable skill to please the gods and pharaoh. It also meant a great deal of pressure for the artists of their day.

The Hollywood myth of Jewish slaves building the cities and pyramids of Egypt are historically inaccurate, although a large peasant labor class did develop to build the cities and pyramids of Egypt. We can see that their cultural belief in their religious system, with pharaoh at the top of this system on earth, brought a great deal of cohesion and solidarity from their shared cultural beliefs as Durkheim would predict. Without this solidarity, none of the cities, sculpture, art, or the pyramids could have ever been constructed. Again, this points to the value of an urban population and urban culture, if the society can be brought together by culture. Then the society could achieve greater tasks than could a smaller, fragmented society. Marxists would disagree and point out that the religious system was exclusively for the upper classes' benefit and that their great achievements were built by an early urban underclass not included in this "cohesive" afterlife.

ancient cities. The Greeks, and later the Romans, will combine these cultural elements into a powerful cultural force known as nationalism centered around the cities of Athens, then Rome. The idea that all member citizens play a part in the nation-state, that this nation-state is a good and powerful thing, and that this nation-state forms part of the individual's identity will all need to be inculcated into the urban city. Art will be the way the elites represent these ideas to a largely illiterate population.

What do artists and art faculty have to say about the production of their craft? In *Calliope's Sisters* (Anderson 1990) the author sets forth a cultural anthropologist's perspective combined with the work of art historians to explain the development, production, and meaning of art from ancient to modern societies. Art for the San (also known as the African Bushmen) served to enhance their daily life by decorating the objects of their day-to-day existence, their bodies, through body painting, scars, and tattoos, and also through their jewelry and clothing. By making household items, their clothing, and their bodies more attractive, they enhanced their lives through using art (Anderson, pp. 12–14). For Eskimo/Inuit/Athabascan culture, art was also important for their religious and philosophical worldview. Art was a way to transform realities and to illustrate a level of reality beyond appearance. Many stories, folktales, and religious parables in Eskimo culture revolve around the transformation of one thing into another, i.e., clay being formed into a man or the mythical raven (a key figure in Eskimo religion) changing into human form (p. 50). Transforming clay, wood, or bone into an artistic rendering of a bird or a bear, or into a toy demonstrated art's ability to transform, not just decorate. The use of art in religion is still one of the most important functions to this day. We use art to glorify our deities, show our commitment to them, and inspire reverie and awe in the congregation. Australian aboriginals to the Aztecs used art for these social functions, making an unseen god or afterlife seem tangible to the imagination of the community, through artistic rendering. The world's most valuable collections and most highly regarded artists have produced religious art for the Vatican (Leonardo da Vinci, Michelangelo, Rafael). This kind of art predates the city and the growth of urban communities, but its power to thrill and bind the masses truly grew as cities grew. Rome's commitment to first pagan, then Roman, and finally Christian art is an example demonstrative of the power art has to promote religious ideas, and the city became the way this art was commissioned, displayed, lent meaning, consumed by audiences, and standardized by the church. The city provided all of the necessary elements for religion's domination of art for centuries.

But what about art lends itself to the transforming religious expression of a society? Art's ability to represent beauty for human beings and its ability to embody the culture's values[2] has made art one of the central methods by which a culture expresses such qualities as beauty and goodness, and then religious evaluations of beauty and goodness through art. West African Yoruba's aesthetics combine the concepts of beauty and goodness as Japanese aesthetics combine the concepts of beauty and bliss and the Greeks combined beauty and truth; all of these cultures relied upon art to inform and educate the populace as to what was considered beautiful and how this beauty was related to other interpretation of art works' social values. Most of the time the representation, display, and education of these concepts were epitomized in a religious work of art. For the religious work of art to be most effective in the society, a city was needed to provide the display and education of the masses. Many of Africa's tribal societies had not urbanized and

---

[2]If a culture values loud, bright colors and random shapes that will be present in the art, the same way that Japanese values of simplicity and minimalism is found in their art.

that is why we find art and the culture varying so much in small geographic areas, while urbanized societies like the Greeks were able to standardize culture for their population.

As the Greek empire became more and more unified, and particularly under Alexander's rule, visible and accessible urban sculpture and art became a part of every Greek city and town. Its highly stylized and realistic looking figures appear in sculptured pillars that held up buildings, friezes that adorned the tops of these buildings, and figures that would stand alone in plazas to inspire the citizens. These sculptures were celebrations of Greek civilizations and achievements. Floors and walls became canvases for frescos and mosaics; art was everywhere in ancient Greece. The production of this art and sculpture was still a very *urban* phenomenon; because of the high cost of employing a sculptor or artist for months to years to complete these projects, only cities could afford these commissions. Few individual citizens could afford this artistic extravagance,[3] so municipalities (the former city-states) were often the patrons of this art and sculpture production. Early Greek states differentiated themselves by the number and quality of their city's public art, contributing to the urban idea that one city was better than another. With the display of art and sculpture in public places, two new urban ideas were being explored through art: first, the distinction between public and private life through the display of public art was explored by defining what we consume publicly, and second, the meaning of place was explored by displaying sculpture and art so people became attached to a place.

Clearly, the ideals of art and learning had an impact on Alexander the Great, who took Greek culture to all of the conquered territories in the known world. The apex of this fusion of Greek ideals in an urban setting would have to be the library at Alexandria in Egypt, often listed as an Eighth Wonder of the Ancient World. This would make Alexandria the most important city of its time in the Western world; it was the largest city of its age, and it contained the museum and library of Alexandria, as well as hosting the Pharos lighthouse (275 B.C.E.) in its harbor. (The lighthouse, 440 feet high, is considered one of the Seven Wonders.) (Asimov 1991, p. 72) While ancient writers have mentioned the Grecian architecture and mosaic floors of the library, it was its holdings of art, sculpture, and literature that made the library famous. Egyptian ruler Ptolemy II (308–246 B.C.E.) is credited with the construction of the library, which became famous for the hundreds of thousands of rolls of papyrus it contained—the sum total of Western thought of the time. Because of the museum and library, Alexandria becomes known throughout the ancient world as a city of learning and culture; in turn, this public image sparks more cultural production as the city provides the tools for cultural production (like the library) and social rewards for intellectuals and cultural artists. It is a reflection of the high esteem in which Greeks held

---

[3]Those that were able would most likely live in the city anyway.

Egypt[4] that many Greek scientists and scholars chose it to locate their research. Gotham's (2002) research into how cities market and promote themselves would point out that Alexandria was the first city to promote itself not as a center of marketing and political power, but as a center of cultural and intellectual production.

After Alexander's death, the Greek city-states fell into a devolutionary period of skirmishing, allowing the island of Rhodes in the Aegean Sea and Ptolemy III in Egypt to become the dominant trade and political powers in the Western world. Rhodes celebrates its trading strength in 275 B.C.E. with the dedication of the Colossus of Rhodes, another of the Seven Wonders of the Ancient World to be located in an ancient urban area. This gigantic urban sculpture was said to have a male figure so large that between his stance ships passed into the harbor of Rhodes. It was destroyed by an earthquake in 224 B.C.E. (Asimov 1991, p. 74) and little archeological evidence, other than written accounts, have been found of the statue. Ptolemy III's rule (246–221 B.C.E.) marks the last period of greatness for Egyptian rulers and Egyptian cities, yet Alexandria's importance as a cultural center never diminishes; despite political blunders made by subsequent pharaohs, its urban image as a center for culture and learning remained.

To summarize, the Seven Wonders of the Ancient World are:

1. The Temple of Artemis at Ephesus (500 B.C.E.?)
2. Zeus at Olympia (437 B.C.E.) by Phidias
3. Mausoleum of Halicurnassus, dedicated to Asia Minor ruler Mausolus (352 B.C.E.)
4. Colossus of Rhodes (275 B.C.E.)
5. Pharos Lighthouse at Alexandria (275 B.C.E.)
6. Hanging Gardens of Babylon by Nebuchadnezzar (600 B.C.E.)
7. Great Pyramid (2530 B.C.E.) built by Khufu or Cheops as it is referred to in Greek

THE ROMAN EMPIRE

With the rise of the Roman Empire (300 B.C.E.–476 C.E.), the Romans appropriated Greek art and sculpture, as well as Greek science, music, literature, philosophy, city planning, and religion. Because of this appropriation of Greek culture, that culture was spread throughout the Roman Empire as the model for urban art. Some have argued that art and sculpture progressed little during Roman times since their artists just copied Greek techniques, but the *scale* of art and sculpture progressed as both the amount and size dwarfed the Greek period. Some of this can be attributed to the city

---

[4]While a point of contention among modern scholars, some researchers like Martin Bernal contend that the Greeks were influenced by contact with the previous Egyptian Dynasties and that Egypt formed the basis of Greek culture.

planning and administration that the Roman authorities imposed on conquered territories. Roman design of plazas, streets, villas, palaces, and temples required sculpture and art to adorn them in Roman style. This increase in the availability of urban art made all art and sculpture more valuable to rural areas and small villages to increase their cultural urban images, thus increasing art and sculpture production and quality.

But it was in Rome that art and sculpture was taken to a new level. As we will see in Chapter Six, Romans became experts in the use of architectural form to drive home the importance of the empire and the need for nationalistic identity. The theme of "the leader is a god" that sculptors used in Egyptian times again resurfaces, as each Caesar is deified in imposing figures, busts, murals, friezes, and triumphant arches. Borrowing and increasing the number of gods from the Greek pantheon, Roman households were replete with gods and goddesses for the kitchen to the outhouse in paintings and figurines. The cityscape was also adorned with statues of gods and leaders; even relatively minor officials could have their image carved and immortalized, if they had the money. During the Roman period, we also see art as an example of conspicuous consumption for wealthy urbanites. Romans competed with each other to display the most current and ostentatious art and sculpture that they could afford. *Theory Break*: Marxists would point out that this exercise in art consumption was fueled by growing class divisions in urban areas, and the display of art was the preferred way of demonstrating one's class superiority.

When Constantine (Roman Emperor from 306 to 337 C.E.) converts to Christianity in 312 C.E., more for political survival than religious fervor, Roman art changes as does all art for many centuries. Art becomes a method of Christian religious expression, and with the state and church as one, other forms of artistic expression virtually die out. Art also becomes a tool for propagating and celebrating the religious state, whether that be the Pope's influence in Italian politics or the Catholic Church's influence on all European politics for two millennia. Sculpture loses its urban influence during this time, since many early church leaders see sculpture and idolatry[5] as the same. When there was some give in this strict interpretation of art, only images of a biblical nature were allowed, often as part of Cathedral construction or ornamentation. Cities themselves fell into disrepair and the glory of Rome's cities and capitals were lost in 1300 years of nation-state wars in what is modern-day Europe; we call this the medieval period and the worst of it is known as the Dark Ages. Cathedrals and the religious adornment of gargoyles, crucifixes, and stained glass windows, as well as manuscript illumination are certainly major cultural achievements in urban areas throughout Europe during this period, and individual talent and regional styles of urban art are allowed to grow in religious art. However, it was the Renaissance and

---

[5]Worship of an image or statue as a god.

the loosening of the Church's hold on art that signaled the next big break-through in urban culture.

THE RENAISSANCE AND CULTURE

Before the Renaissance could happen, European society needed to be shaken up some. The social hierarchy needed to be less ironclad (the rich in their place and the poor in theirs), there needed to be some social mobility

---

THE RENAISSANCE

The Renaissance in Europe (1453–1610 c.e.) is one of those watershed events that most of us today have trouble fully understanding, since the "Dark Ages" that preceded it was so closed (Cooke et al. 1996). There was little artistic change or dynamic talent in this period before the Renaissance because of the church's dominance of art. After the fall of the Roman Empire, when the cities fell, the church and a collection of small European nation-states had to maintain the cities that Rome had left to them. A nation's capital received some attention during this time and the tribute/taxes were often enough to repair and rebuild these capital cities. The church aided some city growth with cathedrals and artists commissioned by the church to adorn the cathedrals. Yet, it was a return to the city-state model during the 1400s in Italy that caused an explosion in art and sculpture. With the burgeoning of trade all over the globe, not just in India and Asia, but also the Americas, certain families began to get *very* rich. One of the things that these newly wealthy families desired was art and sculpture for their houses and cities. Families like the Medici of Florence, Italy, began to exert financial pressure on the art world during this time that could rival even the all-powerful Roman Catholic Church.

The fall of Constantinople in 1453 to the Ottoman Empire removes the last vestige of the old Western Roman Empire. Intellectuals from the former Byzantine or Eastern Roman Empire came westward sparking an explosion of learning, art, and culture in Western cities that had been cloistered by the church (Cooke et al. 1991, p. 96). The next year, movable type is refined by Johannes Gutenberg to meet the growing demand of the Roman Catholic Church's purchasable dispensations (a penitent could buy a church-blessed piece of paper to forgive their sins, a popular item). Trade, printing, and consumerism fueled the consumption of art by important families like the Medici and even less important wealthy patrons who could afford art and sculpture. Having art in one's home and sponsoring art became a sign of wealth and taste, plus the artistic work would cause one's family name to live on in the city where the art was displayed. Still, it must be made clear that the Church and European royal families were the most important patrons during the Renaissance; they commissioned the most important works we have from this period. Marxists would point to this as the Feudal Epoch, in which the nobility and church were complimentary institutions of class supremacy. The nobles ruled the illiterate serfs who worked on the nobles' land as share-croppers and the church reinforced the "godliness" of noble position. Even Lorenzo "The Magnificent" de Medici achieved his position in history as an art patron by first succeeding as a money lender and trading mogul, then becoming the lord of Florence, making the city the center of cutting-edge urban art, sculpture, science, and literature.

It is essential to remember the Renaissance as an age of exploration and discovery not only in art but in world discovery as well. Ferdinand and Isabella combined the kingdoms of Aragon and Castile into what we think of as Spain and launched exploration to the West by sponsoring Christopher Columbus's exploration of trade in India. The European discovery of the American continents was confirmed by Amerigo Vespucci in 1502, opening an entire new World for discovery and, sadly, exploitation. At roughly the same time as Ferdinand and Isabella of Spain were sponsoring new exploration in the Americas, they were starting the Spanish Inquisition in 1478 to punish the suspected "converted" Jews in their urban ghettoes (Cooke et al 1991). Portuguese explorers during the Renaissance found new passages and territories in Africa's Congo, reached Canton, China, and almost succeeded in circling the world, beginning in 1519 when Ferdinand Magellan sailed past South America's Cape Horn into the Pacific before dying in the Philippines in 1521. Yet, this exploration will lead to one of the holocausts of the millenia: the commercial exportation of slaves from African colonies. Cities of the Renaissance became the central organizing points for the new exploration and exploitation as well as the fruits of learning and art. Culturally, major European cities felt a boundless optimism for discovering new places and absorbing new learning. This is reflected in all of the culture of the Renaissance, a sense of "rebirth" in urban learning and culture.

for the talented members of the middle, merchant, and working classes to be able to acquire new skills, education, and wealth. Trade in and out of Europe had to be increased to allow for the importation of new goods and ideas from the Near and Far East so Europe's culture could progress. How does Europe accomplish the "setting of the stage" for the Renaissance? An urban plague. The Black Plague of 1348, combined with other epidemics of the time, had cleared out many of the cities of all classes of citizens. Now, it may seem odd that clearing out these cities could be good for urban culture, but removing some of the old can be necessary before the new can grow. The church and nation-states had tried to nurture these cities as examples of the status quo culture, but an odd thing happened due to the shortage of labor and dying nobility: redistribution of wealth. Unlike other epidemics that had victimized only the wretched masses of medieval cities, the Black Plague was more democratic about who it killed—25,000,000 Europeans, a quarter of the total population, noble and serf alike. Since other viral and bacterial plagues often necessitated human interaction to be transmitted, the nobility, families of the middle class, and wealthy merchant would abandon their homes in the city and travel to the country to avoid the previous plagues, which was a strategy that often worked.

This form of social avoidance didn't work during the Black Plague. Since fleas on the rodents in their house, on their livestock, and in their clothing were carried with the whole population to the country by both noble and peasant, the Plague often came with them. This depopulation of the cities at virtually every stratum of society led to property being shared amongst "poor" relations or squatted on by itinerant strangers when vacant because of the untimely death of its owner. These newly inherited relations and land-squatting strangers drove up the economic demand for fine foreign goods in an effort to obtain a new, expensive, and luxurious lifestyle for this new consumer class that grew at the end of the plague. With a more dynamic and wealthy middle and merchant class in the city, the push to have a wider assortment of goods led to revolutions in fashion—which we will discuss in Chapter Six. *Theory Break*: Functionalist theorists would say this is an example of the equilibrium in society. Things function most of the time with no gross exercise of power, but instead work through consensus of those in society. Until, that is, some disruption, like the Plague, requires new social arrangements.

For the Medici family of the Renaissance, their palaces were revered as architectural achievements (which we will also discuss in Chapter Six), their political power was enough to topple kings or influence the selection of the Pope, and their art and sculpture consumption includes a list of the most famous artists of the time, including Leonardo da Vinci and Michelangelo. Florence's most glorious sculptured figures stand, because of the Medici family's patronage. Florence was the urban capital of the Renaissance and its other great art works stand due to the patronage of the Bishops and Popes of the Roman Catholic Church. Throughout the city-states of Italy, wealthy urban families that survived the plague or became affluent because of the plague purchased art and sculpture for conspicuous consumption, as during the Roman period. This demand for art spurred creativity in the urban sculptors to outshine one another. Functionalist theorists would say that this competition between the artists made art improve in quantity and quality.

The Pope and Bishops could not let mere urban nobles overshadow the Church, so they were compelled to seek the most creative artists and dominate their time with projects for the Church. The art and sculpture from this period has a distinctive *urban* character. Painting frescos and sculptures from Florence became identifiable with the urban character of Florence from the Medici family's patronage. Venice, Genoa, and Rome had their influential families and artistic milestones, but Rome's papal influence was Florence's only real rival in art and sculpture. From an urban perspective, sculpture and art had changed from the Greek to the Roman era, then from the medieval to the Renaissance period, but in the Renaissance period, the urban city-state again became influential to art and sculpture. Like the Greek period, the Italian city-states of the Renaissance pitted urban city-states against one another to claim the best artists for their family, for their noble lord, and for their city. The sculpture of this time glorifies the family, city, and Church that sponsored the art, but also the citizen of the city that displayed the sculpture. Having the citizen identify and experience sculpture as *part* of their urban identity is certainly the new "trick" that Florence's sculptors and artists learn to perform during the Renaissance through the display of art. This identification reinforces the Medici family as the apex of the social hierarchy in the city for sponsoring the art and instills pride in the commoner of Florence, because that art is in his city.

THE BENEFITS OF URBAN CULTURE PRODUCTION

How someone feels about their city is a sociopsychological reaction. *Theory Break*: Herbert Gans (1962) writes that people growing up in a city or urban neighborhood (even a slum) will develop an attachment to and identity with that place. While loyalty to one's hometown might be decided in open warfare, art and sculpture became the means by which nobles instilled civic pride and culture. Now no one has given their life in battle for a sculpture; however, urban art festivals and urban culture can be used by an aristocracy to promote city-state loyalty. It is formed by the social interaction of the individual with the different groups and institutions of the city. Clearly, this is just one of the many identifications an individual can have: family, ethnicity, gender, class, occupation, neighborhood, city, state, and so forth.

The city also has an effect on the individual beyond a simple internal identification. The city organizes the physical environment, and groups of people within the city respond to that organization. This organization and group interaction impacts the individual and their psychological experience. For example, someone who has lived in a small town their whole life might find the buildings and different people and ethnicities of New York City intimidating, particularly the often inconvenient way one has to shop for household goods (having to go to a grocer for fruit, a bread store for bread or bagels, a butcher shop for meat, a fish shop for fish, and all the while having to deal with exotic and different cultures at each of these establishments). They might feel anxious and not feel a sense of belonging in the big city where the smaller, more confining society of a village or town will be more reassuring to them. Someone from New York City, who has grown up mastering the environment and different groups in the city, feels a strong sense of identification and belonging to the city. The inconveniences of New York City that might alienate others become sources of pride for a New Yorker.

A specific example of the impact of neighborhoods and the city on an individual's capacity for identification can be seen in urban gang culture. Many people might consider this a pathological sense of urban identification. In South Central Los Angeles, the streets of Compton and Crenshaw mark boundaries between rival gangs, whose members have determined that these street lines are worth dying for. Even more unusual is that their social and cultural lives also follow these urban boundaries, so much so that friends, dates, and even family members should only be chosen from one side of these boundaries or the other. People living only yards away across a street are deemed to be unworthy to associate with or worse—targets for violence—just because they live on the wrong side of the street.

For the production of culture, these boundaries have been recognized and recorded in the music of these neighborhoods. Musicians, a product themselves of this urban environment, have absorbed the social psychological message that these street boundaries actually mean something important. Rap group Cypress Hill embodies the mixed racial makeup of its neighborhood in Central Los Angeles by having both Hispanic and African American members in the group, and their lyrics speak of the importance of neighborhood (barrio), bilingual language (Spanglish) skills, and group (gang) identity. Tension with the police, random arrests, drug use and drug dealing, gang violence, racial profiling, and police violence that often have neighborhood members seeing the police as just a rival gang that represents rich white interests are consistent themes in Cypress Hill, the community, and Cypress Hill, the music group. Their music, a blend of R&B samples, rap sequences in Spanish and English, and Latin rhythms is also a product of their neighborhood experience. We don't generally think of the lowest urban classes as being able to produce culture, but music and art can come from the city's poorest areas.

Graffiti is the urban art of the disaffected city dweller. Roman cities had graffiti on their walls and arenas 2000 years ago, often scratched or printed there to laud the benefits of a local political candidate or cultural event. Yet, sometimes it was just a name that was scratched, painted, or scrawled there on a Roman wall. Why a name? Perhaps it was to combat the psychological effect of anonymity and anomie that the city can produce. *Theory Break*: Emile Durkheim (1984) discussed in his theory of societal organization a social pathology of anomie that would grip citizens in a modern society that was held together by organic solidarity. This would happen when a person would feel disconnected and not in touch with a group membership or identity in their lives; the city, despite its large number of people, would actually make the condition worse because of its anonymous and faceless set of interactions. So, a Roman citizen feeling anonymous and lonely needed to scrawl his name on a wall to prove his identity and that he was "there."

Today, graffiti is a much more prevalent, damaging, complex, artistic, illegal, and potentially dangerous vocation than ever before. While many might find it hard to recognize as "art," urban graphics called "graffiti" are a visual record of people who proclaim their existence, allegiance, and statements in this grandiose and impromptu style of art. The canvas of the urban graffiti artist is the urban landscape; rather than trying to reproduce the urban environment throughout, he *uses* it as his canvas and gallery; from trains to subways, walls to sidewalks, buses to bridges, the graffiti artists and their message is constantly among us. These public "galleries" of their artwork force the urban public to acknowledge them, and that seems to be a prime psychological motivation for the graffiti artist.

As an urban art form, graffiti has grown and the styles have progressed from writing one's name on a wall to artistic renditions of the artist's neighborhood population and to full mural productions. In many cities, businesses and civic leaders have actually commissioned graffiti artists' work to try and incorporate community cultural values in business or government art projects. The group that used to pursue and prosecute these artists now acknowledges and purchases their work. Obviously, this commissioning of their art work is a legitimization of their efforts *as* art, rather than just defacement.

Another sociopsychological impact the city has on its inhabitants is on friendship and kinship networks. Geographic borders in the city represent the territorial boundaries of neighborhoods; they also represent real distances between people and groups. As the modern city sprawls from the cen-

The urban art of graffiti can be an affront to some people's sensibilities. Is this art or simple vandalism? Here the artists have taken over an urban wall and walkway to display their names in a style called "tagging," proclaiming their affiliation in the large symbolic writing that dominates this photograph. This reflects an urban expression of color and form, though some people may not understand the artists' message. There is also the issue of defacing someone's property with this unwanted art.

tral city to the suburbs and beyond, distances grow between people and friendships become strained to overcome these distances. For our youngest urbanites, their personal relationships are becoming more homogenous in nature because of these growing distances. Young people have their own culture in the city, just like adults; in fact, those Americans under the age of fifteen spend billions every year on their specific kinds of culture. While Britney Spears, Pokemon, Barney the Dinosaur, *NSYNC, the Olsen Twins, and Blues Clues may not be the cultural consumption of most of my readers, it is certainly the culture that very young urbanites purchase every day in our city. Their culture is guided by national consumption that they see on television, but the culture of their friendships is often dictated by who is in their neighborhood. Residential segregation by class has actually *increased* in a recent study of the sixty largest cities in America, while all racial segregation has slightly declined on average (Fischer 2001).

Class segregation of neighborhoods means that children that can't drive will associate only with other children in their class-divided neighborhoods. White middle-class kids will socialize primarily with other white middle-class kids in their neighborhood, and despite buying the occasional rap CD behind their parents' back, the culture that they will develop will be a suburban homogenous culture and worldview. The psychological impact that this will have on young urbanites is to foster a sociopsychological distance between races and classes, because they don't regularly associate with these groups in their friendship network. Despite consuming culture from inner city minority artists on rap records, their daily interactions and social networks are becoming more segregated. The distance that separates neighborhoods separates children too, and the chances of having friendships beyond these distance are diminished by the *increasing* distances we find between the suburbs and the central city. Psychologically, this creates distances between classes and races of children that are separated by the urban environment. Busing inner city children to the suburbs has done little to alter the sociopsychological distance between children in the city. When children go back to their isolated neighborhoods, what few friendships that might be developed at school can't be maintained over the distance between the neighborhoods, so the sociopsychological barriers are reinstated.

Returning to our discussion of the Renaissance, if Florence was the city for sculpture and artistic innovation, then Rome during the Renaissance was the city for artistic legitimatization. The Pope and the Church formally approved a new artist, technique, or artistic movement during the Renaissance through the social legitimizing process of having the Vatican request a "command" performance of the artist. In fact, technically it is the tiny city-nation of the Vatican within Rome that wields the most artistic power in the end during the Renaissance. It is the Vatican that is responsible for the memorable artwork of Donatello, Michelangelo, Bernini, and others; not Rome. After the fall of the Roman Empire, it is the Vatican that becomes the real seat of political power in Italy, and Rome becomes the urban museum for previous artistic works. But Rome and the Vatican together legitimatized the urban artwork and sculpture of other innovative city-states, like Florence. Thus, Rome and the Vatican become the end consumer and patron of many of these urban artists. The city-state during the Renaissance is *the* ultimate patron of the arts, providing both supply and demand. While innovations and styles in art and sculpture come from the artist, the urban influence through patronage and citizen support is undeniable. While the artist creates new culture, it is the city that ultimately approves of and pays for a new cultural product.

URBAN PAINTING

Up to this point, we have concentrated on urban sculpture more than urban painting, because the city's impact on the large and visible medium of sculpture is more apparent. Through the medieval period, the Roman Catholic Church exerted an effect on painting as well, more than any one city or nation-state. As with sculpture, the Church through its power in Rome decided what was acceptable art for public viewing. Those that could afford their own artwork used the same "Church approved" artists to produce the paintings for their consumption. The Church's control of art going into and through most of the Renaissance was absolute. Few artists dared to push the envelope in painting by annoying the Church, because not only was the Church the single biggest customer for an artist, being labeled a heretic by Rome through one's art was an excellent way to become jailed.

This changed with the Impressionist Movement (1874–1886) and the ascending of Paris as a world leader of painting and art. Today, this period of painting and the artists Monet, Manet, and Pissarro are some of the best known and most appreciated of any artistic period in history, even though they only exhibited their work together three times as Impressionists. We would be hard pressed to find any modern calendar shop without at least a dozen different versions of Monet's *Water Lilies* in calendar form for our contemporary consumption. How did Paris influence Impressionism and modern painting? While a city of much history, Paris was transforming itself into a more modern, progressive city after the French Revolution of 1793. Change in art was precipitated by an initial change in the political and social order: the French Revolt in 1848, combined with revolutions in Milan, Rome, Berlin, and Prague, and the writing of the Communist Manifesto all in the same year. Eventually, these political and social changes in Paris allowed artists of the 1860s to explore topics other than castle landscapes and portraits of noblemen. One of these new topics to explore in art was the achievements of men in innovation and design, particularly the innovations and design in Europe's growing cities. Paris's avenues and streets become the talk of Europe as the city's design and lighting make it the toast of Europe, becoming known as the "City of Light" after the revolution ends and a stable government is installed.

The interplay of light, shadow, and color are the hallmark of the Impressionist Movement, and the colleges and art programs in Paris had

Though this painting, titled *Waterlillies and Agapantes*, may not be familiar, it is part of the "Waterlillies" series for which Claude Monet is famous. Even in black and white, we can see that the use of light and color by the nineteenth-century Impressionists of Paris represents a departure from the realism and the religious tone of previous centuries. Paris's art community was intrigued by this new movement and embraced it. Like a fleeting moment in time, this painting reflects the artist's perception of light and color in this scene, rather than a photographic depiction of flowers or a biblical scene commissioned by powerful patrons.

become innovators in the exploration of these new aesthetic elements. Perception of the relationship between light, shadow, and color, rather than the representation of the realistic appearance of objects, becomes the focus of this new artistic style. Impressionism breaks the conventions of previous artistic movements by making choices in color and form that were not acceptable before. The urban component of this movement was the city's political and social environment, which had executed its nobility in 1793, revolted in 1848, endured Louis Napoleon as emperor until 1870, and weathered the Prussian Siege in 1870–71 and the Paris Commune Uprising of 1871. Questioning and breaking the artistic conventions of the previous art regimens seemed a reasonable thing to do in Paris after these tumultuous events. The urban citizen of Paris was more accepting of new art and artists as a result of the death of the aristocracy and the accessibility of art for the middle class. Parisian salon culture was also a part of the Impressionist art revolution as the Parisians who participated in salon culture became a new audience for art. Salon culture in Paris was a movement of wealthy and middle-class intellectuals who entertained themselves at home in their living rooms or "salons" by hosting philosophers, writers, artists, and musicians of cutting-edge or avant garde culture. The first Impressionist exhibit ever held was in photographer Nadar's salon studio in 1874. Functionalist theorists would say that the city's design and the culture's more egalitarian growth allowed the best artists and swelling middle class an opportunity to mingle and make new art.

Paris again becomes the nurturing urban center for a later innovation in painting. The Cubist movement begins in 1907, and just as artists questioned realism during the Impressionist movement, Cubists questioned the whole process of artistic representation by showing their subjects from several angles at once in angles and planes (Hartt 1985). Paris's history and culture formed the artistic revolution that is Cubism by first having a gallery devoted to Cézanne (1906), whose work the cubists most often cite as their biggest influence. Breaking the artistic convention of realistic representation by replacing it with fanciful angles could only be embraced in a city with art critics, intellectuals, and audiences accustomed to challenging new artistic visions. Cubism's eventual acceptance into the institutions of art criticism and education in Paris allowed the later acceptance of abstract art and movements such as Futurism, Constructivism, Dadaism, Surrealism, and Abstract Expressionism that followed.

Pablo Picasso (1881–1973) moved from Barcelona to Paris in 1900 and endured eight years of depression and wandering artistic influences before developing Cubism. For Picasso and Georges Braque, Cézanne's work and acceptance in Paris helped to inspire the Cubist movement.[6] Few other cities were as accepting of new art and new intellectual ideas as Paris was, a quality that allowed Paris to embrace the challenge of Cubism beginning in 1908. The salons and intellectuals of the city were so numerous and influential that the artistic knowledge and appreciation of the average person began to be elevated. Cubism in both stages, analytic and synthetic, only lasted as the vanguard art form for six years, until World War I broke out in 1914. Although Paris hosted many other art movements over the next eighty years, Cubism's effect on Kandinsky, Duchamp, Mondrian, Rivera, and others up to the later Abstract Expressionism of De Kooning and Pollock is immeasurable. Paris

---

[6]As well as Picasso's fascination with African art that was being featured in Paris's museums and salons at the time.

Pablo Picasso's painting titled *The Dream* employs an innovative painting technique called Cubism. Cubism represents an even more dramatic departure from the religious themes of earlier periods and the Parisian art community welcomed it. Realism is completely discarded here, as is traditional perspective. Using this technique, Picasso tries to enable the viewer to see the figure from several angles, including through her head.

understood and embraced art as part of the Parisian "psyche," in which even those that could never afford their own artworks went to museums or salons to soak up the current trends in art. Manuel Castells argued that city's don't have characters or cultures, but clearly, from this example cities do develop cultural character.

New York City in the 1950s became another environment to have an urban impact on painting. Both Pollock and De Kooning were drawn to New York as the site of a new direction in painting that would abandon naturalist representations of reality or form. New York emerged as *the* international city after World War II, outpacing Paris, London, Moscow, and Berlin, which were all rebuilding after World War II. New York's art schools and teachers, including some European immigrants who had fled before the war, were still alive and eager to teach a new cadre of young artists who dared to break with all of the previous European art conventions. The war robbed these other cities of their artists, art schools, and art patrons, but their loss was New York's gain. It could be said that most New Yorkers, during the 1950s, were *not* supporters of abstract expressionism; it was still too wild and disturbing to most viewers. However, New York had a small, committed community of art gallery owners and patrons that did respond to this new art movement.

Like our earlier discussion of classical music in New York and the three different music worlds of classical musicians and patrons, the art appreciation world of artists and patrons is also separated into different art worlds. The traditional community of wealthy patrons centered on the midtown museums of Manhattan, as opposed to the more experimental and avant-garde artists of Soho in the downtown area of Manhattan (Gilmore 1990). It was in the Soho area that Pollock and De Kooning found some acceptance, if not immediate financial reward, for their work; first from fellow artists and later from patrons of their abstract work. New York City became the economic, political, and cultural center of post-World War II, the desire to push boundaries of culture to new areas became part of the Soho art community's character in the bigger environment of New York City.

The city's growth in international stature for trade, finance, fashion, media, and art increased the acceptability for avant-garde items and also increased the market forces to explore new themes in art. These urban factors that pushed artistic culture in New York might have been explored in Paris before that city's devastation in World War II. New York's distinct art worlds[7] and myriad of ethnic communities were clearly an influence on the often chaotic production of Abstract Expressionism at this time (at it's peak from 1950 to 1960). The evidence of this ethnic influence is in the multitude of ethnicities of the artists in the downtown art community. Recent artist immigrants to the city began exploring the territory beyond Kandinsky's work in Abstract Expressionism toward Lichtenstein's elevation of low culture forms like comic book illustrations to the highest art gallery.

Pop art, as innovations of this genre are sometimes known, might be among the last identifiable "urban influenced" periods of art production. Andy Warhol, Claes Oldenburg, and other artists took everyday objects and commercially mundane processes of art production, like silk screening and lithograph methods, and began to explore the "art" in everyday life. The "pop art" period (1960s to 1980s) had an impact on urban art production

---

[7]An art world is composed of the unique artists, patrons, and venues of a specific urban community. Soho artists possessed different norms of production and interactions than the other art worlds in New York City.

and consumption. Pop artists bring art into everyone's home by finding art in everyday objects and utilizing mass production techniques to make art reproductions financially accessible to any urban home. If an everyday telephone or can of soup was art (which seemed absurd to most Americans), then what is art? For most urbanites, art was not the ability to hang a Renoir in your living room—that was more art consumption than art appreciation. A Renoir is still high art, but *possessing* the painting became the obsession of moneyed Wall Street types, many of whom hadn't the foggiest idea of the painting's artistic meaning. Since most urbanites didn't know the artistic meaning of Renoir either, art became more firmly rooted in urban living as ornamentation and decoration, rather than genuine art appreciation. The painting or poster that matches the carpet or the couch in one's apartment is often more important to today's urbanite than its artistic merit.

In fact, the over-reproduction of Monet's *Water Lilies* has actually made this masterpiece an example of modern kitsch.[8] The difference that pop art made to urbanites was the accessibility of the techniques of mass reproduction devoted to making copies of high art like that of Renoir, Monet, or Leonardo da Vinci. Now, of course, every home can have a poster-size reproduction of the great masters of painting—not the original painting, but a high-quality reproduction available on most urbanites' budget. Even more to the point, every home can possess a version of Edward Hopper's haunting classic *Nighthawks* or an updated version of the picture with pop artist Heinlein's addition of pop culture icons James Dean, Marilyn Monroe, Humphrey Bogart, and Elvis Presley as the characters in the new painting, now called *Boulevard of Broken Dreams*. With this painting, the great masters' tradition of painting is blended with pop culture to make new "pop designer art" in the style of a great master painter. One can also pick a neon color accent for the poster that goes with the couch.

THEATER AND LITERATURE

Writing for the public's amusement in theater, and to a lesser extent literature, is also an urban phenomenon, because the city is where the primary audience for the theater is located. The urban community of Greek playwrights and philosophers in Athens stands out as one of the more literate and influential periods of Western literature; Socrates, Plato, and Aristophanes wrote plays and books of social and political significance for their urban audiences, and the stage for their plays was the urban environment of Athens. The Mediterranean world changed during the Greek and Roman Empire periods to include the culture of the playwright and author in the brave new cities the two empires built. In fact, these literary culture producers changed the

---

[8]Kitsch is tasteless or bad art, furniture, or decoration.

design of the ancient city. No Greek or Roman town, no matter how small, was complete without an amphitheater built for the entire town as an audience, and the amphitheater's location was central to urban life. Politics, religion, philosophy, and theater each had a place in the amphitheater as each of these cultural forms played out their dramas in front of their urban audience. The public gathered in this central place to bear witness and play a part in these dramas, and the feeling of community was reinforced by their participation. For Greeks, the amphitheater was central to their social solidarity, as well as to their city design, and they passed this institution to the Romans.

The Roman Coliseum was so central to Roman citizenship and solidarity that the nation's leaders (and by proxy the city's leaders) had over one hundred days of holidays and festivities in the Coliseum just to keep the mass of Roman citizens content. It wasn't enough to give this group the day off from work; many spectators in the Coliseum were already unemployed and enjoying another urban invention: the dole, or what we call welfare. The Roman citizen demanded diversion constantly. The masses wanted to be entertained, and they felt it was their right as Roman citizens[9] to be sufficiently distracted, fed, and amused during those holidays. Religious temples would often employ some of the 30,000 registered prostitutes in Rome to service festival revelers as adequate amusement for the holiday's celebration (Little 1989). In the Coliseum itself, the architecture was so large and versatile that it could be used to execute prisoners by wild animals in the morning, reenact a historic chariot battle at lunch (complete with bread and wine for the crowd), fill the stadium with water for a naval battle reenactment in the afternoon, and finish the spectacle by torchlight with a translated Greek play at night. The theater and spectacles of the Coliseum were used by elites to control and entertain the masses, who couldn't be toppling the government if they were warming a chair in the Coliseum. *Theory Break*: Karl Marx once said that the best form of social control was a job. That may seem cynical, but, from a pragmatic point of view, while at work the urban citizen can't commit crimes, riot, or cause political dissention. With not enough employment to go around in Rome, the government used culture as social control to maintain order through this central urban institution.

When Rome fell, it had been the central point of organization for literature and theater; its gods, myths, and legends were the cultural basis for all literature and theater, of the time. The Middle Ages were unable to replace Rome's influences in literature and theater, and since the Church was suspicious of non-Church writing, all previous forms of literature were banned and filtered through the Church hierarchy. No Roman state salaries for playwrights, philosophers, or writers in the Dark Ages meant that acting and theater became a wandering nomadic existence as troupes of entertainers went

---

[9]Being a subject of Rome and being a Roman citizen were very different things. Unlike Americans, who feel that being from Boise or Boston isn't as important as being an American, Roman citizenship had a great deal to do with whether you were actually from the city of Rome versus one of the conquered territories (who were treated as less important).

from village to village, along decaying Roman roadways, to play and perform for tips. The Roman Catholic Church was no more kind or respectful than the barbarians that sacked Rome when it came to the written arts, and the church set about destroying or segregating all written literature, theater, and philosophy that it did not have a hand in creating. Most Greek and Roman literature that wasn't destroyed by barbarians was lost during this period as the Church became the sole proprietor of education, and the Church was intent on the Bible and its own dogma being read and recited, rather than troublesome ancient texts. When cities fell into disrepair, the art and literature communities in these cities did also with no audiences or theaters to sustain their work. It wasn't until the reestablishment of Eastern trade routes in 1200–1300 c.e. that contact with Islamic countries rediscovered ancient Greek plays and literature that had been saved in the Islamic cities of learning. Rediscovering the lost Greek and Roman plays helped to spark the Renaissance, and once out of the bottle, the Church could not contain the artistic and scientific explosion of new ideas brought by the Renaissance.

It was in the Italian city-states of the Renaissance that urban culture again flourished, as we have already mentioned, and the painting and sculpture of urban artists in Italy grew during this time. Trade between city-states and the growth of artistic production seemed to be interrelated as artists and artistic technique moved from city to city. In this way, the arts and artistic innovation wasn't confined to one city but could circulate as economic demand for art increased. Literature and academic thought grew as well during the Renaissance with Leonardo da Vinci contributing to inventions, military tactics, and the study of anatomy; Machiavelli changing political thought with *The Prince* (1538); while Brahe (1546–1601), Kepler (1571–1630), and Galileo (1564–1642) changed astronomy and cosmology, and Shakespeare (1564–1616) changed theater in London.

Cities along trade routes in Western Europe were the first to share in the new explosion of culture. Budapest, Paris, Moscow, and London were centers of trade and government, and thus culture production that was stimulated by cross-cultural contact. But, it was the dissolution of the Church's control over culture that really allowed these city capitals to begin producing culture after the Renaissance. Dante Alighieri's *The Divine Comedy* (1321) stands at the apex of social, political, and religious commentary from any age, that its seamless poetry was written before the Renaissance in the early 1300s is truly amazing. Dante's writing sets the stage of artistic commentary on society, and the political intrigue of Florence and Rome of his day influenced this work. After being exiled by a rival political party from the Florentine magistrate's office, Dante reserves the ninth level of hell for traitors of all kinds. Clearly, Dante's political experience in Florence shaped his work, not only to locate political traitors at the bottom of Hell, but to discuss Paradise in such longing imagery, much like he longed to be able to return to Florence. Another literary giant who set the stage for the Rennaissance was Chaucer, whose famous *Canterbury Tales* (1387) was a romanticized tale of pilgrims traveling in the fourteenth century along one of these trade routes to attend St. Thomas of

Canterbury Cathedral and Shrine. Cities were bringing people together in trade and other relationships, and Chaucer's tales are a frank and sometimes bitter portrayal of the social class system of the time. The corruption of the clergy, the immorality of the merchant class, and the excellence of noble action for unsung ethical men, *The Canterbury Tales* was a social polemic dressed as satire. This type of popular social critique would have been unheard of prior to the growing urban populations that came after the Black Plague.

Niccolò Machiavelli's *The Prince* is still studied in political science classes today, because of his ruthless clarity when discussing political virtues. Not just virtues of a monarch, but of all leaders and the political system itself. Again, Florence, Italy, begins Machiavelli's political and urban education in 1494 as he is part of the city-state's "war department" and "state department"—handling military issues connected with Florence's war with rival city-state Pisa, diplomatic relations with the Vatican, and intelligence intrigue with the French (Machiavelli 1538). From these experiences, Machiavelli begins to construct his conception of his ideal "Prince" from the experiences he had in Florence. This archetype of a leader is definitely not the primitive agricultural king of ancient days, but an urban city-state ruler who has to manage a population of urban citizens that need services and municipal structure from their leader. This handbook for leaders discusses all the important urban institutions to be dealt with—the military, the church, the mob, and even a section on basic human nature. Kindly put, Machiavelli's view was a kind of urban pragmatism, in which people were meant to be led and leaders had to lead at all cost. This urban pragmatism was necessary because the city creates a culture of removed, distant urbanites, and both citizens and leaders need the rational, pragmatic leadership Machiavelli describes. *Theory Break*: According to Georg Simmel, being in a crowded city overwhelms an urbanite and this leads to what Louis Wirth labeled a wealth of secondary or impersonal relationships (Simmel 1908; Wirth 1938). The political culture of the city, which Machiavelli's Prince wishes to exploit, relies upon this numbed, selective, and impersonal urbanite culture to dominate a large number of urban workers by a small number of urban elites.

On the other end of the spectrum from pure pragmatism was William Shakespeare's forays into theater, poetry, and literature. England's playwright centered his activity at the Globe Theatre in the heart of London's entertainment district, and his work was filled with the urban character of London. Tapping into both the illiterate urban dwellers of London's tenement district and the well-read aristocracy of the nobility, Shakespeare's urban audience inspired him to write his classic stories with clever literary references for the noble class and raunchy, bawdy humor for his other urban audience. Sexual escapades, political intrigue, nobles versus peasants, good versus evil, Jews versus Christians, Christians versus Moors, and even black versus white can be found in his stories, and most of the time Shakespeare's story is framed on an urban stage (Romeo and Juliet's Verona, a merchant in Venice, Julius Caesar in Rome, Richard III in London). Traveling minstrels prior to London's theatric ascendancy were a pleasant distraction for those in English villages and cities as touring troupes made periodic stops in almost any city or village that would draw an audience. Opera and stage productions for noble and wealthier classes were held by more professional (and government approved) acting troupes in theater houses in the bigger towns and cities. Obviously, it was to these more illustrious and lucrative venues that playwrights and actors aspired, but not all work or every actor met the tastes or censor's approval. It was the popularity of Shakespeare's work to the urban masses that first made his plays attractive to the courts of London and Europe, the urban edge of his plays would have normally made Shakespeare's work too controversial for the noble classes. In fact, Shakespeare's popularity both with his modest urban audience and his privileged noble audience made some of his more scathing political plays palatable when similar works faced strict censorship from the Crown.

As the Roman spectacles were good for the urban masses at the Coliseum, plays and minstrel shows became entertainment for the English urbanites tired of plagues, wars, famines, and fires. Sadly, it is the lack of adequate urban crisis culture (i.e., a fire department) that causes the loss of the Globe Theater and half of London in a large fire in 1666, but not before Shakespeare's body of work becomes the standard we use today for evaluating modern theater. It might be hard for us to think of Shakespeare's work as having an urban component, but the audience and the theater he worked with were definitely urban products. Even more urban adaptations of Shakespeare's work continue to be popular in our modern theater and cinema. *West Side Story* (1961) graced the screen after winning awards on Broadway, and its musical update of Shakespeare's *Romeo and Juliet* included urban themes of rival street gangs and ethnic tension in New York City. Director Woody Allen updated *A Midsummer Night's Dream* in 1982; Mel Gibson modernized and shrunk *Hamlet* in 1990, as did Kenneth Branagh in 1996, though he kept the length after modernizing the sets. Also, teen heartthrobs Leonardo di Caprio and Claire Danes did another update of *Romeo and Juliet* in 2000 with a Los Angeles street gang motif. The literary themes of Shakespeare's work translate into our modern time because of the urban context of his original plays.

The Enlightenment in Europe (1660–1770) celebrated the power of reason and intellect in its culture and the expression of these ideals in its capital cities. Despite Thomas Hobbes's (*Leviathan* 1651) insistence that the social contract between ruler and rules arose from the people's need for leadership, rather than divine ordinance, the people's ability to change their leadership through force[10] made noble rulers of the Enlightenment less secure in their position. London had gone through two such changes in leadership in fifteen years before Hobbes wrote those words. People of this time were placing greater faith in the scientific ideas of René Descartes and Isaac Newton rather than the pageantry of the church or the royalty of kings; they found these new ideas in the burgeoning capital cities of Europe. Natural and scientific

---

[10]The English executed their king in 1649. Later came the American Revolution and the French Revolution.

laws also influenced the view of society and its collection of classes by the Enlightenment's social and cultural critics, who often expressed themselves through the theater and literary arts. Paris becomes the center for much of the artistic criticism of society during the Enlightenment, as a disenfranchised Parisian public begins to question the noble position of its leaders—questions that come to a bloody end for the French Monarchy during the French Revolution, as Paris again swirls around the epicenter of social revolution. Following the urban riot's storming of the Bastille and executions of the monarchy, capital cities became the center for the growing ideals of political participation of the masses and for a biting satire of the current system.

Jean-Baptiste Molière (1622–1673), like most theatrical social critics of the Enlightenment, employed comedy in his play *Tartuffe* (1664) to comment on the state of the social classes in France. Ideals of social inequality and the corruption of the church and nobility were introduced to wider groups through his plays. Louis XIV bowed to pressure from the church and banned *Tartuffe* because of the biting satire that the church said would stir antigovernment and antinobility sentiment in the city's streets. The Paris theater community had nurtured the troupe of actors that Molière had first gained notoriety with, and his loyalty was with his audience. Molière's use of biting satire continued in his work, despite the church's censure of *Tartuffe*, and his plays became the common language of Parisians to discuss the failings of their government. Paris's community of artists and patrons were sophisticated enough to embrace the neo-Greek drama of playwrights like Racine (1639–1699), as well as Molière's satirical urban political comedies, showing the depth that the urban arts community had in Paris. Racine's work delves into society's struggle with the growth of reason and science in a stratified society, but he escaped the wrath of the church's censure by placing his work in ancient Greece instead of contemporary France. *Theory Break*: Because of the success of these French literary giants and the education of the Parisian audience, an agglomeration of talent in the literary and theater arts was started in Paris. This agglomeration process drew actors and playwrights from all over France.

François-Marie Arouet de Voltaire (1694–1778) combined satire and dark comedy in his work, but the Paris that nurtured Voltaire wasn't always able to handle his work. Combining a range of theater, drama, philosophy, fiction, and even history to bite at the ruling powers in France, Voltaire spent years in the Bastille and eventually was exiled for his sharp satire of French society. Despite his travels from England to Switzerland, Voltaire was a Parisian writer and his works reflected his Parisian influence in both style and topic matter. *Candide* (1759) shows characters losing their naiveté, the way Paris had lost its naiveté in its social revolution of the classes. But, the characters in *Candide* also suffer terrible deaths that add the element of a sinister reality to the world of theater. This fantasy combined with reality technique of narrative shows the influence of the urban Paris backdrop that Voltaire grew up in, the bleak desperate reality of the lower classes posited against the opulence of the noble classes. By 1789, the French Revolution had written a bloody chapter to the end of the Enlightenment with the storming of the

Bastille and Madame Guillotine's darkly humorous method of leveling the classes in Paris. We cannot conceive of Paris without this period of violent revolution and the preceding theater and literature that set the stage for social commentary, satire, and criticism in the city of light.

This period of class conflict is related to us through later literature in Charles Dickens's *A Tale of Two Cities* (1859), which takes place in Paris and London. London also generated challenging prose during the Enlightenment with the work of Jonathan Swift (1667–1745), who was the most distinguished social critic in printed form. Today, *Gulliver's Travels* (1726) is thought to be a charming children's tale of a voyager's journey through enchanted lands of little people, giants, and talking horses. In a way, the story is so well written that many modern readers can enjoy the story at that fantasy journey level, with no idea that Swift's goal was not to write a children's tale, but to render a social polemic against the British Empire. *Gulliver's Travels* was another work of the Enlightenment's combination of narrative styles (satire, political analysis, social analysis, fantasy fiction, and children's stories) in which Swift's experience growing up in Dublin, Ireland, colored his written opinions of class relationships in London and abroad.

London's relationship with Dublin and all of Ireland was one of an absolute master to a sharecropping tenant. Cities have power relationships like people do, and London was in charge of Dublin. Both cities embodied the spirit of their people, but the political reality was that the British had conquered Ireland and dictated policy. London was the perfect picture of an Imperial Capital built rich on the plunder from its colonies in Ireland, India, Africa, and America, while Dublin's proud history and people had to be content with a culture made half from England's conquering nobles and half from its indigenous Celtic Catholic rebels. The literary history of Dublin is a combination of English and Celtic traditions.

As the political lords of London issued each new set of disastrous policies to the "serfs" in Ireland, the Irish in Dublin and the Irish in London become more and more resentful. *A Modest Proposal* (1729) is the most versatile use of satire in the English language, and it bites at the London political establishment, who were crippling Ireland and the Irish people with punitive domestic policies, taxes, and absentee landlords. The "modest proposal" of the narrator is for the English to eat the children of the Irish as a meat product to save these Irish families from the burden of too many children. The furor this proposal caused in the papers and inner circles of London society lifted the hypocrisy of the English establishment to unparalleled heights, as those that railed against the outrage of this "modest proposal" were the same elites who created the policies that starved Ireland. Dublin couldn't battle the English empire or even defeat London's empire with prose and satire. Perhaps Swift even changed some of London's social landscape with his writing talent. Using the literary institutions, of London, an Irish sympathizer calls attention to the plight of the subservient group to shame the English. He had to use London's powerful literary institutions, because Dublin had few of its own that could affect the English landowners.

Writing can be a very urban art form, but this can be hard to see because of the type of urban space used in literary production. The theater writing and performance, for instance, occupies a theater space and a venue in the city, which we can see as being "urban," while literary composition often has no venue in the city. But, we should look a little deeper at the urban component of literature in the Enlightenment to ascertain its impact on the city. For Swift, there was an entire community of London writers, printers, newspaper men, philosophers, and critics that he interacted with that we don't see. History has concentrated on the one or two authors from that period and so we lose the urban context of the author's work. Swift wasn't writing sequestered in the Yorkshire countryside about rural topic matter; his was an intensely urban literary world. Instead, he was writing about London's political establishment and the impact these policies had on British colonies in the intensely urban community of fellow writers in London. For urban sociologists and anthropologists doing historical research, it is our responsibility to uncover the urban influence on culture production. *Theory Break*: To accomplish this, we must use the writings of this time (books, journals, newspapers, and even paintings and photos) and historical accounts as data to uncover the hidden meanings to historical literature.

The Parisian example is a much easier exercise to analyze for urban influences than London's complex social and political intrigue. With the dawn of the Enlightenment, Paris was abuzz with new scientific ideals. The Parisian Royal Academy of Science benefited from the King's indulgent interests in math, science, and philosophy, drawing the best minds in Europe to Paris. *Theory Break*: This is another example of agglomeration. Unwittingly, the Cartesian philosophy that grew from the Academy became the logic and rational critique that the sociological philosophy of Comte and Durkheim was built upon. The immediate time frame of the King's interest into science allowed a certain degree of social and political criticism that had not been tolerated before in the social sciences.[11] Paris and its citizens were allowed a certain amount of general criticism and questioning in their philosophy and literature that was not going on in Lyon, Calais, or Gascon. The reason for this critical latitude was Paris's dominant function for arts and learning in France and mainland Europe at the time. As Paris began to share in the accomplishments of its artists and writers (see our discussion of music in Chapter Four), the city began to draw literary and theatrical talent from elsewhere in Europe.

Our modern world of literature and theater also has an urban component to its production, but instead of royal patronage for authors, it was capitalism's competition in New York City that fueled literature and theater. From the Vaudeville period (1890–1920), New York has been the theatrical center for the Americas as actors, playwrights, authors, composers,

---

[11]Molière's and Voltaire's works might have been banned, and Voltaire exiled for some of his theatrical liberties, but in previous days, the church may have required more serious punishments.

and lyricists flocked to the city to create new art. Boston, Philadelphia, and Washington, DC, supported theater and literature as well, but often the communities of artists they supported, from the American Revolution to the Reconstruction, recreated theater or literary works from Europe, rather than creating new work. New York City's stage and theater community has a long history of over one hundred years creating new American theater. A community of theater owners, booking agents, stage hands, actors, managers, writers, lyricists, musicians, lighting crews, and ushers grew from the Vaudeville period in New York City and, combined with the more European-influenced opera and stage period that preceded Vaudeville, began to coalesce into the New York theater community. Focused on American stage and musical works, this theater community has in general occupied the area surrounding Times Square extending from 40th Street to 52nd Street and bordered by 7th and 8th Avenue, and since the turn of the twentieth century it has been referred to as the theater district. Leaving European-styled opera and music to the Lincoln Center area, the theater district focused on original American stage productions about American themes. Vaudeville proved that there was an audience of working-class to middle-class theatergoers that were willing to pay for entertainment, just not at the prices of the opera houses or of the themes of Italian or German operas and symphonies. This new American audience wanted theater entertainment that they could relate to, not opera, but also not the campy, base humor of Vaudeville either. New Yorkers responded to the theater district and Broadway's lights, its cultured musicals, dramatic urban theater works, and witty stage productions, by attending its productions regularly and enthusiastically.

Today, New York's theater district is the dominant urban theater scene in the country, drawing actors, producers, and audience members from every city in the country and the world. *Theory Break*: Like a *music scene*, the *theater scene* in New York City organizes the production of theater culture in a specific area of the city (Broadway), spawned ancillary businesses (lighting companies, theater agents, prop companies, ticket sales companies), and as the scene comes to play a dominant function in a region or country it draws both culture producers and culture consumers to the area of production (actors and audience members being drawn to New York City). Theater and musical production has become so centralized in New York's Broadway Theater District that it has spawned secondary theater scenes, like the off-Broadway productions, theater in the parks, and theater communities in other cities that wait for the Broadway productions to go on the road. All of these urban culture production elements for theater hinge on capitalist elements in the city, driven by financers that promote theater productions and the taste of audience members that support them with ticket stubs.

New York City is also the center for capitalist, corporate literary production in the United States as well as for most English-language books in the world. All of the major book publishers in the United States have a headquarters in New York City. While many themes in the tons of books published in New York City have urban themes, there is little about this literary production that can be called "urban centered" or corporate centered. This may be somewhat confusing, since clearly the urban publishing businesses in New York City are performing a key function by drawing writers to New York and dominating the industry. However, this function has drawn mainly the financial and business elements of literary publishing to New York City. While possessing a strong literary community and several publishing houses in New York City, the corporate publishing business draws from authors all over the United States, who do not have to move to a specific urban environment to create their cultural products. Authors only need to send their finished manuscripts to New York to have them published, and then they are physically printed into books wherever that printing process can be done the most economically. So, for modern writers, the need to be physically present in a specific urban environment or to incorporate the urban themes of that city to succeed in literature are unnecessary. Stephen King, Tom Clancy, and James Michener have written their books while at home or traveling, and the books have very little to do with any specific urban environment other than that they were published in New York City. Like finance, literary production is centered in New York City for corporate reasons, which are urban in nature (being near the competition, transportation hubs, communication centers, having the corporate culture that facilitates literary production), but the actual writing does not create the culture in a city.[12]

References

ALIGHIERI, DANTE. 1321. *The Divine Comedy.* Trans. Thomas Duncan. Cranton Press (1926): London, England.

ANDERSON, RICHARD. 1990. *Calliope's Sisters: A Comparative Study of Philosophies of Art.* Prentice Hall: Englewood Cliffs, NJ.

ASIMOV, ISAAC. 1991. *Asimov's Chronology of the World.* Harper Collins: New York, NY.

CHAUCER, GEOFFREY. 1387. *The Canterbury Tales.* Oxford University Press (1998): Oxford, England.

COOKE, JEAN et al. 1996. *History's Timeline.* Barnes and Noble: New York, NY.

DURKHEIM, EMILE. 1893. *The Division of Labor in Society.* The Free Press (1984): New York, NY:.

FISCHER, MARY. 2001. "The Relative Importance of Class and Race in Determining Residential Outcomes in U.S. Urban Areas, 1970–1990." Unpublished work presented at American Sociological Association Meeting: Los Angeles, CA.

GANS, HERBERT. 1962. *The Urban Villagers.* Free Press: New York, NY.

GILLMORE, SAMUEL. 1990. *Art Worlds.* University of Chicago Press: Chicago, IL.

---

[12]The same way finance may be centered in New York City, but money is spent, traded, and printed in other places, and New York City has only a small role to play in the way it is spent, traded, and printed in the nation or world. In other words, fluctuations in the market or currency happen in New York City, but they have very little to do with the character or culture of New York. These fluctuations have more to do with falling gold prices in Zurich or cattle disease in Britain; they are just reported to the markets in New York City.

GOTHAM, KEVIN. 2002. "Marketing Mardi Gras: Commodification Spectacle, and the Political Economy of Tourism in New Orleans." *Urban Studies*. Sept 2002, Vol. 29, No. 10, pp. 1735–1757.

HARTT, FREDERICK. 1985. *Art: A History of Painting, Sculpture, Architecture*. Prentice Hall: Englewood Cliffs, NJ.

HOBBES, THOMAS. 1651. *Leviathan*. Touchstone Books (1997): New York, NY.

LITTLE, CHARLES. 1989. *Deviance and Control: Theory, Research, and Social Policy*. Peacock: Itasca, IL.

MACHIAVELLI, NICCOLO. 1538. *The Prince*. Trans. Neil Thompson. Barnes and Noble (1999): New York, NY.

SIMMEL, GEORG. 1908. *The Sociology of Georg Simmel*. Kurt Wolff (ed., 1950 edition). Free Press: Glencoe, IL.

SWIFT, JONATHAN. 1726. *Gulliver's Travels*. Penguin Books (2001): New York, NY. Originally Published Benjamin Motte, Jr. Publisher: London, England.

WIRTH, LOUIS. 1938. "Urbanism as a Way of Life." *American Journal of Sociology*. Vol. 44, pp. 1–24.

CHAPTER SIX

Architecture and Fashion

Architecture is the design and ornamentation of a structure. Our first dwellings were probably caves, which if course we didn't make, but we certainly ornamented.

Lean-tos of earth and brush or twig dwellings followed and were also used as homes, eventually developing into bricks or stones as our settlements became larger. In the first proto-urban areas at the crossing of trade routes or on the edge of some natural harbor or inlet (c. 3000–1000 B.C.E.), these structures that people lived in became signs of wealth and status for the occupant. The appearance and design of one's dwelling took on a social meaning. The better and stronger house you built, the more important you were. As the early settlements grew, the size, position, and decoration of one's dwelling were an insignia of your rank and status in the social order. If you could afford a large house on the main thoroughfare and decorate, paint, and ornament the structure, then clearly you possessed superior status. The smaller the structure, the more inferior one's social status in the city.

Fashion, the style of ones clothing, can also denote status, and in traditional societies what one wore was also a sign of their position. Later in this chapter we will discuss the urban rules and development in fashion. For now, we will just keep in mind that clothes were often a uniform of one's position in ancient and traditional societies, the same way one's house could be a sign of one's social status.

ANCIENT URBAN ARCHITECTURE

As the first settlements turned into small cities, the division of social labor and hierarchy of position in the society were expressed through fashion and

Prehistoric cave painting from Lascaux, France. Decorating their living space was obviously one priority for these prehistoric people, but we can also see from this painting *what* in their environment was important to them. The horse that this artist immortalized on a cave wall thousands of years ago must have had some significance to the artist to warrant the time and energy devoted to this painting.

architecture. The simplest example of hierarchy expressed through architecture would be the king's palace. Bigger and more ornate than other homes, it was most often located in the center of the ancient city. The king's palace was the most important family dwelling in the city, and local ordinances ensured that no other homes were allowed to be built larger or more ornate. In ancient China, for example, homes in the capital city had to conform to a strict code. First, nobles were allowed to have homes of up to two stories, but no larger because it would have interfered with the emperor's special visual space within the city. Second, the nobles could use purple or yellow to adorn their homes, but not red. Again, this special color was reserved for the emperor. Third, by implication, peasants could not have any dwelling taller than one story or with any noble ornamentation whatsoever. It was the Chinese culture that gave red its special place as the emperor's royal color, and it was through the urban environment that Chinese culture expressed its social hierarchy through architecture (Macionis and Parillo 2001).

The second group of citizens to have a special place in the social division of labor was the military. In the design of their barracks, which were also located in the city center, usually across a town square or plaza from the palace, their building's form followed its function. The design of military housing was often stern and austere, built to appear imposing. The troops were kept close to the palace to quell disturbances and maintain the king's power. Military barracks also served as the military's training ground and the jail for political prisoners. Periodic displays of the military's muscle and the might of the military's armory around the barracks have become our modern-day parades. The specter of the military's power to silence the political opposition was also embodied in the imposing physical form of the barracks building; it was made to look impregnable.

The third group of special citizens with their own building and architecture in the ancient city were the clergy or religious class. Often a key distinguishing cultural feature of a society is its religious beliefs, and for early societies the nobility's hold on power was often legitimatized through the church or clergy, i.e., God has chosen the king, which is why he is king, and this is why the king says you should worship God. Sometimes larger and more ornate than even the palace, the religious temple, ziggurat, or cathedral was meant to inspire awe and obedience from the citizenry. Think of any medieval cathedral and the psychology of urban architecture becomes clear. Ornate spires that reach toward the heavens frame archways with pictorial representations of biblical stories[1] that are meant to emphasize the importance of God and the insignificance of man. Gargoyles on the facade inspire fear, while stained glass windows provoke reverence inside the cathedral. The inside decoration of a cathedral itself has a psychology of hard-back pews to keep the audience awake, uncomfortable, and penitent, with the priest's pulpit suspended above the crowd to instill the authority of the priest's words.

The peasantry of the city lived where there was space to find shelter, and often if they had a business or craft they resided in their shop space. Comfort, sanitation, and quality of life were not considerations for the urban dweller that did not have a noble title. So, why stay in the city if it is dank, crowded, unsanitary, and dirty? Most people chose to stay in ancient cities for its most imposing piece of architecture—the battlements and walls. Most ancient cities had some walled or gated defense system that was crucial to its survival. From Jericho and Jerusalem in the East to Rome and Athens in the West, an ancient city's first organized urban architectural project was the construction of walls. The cities of Peking in Asia and the Mayan cities in the New World also employed a walled defense model. While many urban areas spilled outside of their urban walls, the space within the walls was a source of urban conflict for those wanting a safe place to live.

Walls were often necessary to prevent the plunder of wealthy cities by neighboring city-states, societies, or wandering nomads. Cities were the accumulation of all of the region's wealth and trade, but they also were seen as a source for raw goods (food, horses or camels, women, clothing, jewels and

---

[1]Most medieval peasantry and some nobles were illiterate, so often art and relief sculpture told a pictorial story for their understanding.

gold) to either expand a conquering society or sustain a nomadic one. Unfortunately for a city's architecture, warfare culture often proceeds faster than the height or width of the city's walls. City walls easily thwarted small bands of marauders, but armies with battering rams, catapults, and later cannons often forced a city's capitulation either through destruction or through starvation and thirst. A further reinforcement of the social hierarchy, even within a city under siege, was the European castle keep. This tall, inner city defense was only for the noble family and the last of the defenses to try and keep the nobility's wealth from the invaders. *Theory break*: Marxist theorists would point out that class was meant to be *very* visible in the design and placement of structures in the city, right down to the elite class's control of the urban space and the laws about what could be built and by whom in the city.

MODERN URBAN ARCHITECTURE

The Industrial Age brought a new sense of urban architecture; instead of castles for nobles and hovels for the peasants, a middle class was growing in the city. The middle class, often composed of merchants and service providers, were urbanites with homes that reflected their social stature in the city. Tall Victorian-style houses with ornate shutters and porches began to appear on the East Coast of the United States as early as 1870 for the urban middle class. These were not the plantation mansions of the South or the robber baron palaces of the North, the new middle class lived in a two or three story house with a modest lot within the city limits or a newly growing suburb. As a country, the United States begins to realize the value of the middle class (stability, class cohesion, economic prosperity, dependable political patronage) and all levels of government (federal, state, local) begin to promote a vision of the "American Middle Class." This quickly becomes an important part of American culture. The expounding middle-class presence is felt in every U.S. city through their domination of suburban housing and is greeted by most as a uniquely positive American trend. For the urban government, subdivisions with paved streets and sometimes streetcar services, water and sewer connections, and progressive school districts were demanded by middle-class citizens, and local politicians rushed to meet these demands in the 1900s. Sustaining a middle class in one's city became a priority for urban leaders who wanted the taxes and patronage of this group.

A modest-sized lot, rather than a huge estate, became associated with the urban middle-class homes of North America. Yet, the growing number of middle-class urbanites began to dominate the city space through sheer size and numbers. Despite its ornate facade or large and well-appointed interior, the lots for these homes were small, because transportation options to get to the jobs downtown still made small lots in city neighborhoods the norm. The reason for these small lots was to keep the travel time by walking, horse, trolley, or Model T to a minimum. At the same time, smaller lots increased the profitability of the land owner, who initially subdivided the land to sell to several families.

The growth in automobile ownership changed urban architecture, particularly for the new middle class, as roads to the suburbs led to larger homes on larger lots with a horizontal flair versus the vertical flare of the old urban middle class. After World War II, suburbanization becomes the national trend as even mid-sized cities pushed their boundaries out to suburbia to accommodate middle-class lifestyles. Cities and land developers also wished to increase the category of "middle class" by making suburban middle-class housing more accessible.

Levittown is the archetype of post WWII mass suburban construction. Primed by government subsidies to provide housing for returning soldiers, large subdivisions like Levittown grew with direct government building money and affordable Veterans Administration housing loans for GIs returning home. The speed with which they grew led to few options or amenities available in the housing. Referred to as "cookie cutter" houses for their pattern-like construction or "cracker boxes" for their small, one-story design, these homes signaled a new construction paradigm for suburbia. Suburban architecture was clearly going to be a dominant urban architectural force in the coming decades, and the category of people who could afford suburban housing was growing.

"Cookie-cutter houses" of Levittown, Long Island in New York, circa 1954. One can see how this term applies to this block of almost identical houses with little individuality or architectural uniqueness. Few choices were available for the new buyer of these Cape-Cod-style two-bedroom, one-bathroom homes—each having a covered carport, a windowed room on the second floor, and a paved driveway—yet thousands of young homebuyers flocked to neighborhoods such as this in the 1950s. These unremarkable dwellings, however, represented a social revolution as government subsidies and direction made home ownership a possibility for working class GI's—albeit white GI's.

The "ranch-style" home of the Levittown period becomes the standard one-story format house for the next forty years. No matter where you live in the United States, there is a middle-class suburban neighborhood that has as its primary model some variation of the ranch-style home. Affordable to build and buy, these quickly constructed homes, combined with the assistance of VA[2] and FHA[3] loans, actually helped the middle class grow by making housing more affordable. For many years, cities have maintained this architectural style in the suburbs, but recently the middle class has felt that this style has become too predictable. Obviously, the "predictability" of suburban middle-class architecture is a negative opinion held by some social critics who found the suburban housing culture of the 1950–70s repetitive. Happily, several new types of home designs have been crowding out the ranch style in the past decade, but the desire to please middle-class tastes continues to drive architecture and housing in the city.

HOUSING DISCRIMINATION—RACE AND CLASS

Discrimination in the ability to purchase housing in the suburbs unfortunately is a reality in every major American city. The suburbs have become all too often exclusively white by a combination of racial steering by real estate agents, redlining minority areas by banks, and outright racism by the Veterans Administration. The "whiteness" of suburban architecture and schools is an outcome of institutional structures that have restricted minorities and the lower class from moving to the suburbs. Not only were there restrictive covenants[4] and Jim Crow laws in many cities before 1960, but the VA actually wrote discrimination into its loan program after World War II. Loans to African American servicemen were only to be made for homes in "racially homogeneous" neighborhoods and where racial conflict would be minimized. In other words, white servicemen could take their VA loan and move to one of the new homogeneously white suburbs, while African American servicemen could only use their VA home loan benefits in existing minority neighborhoods. This effectively forced African American, Hispanic, and Native American vets returning from service into existing segregated neighborhoods and not in the new suburban housing developments for white soldiers. Suburbia remains primarily Caucasian today by informal methods, like racial steering, where real estate agents steer or encourage minority homebuyers away from white neighborhoods, and redlining by banks or insurance companies, where these minority areas are denied loans and services or are charged exorbitant fees.

---

[2]Veterans Administration

[3]Federal Housing Administration

[4]A restrictive covenant is an agreement between homeowners not to sell their property to other racial groups.

This is not to insinuate that suburbia is the only location of bland architecture, because of the popularity of the suburban ranch-style home. In fact, the architecture that is most often easily identified and universally hated is government-built inner city housing for the low-income citizen. From about 1960 to 1980, public housing was built in America like warehouses. Find the cheapest land, build the cheapest and largest building that the budget can sustain with the fewest optional additions (air conditioning, carpet, and so forth), and then pack as many people as possible into them. Unfortunately, most urbanites can identify the public housing (euphemistically called "the projects") in not only their own city, but any other city as well. This becomes part of the visible urban stigma of government housing and government architecture.

Not surprisingly, poor residents do not have a great deal of affection for these faceless, soulless, high-rise human storage facilities and, therefore, they have shown little respect for them. Trash, graffiti, and violence have long plagued America's public housing projects in every city where they have been built, until social service researchers and public officials began to do something radical . . . talk to the residents.

Theory Break: A perspective that starts from the bottom up, in this case, the resident's viewpoint, rather than from the perspective of the Housing Authority or HUD office is an example of a Marxist paradigm. Placing the working class's life world[5] first, rather than the life world of the elite classes, government, or municipal authority is one of the goals of socialism. Both Marx and Engels were inspired by the plight of the city worker and the conditions in which they labored to write and become activists to change the elite viewpoint of those that govern. Marx's model for a government run by the proletariat was inspired by the Paris Commune uprising of 1871, and Engels's description of living conditions in Manchester, England, was his inspiration for the range of services a socialist government should supply its citizens (housing, education, food, water, and sewer). Providing housing for the poor or working class is a socialistic urban goal; a purely capitalistic society wouldn't provide housing for those who can't afford it. The United States isn't a socialist government or economy, but neither is it a purely capitalist economy; referred to as welfare capitalism, many Western Industrialized nations have a hybrid economy. There is private property ownership and influence in the market, but it is regulated by the government and a safety net is provided for the poor.

When researchers and housing authorities took the radical step of actually *talking* to the "lowly poor," they found some interesting things. First, researchers found that architecture did matter to the residents and the community. Residents didn't want to take the time to fix up and protect a building that they didn't own, couldn't control (all decisions regarding rentals, evictions, décor, and the like were made by the housing authority), and that looked awful to begin with. In addition, being a resident of public

---

[5]Life world is the total of culture, class, and experiences of a group. Not just the wages, education, or neighborhood, but the entire world of that group.

SUBURBAN GANGSTA

Strangely, it may have been the lack of diversity in the suburbs that has led to white suburban teenagers' fascination with urban African American culture. Despite all of the media hype and predictions of imminent disaster due to kids listening to "Gangsta Rap," there has been no rash of rap-related crime in our cities. In fact, this is a good time to remind ourselves that consuming culture and the meaning that we attach to that culture is a choice. Culture has an impact upon us, but it does not program us like robots. A good example would be the expectation that Gangsta rap would be consumed mostly in the inner city. Consump-

Gansta rap star Snoop Dogg performs in Illinois at a sold-out show. Gold chains and baggy clothing are the visual trademarks of this urban music. Much of this image is about street crime and street culture, reflected in the lyrics and appearance of the stars. Snoop Dogg's own street credibility and record sales increased when he was charged and acquitted of murder in 1999. Many fans of his music and his dangerous "street image" tend to be white suburbanites who are clearly rebelling against their comfortable, safe surroundings in their search for some identity to mimic.

tion of rap music is more prevalent in suburban areas and is purchased by white children more than by inner city kids. But why would this be? Culturally, inner city kids supposedly come from the environment of Gangsta rap, some would expect them to purchase this music and suburban teens to purchase pop music. White suburbanites have a lot more disposable income, though, to buy CDs in the first place, and they enjoy sharing the feeling of power that urban black rappers communicate through their music. The disconnected nature of suburbs from cities, the banality of their design and architecture, and the lack of ethnic and cultural diversity has provoked suburban teenagers to reach out for what appears to be "authentic gangster" culture. The sad irony is that while much of the first rap gangster culture was begun to give voice to the poverty and violence in inner city neighborhoods, the popular Gangsta rap most kids listen to now is performed and packaged by rich men that live in the suburbs themselves and have become disconnected from the "real" inner city life.

housing created a social stigma for its residents. The buildings looked like ugly boxes, deteriorated quickly after being built, and quickly became covered in graffiti and trash. No one liked them . . . the community resented the buildings as eyesores (including the residents), and the residents despised being forced into buildings that they had no agency to control. It bears mentioning that the "projects" were perceived as being extremely dangerous, as well as ugly, because of drug and gang activity. The projects became a "no-man's land" controlled by the most violent gangs, who turned to drug dealing in areas where jobs are scarce. Being from the projects carried with it a label of broken families, unemployment, poor education, criminality, being from the "bad" side of town, and all-around negativity.

Urban sociologists from the Marxist perspective analyze how the urban environment affects the working class and how the working class affects the city. *Theory Break*: Politicians and Functionalists in the United States would say they provide low-cost housing for the poor out of charity; Marxists would say this housing is to appease a working poor that could become violent without some accommodations being made for them. Regardless of one's politics, the architecture of public housing in the United States and Russia look very much the same.

Both systems approached subsidized public housing in the same "warehouselike" fashion. Socialist housing engineers in the former Soviet Union felt that fancy or unique architecture was too bourgeois,[6] and American housing authorities felt that the low-income poor didn't deserve nicely appointed and maintained buildings with aesthetically pleasing architecture. The problem is that, regardless of where one falls on this issue, we do all have to *look* at the buildings and *share* our communities with them. As long as the projects must be built, it doesn't seem it would hurt the elite too much to make them look nice.

The last effect of the urban architecture of public housing is not only the warehousing concept of putting undesirable people in our society away from public view, but also warehousing the problems of the city. Drugs and

---

[6]According to Karl Marx, the bourgeoisie were the class that owned the factories, banks, and housing of a society and the proletariat were the workers of a society that owned very little and survived by selling their labor to the bourgeoisie.

This bleak scene is from a Moscow housing project built by the government of the Soviet Union and photographed in 1988. The modern high-rise apartment building is supposed to demonstrate the superiority of the socialist state, where even working-class people could afford a Manhattan-style dwelling provided by the government. Yet like those New York skyscrapers, the people and families look strangely out of place next to them, as if the eventual inhabitants were a mere afterthought by the architect. This sterile, institutional design served to alienate the residents from their own urban living space. Lugging groceries up flights of stairs or into cramped elevators, being surrounded by little green space, having no solitude, and having only one playground for all of the children are the realities of life for residents of this government housing.

violence do not drop out of the sky, land in a place, and infect the residents. For a neighborhood to decline into drugs and violence takes a long time and a period of profound neglect. The poor are no more prone to violent criminal activity than any other group, but if we, as a society, stack the poor in concentrated areas of town, the few among them that are violent will use that concentration to prey on the rest. Most members of housing projects are law-abiding citizens, but an architectural edict to stack the poor on top of each other has multiplied the effect of the few with criminal problems into a terrible stigma for the projects.

SEEKING SOLUTIONS: PARIS, FRANCE; ST. LOUIS, MISSOURI; AND BALTIMORE, MARYLAND

Paris, France, has a similar problem as America's cities with the government struggling to fund enough affordable housing for the working poor. The Parisian solution in the 1950s and 1960s was much the same as the American high-rise apartment projects of Chicago's Cabrini Green. The solution was to stack the poor in the most efficient and least attractive manner possible on the outskirts of Paris in high-rise buildings called the Grand Ensembles that connect its 60,000 residents to the city by road, bus, or rail (Castells 1983). Architecture can provoke a variety of cultural reactions; in Paris the poor and working class in these urban warehouses organized and actually pushed the government to provide *better* housing. Their efforts paid off, and the Parisian government found land outside of Paris and constructed new housing with an architecturally pleasing look. New buildings with contemporary architecture don't immediately eradicate poverty, crime, or social problems, but the lesson the French learned was not to have the design of low-cost housing *multiply* the problems of the poor. A new organizational culture stemmed from the success of the working-class housing demonstrations, and since the new housing projects have been occupied the grassroots organizational culture of the residents continued to demonstrate for more facilities, better transportation, and more civic amenities (Castells 1983).

A scene almost identical to the Moscow apartments in the photo on page 128 comes from the Cabrini Green housing project in Chicago, circa 1995. Torn down five years later, this set of government-run, low-income high-rises came to represent the worst of dilapidated, dangerous, drug-infested projects. Housing projects often serve as laboratories for man of the social problems associated with inner city life in America. A recurrent theme in both this photo and the one on page 128 is how out of place human beings are next to these sterile, boxlike structures. Although they are efficient and economical designs for cities, their lack of space may not be the best design for the people that live in them.

In St. Louis, a different urban social experiment took place in which the tenants were put in charge of the tenant leasing, eviction, security, and grounds maintenance. When given the control of their housing projects, the tenants were found to be more strict and draconian in applying the rules to their fellow tenants than the housing authority had been. A culture of victimization, disempowerment, and crime was replaced with a new culture that can often resemble the restrictive homeowners' associations of suburbia. Owning the former low-income housing unit was the next step in this new cultural "catharsis" that urban housing authorities were trying. Support by the government housing administration to have the residents purchase the units they were living in was an attempt to turn the lowest rung of the working class into respectable and safe middle-class suburbanites. This cultural change has met with lukewarm success, because ownership of an often distressed low-income apartment isn't a panacea for disintegrating neighborhoods, high crime, high unemployment, single-headed families, low education, or low wages. White, middle-class suburbanites still found fault with the ownership program, because the poor neighborhoods weren't immediately transformed into beautiful, safe communities.

The problems of the poor are still being densely packed on top of each other, along with the problems of their neighborhoods, and despite the benefit from owning (versus throwing money away on rent) their own residences; ownership alone isn't enough to combat all of their problems. To combat this, the Baltimore Housing Authority decided to place their low-income homeowners in repossessed, foreclosed properties throughout the city in middle-class and working-class neighborhoods. This leads to a more random placement of the urban underclass poor, since this program doesn't intentionally densely pack the poor on top of each other. Yet again, the housing culture of the underclass came into conflict with the expectations of their middle-class neighbors when issues of ornamentation and décor put the new homeowners at odds with their Suburban Homeowner's Association. The charges lodged against low-income residents ranged from some as trivial as the color of a painted fence to more serious charges like drug dealing from their homes. Critics also returned to an old argument that the culture of the poor was so different that they couldn't possibly assimilate to the middle-class culture of the suburbs. That type of critique has been labeled racist because it blames the mostly minority poor for not being able to participate in the "mow your yard—buy a Lexus" middle-class culture of the white suburbs.

CITIES BUILT TO SUIT

Some of the world's most interesting cities are not the compilation of decades or centuries of architectural design, but were created for a specific kind of urban culture. The Forbidden City of Beijing, China, and the surrounding neighborhoods were created and guided by the Emperor for his needs as head of state and supreme being. The design of the buildings and ramparts are to reinforce the authority and deity of the emperor; the oddity of this was that the general public were forbidden to enter the Forbidden City. The emperor's guards, servants, and civil officials must have been the direct audience for this striking and awe-inspiring architecture, but the indirect audience were the peasants and other citizens, who could only see the tops of the ornate buildings from behind the imposing walls.

Japan also has a ceremonial section of Tokyo for its emperor, but it is the city of Kyoto that stands out for its specific contribution to Japanese urban architectural culture. Referred to as the cultural heart and soul of Japan, Kyoto is the home of numerous Shinto shrines and was the capital of Japan for a part of its feudal history. It was planned and designed to be a feudal capital and a showcase of noble power and design. The traditional feudal Japanese architecture is present in many of Japan's cities, but Kyoto has been constructed and maintained as a living museum of Japan's cultural past. The influence on modern Japanese architecture is the use of Kyoto housing styles in the modern suburbs of Tokyo and Yokohama. In fact, when modern designers think of Japanese design they are most often envisioning the structural elements of Kyoto's architecture. So, important was the city to Japan's people and culture that it was removed from the list of atomic bomb sites by the American military at the end of World War II, despite the Americans' burning desire for revenge after Pearl Harbor. The animosity that would result in the Japanese public if Kyoto was destroyed was judged to be too great a risk (Kurtz 1988).

Washington, DC was founded in 1790 to be the nation's capital out of a drained swamp. The architecture and design of the city were to play important roles in its urban function as our capital city. Our founding fathers felt a sense of inferiority when visiting the grand cities of Europe with their history and intimidating architecture. The infant cities of New York and Philadelphia could not adequately host the political leadership and royalty of Europe considering the imposing European capitals and the lack of grand design in the early American cities. Surveyed and drained of its swamplands, Washington, DC was planned to be intimidating to visiting heads of state, with a huge white dome in the Congressional building and the Greek revival columns of the White House.

Parks and streets further the majestic impression of the city, which has been enhanced by the Egyptian obelisk design of the Washington Monument, the tranquil reflecting pool of the West Mall, and the brooding Lincoln Memorial. These architectural wonders are in a style that was foreign to the American colonies, but was adopted for the grand and intimidating look of the buildings to potential visitors. Even jaded modern visitors are awestruck during tours of older government buildings in Washington, DC, due to the grandiose and expansive nature of the buildings. The change to the capital and American culture since its founding is evident in the centrality our capital city plays in all world events and how Americans have come to expect its cities, culture, and viewpoint to always be critical to all world events. Yet, today the city that holds the world's most powerful government is also home to an urban environment racked with crime, drugs, and poverty.

This darker history of Washington, DC is also one in which architecture played a part. The buildings of government made a social psychological impact on the city's poor, minority citizens that communicated to them that this part of Washington, DC was not theirs, but instead was a part of government (white elite government). The government was clearly in charge of these areas of the city, and the rest of the city was left to the local municipal authority. But, without the ability to tax the suburbs in Virginia and Maryland or adequate funding from the federal government, the nongovernmental areas in the District of Columbia began to deteriorate fast after the 1900s. Before that date, Washington, DC was the shining example of a capital city with its bureaucratic mandarins living in townhouses or middle-class Victorian houses near the proud governmental buildings that these government employees and lobbyists wished to be near. After the 1900s, all cities were beginning to grow with the influx of former rural citizens looking for jobs and opportunities, and the competition for housing, precipitated on a decline in housing maintenance, generated areas of dilapidated housing. Government took little interest in this situation, considering it a local matter of concern and not a national issue. This situation was easy to ignore for the local bureaucrats when the government-maintained office buildings, like the Capitol and White House, were doing fine and were kept architecturally and spatially isolated from the rest of the city.

In fact, the Senate enacted a plan in 1900 to continue to beautify the government's buildings and parks in Washington, DC from an original design by Pierre L'Enfant left from 1791. Yet, the city's nongovernmental areas were left to flounder as roads, canals, and railroads that were promised to the city were left unbuilt by a lack of federal concern for the city. Sadly, this lack of concern has lasted another 100 years, as Washington, DC detoriated into one of America's most dangerous cities.

Can architecture really intimidate and produce a "feeling" in people? Obviously, the architects of Washington's city and buildings felt that the majestic nature of the city, Congress, and the White House gave the American president a "home field" advantage when negotiating with foreign dignitaries.

Another enthusiastic believer and designer in the social psychology of urban architecture was Adolf Hitler. Not only the builder of death camps that attempted to exterminate the Jewish, Communists, mentally ill, mentally retarded, physically disabled, homosexuals, and Gypsies, Hitler was obsessed with the design of a new Berlin from the ground up in collaboration with one of his few close acquaintances, urban architect Albert Speer. This was no "pipe dream" by Hitler, he had already impressed the world with the 1936 Olympics in Berlin that startled even casual observers with its totalitarian design, and he had dwarfed previous German monuments with his coliseum design in Nuremberg and Autobahn roadway system. Hitler was a believer in the lasting power of the Third Reich through the construction of huge buildings dedicated to his ego and mania. He was also confident in the ability of those buildings to dwarf the German individual and encourage conformity. Certainly other factors contributed to Hitler's rise to power and the acquiescence of the German people; the urban architecture of Berlin was just one of many weapons of the Nazis that were used to coerce the German people into conforming to his twisted worldview. *Theory break*: Marxists felt that Hitler's fascist goal of total human conformity was a primary goal of his architecture and political planning. Critics of Marxist soviet politics in Russia and East Germany would point out that the architecture and secret police policies in those two countries bear a striking resemblance to Nazi Germany's obsession with controlling its citizenry.

In the modern age, Brasilia, the capital of Brazil, was hewn out of the jungle in 1955 to become the political center of Brazil. Created by president Juscelino Kubitschek and planned street by street and building by building by architect Oscar Niemeyer, urban planner Lucio Costa, and landscape architect Burle Marx, the capital's architecture is a product of the culture and time that it was constructed.

The futuristic building design of Brasilia is reminiscent of the 1950s and 1960s, because it was finished in 1960, but it was also an attempt by politicians and designers to promote the idea that Brazil was a modern, progressive country. The urban architecture was meant to promote this modern Brazil to visiting heads of state, the new professional governing bureaucracy, and to the people of Brazil. Traditionally, the cities of São Paulo and Rio de Janeiro have been the centers of economic and political power in Brazil, and it took salary increases combined with housing subsidies to lure government

No city can boast more of a futuristic design than Brasilia, Brazil. A government culture unleashed on an urban environment, this city was created by the state to be its capital. Cut out of the jungle in central Brazil, an architect and landscape artist planned the buildings and roads from scratch to serve as an urban message to the rest of the world: "Brazil has arrived." No one could have a backward or third-world view of the country after being to this ultra-modern city—a new, sleek phoenix rising from the ashes of the jungle floor to be Brazil's international calling card of progress.

workers over 600 miles into the jungle to Brasilia (Noble et al. 2002). These older cities have also been associated with the corruption and ineptitude of the previous governments dating back to colonial times. In an effort to bring confidence in their government and create a new cultural direction for the country, the unique step of building an entire new capital city was taken, and considering Brazil's dominant position in South American economics and politics, it may have paid off.

A city with a millenium of history that embodies a past colonial urban design in a state of constant conflict with a modern sense of planning and urban architecture is Mexico City. A twenty-mile-long, seven-mile-wide mountain valley is home to nearly twenty million people that have to work and survive in an urban environment that is at war with itself (United Nations 2000). Perhaps to some this sounds overly dramatic, but consider that twenty million Mexicans in Mexico City is a population more than the 18.1 million New Yorkers in all of New York or the 18.3 million Texans in all the state of Texas. That is a prescription for trouble, and Mexico City is never short on urban problems. *Theory Break:* Marxists would point out that Mexico City is a city of two extremes: ramshackle cardboard homes of the poor in the "Villas Miserables" and the gated mansions of Mexico's powerful upper class. Not only do the gates and bodyguards mark the cultural differences between the classes, but the architecture of the city demonstrates a totally different orientation to obtaining and maintaining housing.

The class relationship in the city is aggravated by the previous colonial relationships in the city. The design of the old colonial city didn't just provide a central plaza and cathedral, but it provided the first living arrangement in the city as well. The large colonial-style apartment buildings with central, open atriums were built in the 1920s to house the growing urban population of Mexico City. Originally, these apartments provided spacious accomodations to the urban dweller of modest means, but they have been subdivided into smaller and smaller units over the past fifty years as the numbers of potential occupants have grown. This plan of centrally located apartment buildings was thought to be sufficient to take care of the poor's housing needs by seventy years of Mexico's leaders (Ward 1996). With their own distinctive architectural look, these inner city apartments have actually become too expensive for Mexico City's poorest citizens, forcing the poorest urbanites into creating an entirely new form of urban architecture for their housing—the squatter camp.

To understand the significance of the squatter movement, we must have an understanding of how powerful the issues of land and housing are to the Mexican people. There are not two more culturally powerful ideas to the Mexican citizen than land and housing; in fact, the right to land and housing are guaranteed in the constitution, a constitutional right American citizens do *not* have. The 1917 Constitution was written in opposition to the old colonial dictatorial style of government in Mexico. The nine years of revolution that led to the new constitution was fought by figures like Emilio Zapata, Pancho Villa, and Álvaro Obregón, and the principle rallying cry for the peasants that they organized was land reform for agriculture and housing. "Ejidal land" is the constitutional ideal that each village, town, or city would have a communal section of land that the peasant poor could work on and grow food on for survival. This idea of communal land for the landless poor has become part of the national culture. Sadly, many Mexicans do not have adequate housing because the economic and political forces have changed the government's focus from helping the poor after the revolution, when nearly a third of Mexican citizens were granted redistributed land, to a focus of consolidating power by appeasing the nation's elites.

Yet, the constitutional right to housing has led to a unique, urban culture regarding architecture in Mexico City. Squatting is seen by many Mexicans as a noble thing for the urban underclass and peasant class to engage in, and city efforts to remove squatters are met with public protest. A much different culture exists in the United States, where squatters are seen as trespassers that need to be irradicated to maintain the sanctity of private property, and the homeless are just the undeserving poor that annoy the good American citizen by panhandling. Much of this cultural difference is attributable to the two culture's conception of urban space and place. In the United States, no one has a right to space in the city, making place (or the ability to occupy a certain area) something that a citizen has to achieve. In Mexico, space (particularly public land and space) is thought of as more in community ownership terminology, making place and urban geography a struggle for constitutional rights in their culture.

One of the most innovative cultural solutions the poor have come up with is squatting on public land and then forcing the government to provide essential neighborhood services, like power and water, to these settlements. Urban poor activists found that squatting on public land avoided the hostility and legal entanglements of private landowners. Any small plot of public land from freeway overpasses and highway medians to landfills will be occupied by these housing activists to fill the need for housing and raise public awareness about the housing crisis. Once the squatters have taken possession of the land, an architectural resourcefulness ensues with cardboard and tin for building materials, trenches for sewers, stolen power cords for power, and buckets of water for thirst. The urban poor construct and even decorate these cardboard and plywood shacks. While the architecture won't make *Better Homes and Gardens,* the residents place doors, gates, and windows in their homes, and even construct two-story homes out of the discarded building fixtures and materials they can scavenge from landfills. From these humble beginnings, not only grows a specific kind of urban architecture, but an urban culture of demonstrations and organizations centered around these neighborhoods that can be in the middle of landfills and under highway overpasses.

For the city to recognize the land deeds of the squatters and provide the necessary services, the residents *must* organize and carry a culture of grassroots organization within their neighborhoods to the often reluctant municipal leaders of Mexico City. A grassroots organization culture becomes directly linked to urban architecture in Mexico City. (For more information on Mexico City, see Peter Ward's *Mexico City* (1996) and for more information on grassroots organizing in the urban environment read Manuel Castells' *The City and the Grassroots Movement* (1983).)

An undeniable form of architecture that is synonymous with the modern city is the skyscraper, and the city of skyscrapers is New York City. No other city has such an impressive skyline as New York City and a unique set of social, urban, architectural, and historical factors pushed the city's skyline upwards. The first factor that drove the structure of New York City skyward is the most obvious, land. Manhattan is an island, and while the five boroughs that make up New York City have steadily sprawled outward, the desire for business to be downtown in Manhattan has remained a constant urban factor. Architecturally, the steel frame building was becoming accepted by urban architects in the 1900s as a way to free building designers from the limits of brick and masonry construction. Unknown to most of us, brick construction will crumble under its own weight after only five or six stories in height. The Fuller (or Flatiron) building with its 22 stories at twenty-third street where Broadway and Fifth Avenue intersect was one of New York's first skyscrapers, and while its modest height might make us wonder if it would be called a skyscraper by today's standards, in 1902 its unique triangular shape and size made it something to behold.

The building that was the jewel of the skyscraper age in the first half of the twentieth century was the 1,250-foot-high Empire State Building. It took sixty thousand tons of steel to complete the eighty-six-story (plus a sixteen-story observation tower) office building by 1931, and though many thought it was going to be a foolish gamble to build something so extravagant in the depths of the Depression, the Empire State Building remains a triumph of planning, architecture, and design for New York City.

Attracting over one million visitors a year to its Art Deco interior and eighty-sixth-floor and 102nd-floor observation decks, the Empire State Building was going to embody the future for city architecture in the United States. From somewhat dated concepts like a port for Zeppelin docking to its innovative use of seventy-three elevators to move people up and down without causing delays, the Empire State Building created a standard by which all other skyscrapers are judged.

In fact, we should make special mention of the creation of the elevator as another key historical event that made skyscrapers possible. The idea of walking up eighty floors to an office is laughable and would have made skyscrapers highly impractical for workers and clients. However, the elevator made the eighty floor journeys take mere seconds and made skyscrapers plausible. The elevator is an urban innovation that would have only come about if land was in high demand and steel construction allowed buildings over six stories. The Chrysler Building, Rockefeller Center, and ultimately, the World Trade Center towers all were built using the steel frame concept, and because the price of real estate in Manhattan's desirable downtown area makes building "up" an affordable option. The multimillion dollar price tag of these buildings is still a sound business decision. *Theory Break:* Skyscrapers bring up a classic conflict between Functionalists and Marxists regarding urban planning and urban space. For Functionalists, the development of the skyscraper is an innovative yet logical solution to the issue of rising real estate. Marxists, on the other hand, view the skyscraper as an example of elite classes controlling urban space and using innovation for profits, rather than for people, wasting technology on constructing tall buildings for rich businesses instead of housing for the poor.

Oddly, ever since the Empire State Building's construction, cities have battled over the highest skyscraper. A competition for image and stature has driven the construction of the Sears Tower in Chicago, the Transamerica Pyramid in San Francisco, and eventually the tallest buildings in the world, the Petronas Towers in Kuala Lumpur in Malaysia.

The cultural image of the city of Kuala Lumpur and the nation of Malaysia is particularly evident in the Petronas Towers construction project. As the city and country became engaged in the project of having the world's tallest building, the city's elites and ordinary citizens became energized by the thought of having such a building in their city and nation. There can be no clearer example of urban architecture affecting urban culture than the city leadership, municipal officials, business leaders, and city dwellers themselves becoming excited about the project and possessing a shared sense of identity due to the tower's construction and location. *Theory Break:* In a way, one can't escape the Marxist critique of a false sense of consciousness[7] that the municipal elites created for Malaysians regarding the Petronas Towers. False, because a foreign conglomerate owns the buildings, most city dwellers won't get a paycheck from either the construction or employment in the Towers, and most citizens of the city won't even get an opportunity to go into the security conscious buildings. On the other hand, Malaysia pushed for the building and the unique Islamic star design because it would bring an image of a progressive and advanced nation to this peninsula. This project would change the world urban culture regarding Kuala Lumpur and Malaysia; no longer would it be a backward Third World island nation with a "suspect" Muslim culture and a repressive government. The Petronas Towers were clearly a sign that Malaysia was technologically developed and looking to engage the world, while the design of the towers holds an Islamic design motif important mainly to its Muslim urbanites. To ascertain the extent that a piece of urban architecture could change world opinion and spark further world interest in Malaysia is self-evident, because without the world's largest buildings we wouldn't be discussing Kuala Lumpur.

---

[7]A distorted or false belief that the elite or bourgeois class creates and maintains for the working class to pacify or distract them. An example would be the widely held belief that most people are middle class when in fact there is a sizable working class in America that is overlooked due to the false consciousness in America that we are all middle class.

Petronas Towers in Kuala Lumpur, Malaysia. These are the largest buildings in the entire world and like Brasilia, their construction has a great deal to do with an underdeveloped country using urban culture to create a new image. A nation can't be technologically retarded if it has the ability to build such amazing structures. Two uniquely Malaysian elements exist in the towers as well. If viewed from the top, we would see the presence of an Islamic star in the towers' design. This gives the towers their odd side ridges, visible in the photograph. There is also an Asian influence in the tapered tops of the buildings that is architecturally similar to the temples at Angkor Wat.

FASHION

When we were still living in caves, clothing was functional—it existed as a primitive form of technology and culture to keep the wearer warm. However, as our societies became more stratified (a difference between the power and wealth of specific groups is evident) and the division of labor increased (individuals have specific roles and duties to perform in the economy and society, i.e., priest, king, baker, soldier, merchant), clothes became a way to identify an individual's status. Special robes of special material denoted the priestly class, as they do today; royalty wore an even more specific garb and crown, which was denied to any other group or class. This clothing difference was a visible sign of the individual's class, status, and power, or, as was the case for most people, their lack of class, status, and power.

The urban component of these fashion realities of the past was initially that more people in a city meant more statuses and identities to keep up with, thus clearer signifiers of status were needed for the city versus the rural areas. Rome's code of fashion for emperors to slaves is an excellent example of a city writing down and codifying fashion's importance to the city and the urban environment. The emperor was the only Roman allowed to wear purple, an official Roman citizen (not all residents of Rome were actual citizens) was the only group allowed to wear a white toga, and the nobility could accent their toga with red or gold fabric. Europe's cities and countries also had formal laws of dress to separate the classes, and as cities on trade routes grew more powerful, the need to codify and enforce these rules for a more mobile population became evident. Now merchants, as well as nobles, moved and traveled from place to place in Europe and could acquire fine fashion; thus producing a need to officially classify fashion standards (again, certain fabrics and colors were reserved for nobility).

PUBLIC HEALTH AS AN IMPETUS FOR URBAN CULTURE PRODUCTION

One of the things making populations more apt to move from their home region or town were the plagues that attacked Medieval Europe's towns. Science and medicine provided no answers or relief to these pestilences, so those that could abandoned the cities, often for superstitious reasons (the city is cursed). This superstition saved many lives, because it was often the close and unsanitary conditions (open sewers, no reliable drinking water, standing puddles of liquid, animal excrement, and the close quarters of livestock) of cities that led to the outbreaks of various plagues like cholera, typhus, and yellow fever. There is one plague in the Middle Age's cities of Europe and another plague in the modern age that bear examining for their impact on urban cultural fashion.

The Black Plague (or Black Death) began in Italy (1346–1347) carried by fleas that infested rats aboard ships that made it to Italy's shore. While not a very "hearty organism," *Bacillus pestis* needed a live host and to be transmitted through the blood or another bodily fluid to be carried from host to host. Nevertheless, it thrived in the flea, lice, and bedbug population of Italy's teeming cities and was soon infecting humans. Hitching a ride from animal to animal or animal to human through the bites of these blood-sucking vermin, 25 to 30 percent of the population of Europe died in the two years after its rampage through Italy. Aside from emptying by half many of Europe's largest cities through death and population flight, it also redistributed a great deal of wealth. Since fleas liked to bite the upper class as much as the lower class, family fortunes were often going to the next of kin several times removed, or family estates were abandoned altogether and left to squatters.

The effect of urban fashion, since rural areas were not as focused on these matters, was twofold; for the first time in centuries, there was upward mobility of those that survived the plague and they wanted to spend money in a conspicuous manner, and secondly, surviving meant celebrating. The new, small middle and merchant class combined with those recently made wealthy through inheritance created a demand for better clothes and fabrics that challenged many of the old rules of dress for people of undetermined status (i.e., not born to nobility, but now wealthy). These new fashions could only be obtained in the trade route cities, which began to grow again after the plague, and the new fashion was bright colors and fabrics to celebrate the living's triumph over the plague.

Modern Americans tend to think of plagues as an ancient word and concept, something from the Dark Ages of humanity with no place in today's world. We sadly have a very short memory. Tuberculosis, cholera, typhus, and diphtheria have ravaged the East Coast of the United States, while outbreaks of malaria have ravaged the Gulf Coast states and New Orleans colonial history in particular. The Spanish influenza of 1918 killed more people than World War I (20–40 million worldwide), and in America alone it took 1.5 million lives (Kolata 1999).

But, the modern plague for America and the world is Acquired Immune Deficiency Syndrome (AIDS). Of the 33.4 million known cases of AIDS in the world in 1998, 29 million are in Africa and Asia, where the spread of the disease is through heterosexual use of prostitutes, often in the brothels of the biggest cities, where infection rates have reached alarming proportions (Flint et al. 2000). Since AIDS is spread through the intimate passing of bodily fluids, *anyone* engaging in high-risk behavior, such as unprotected sex or sharing intravenous needles, is at risk for contracting AIDS. A city's larger population increases the risk of encountering someone with the disease, particularly in Third World cities where an urban population does not mean a more educated or healthy population.

America has had a peculiar cultural reaction to the AIDS outbreak in the United States, because the first identifiable community to show high infection rates was the male homosexual community in the early 1980s. At this time, a promiscuous attitude toward sex in America expressed itself in the bathhouse culture of male homosexuals and in the heterosexual discos of the late 1970s in the large cities of America. Anonymous, unprotected sex with multiple partners was common in both discos and bathhouses and led to high STD and AIDS infection rates. Due to the initial infection of predominantly gay men in the United States, AIDS became known as a gay disease rather than just another sexually transmitted disease. The urban gay communities of New York and San Francisco were the only groups talking about this new disease as it spread across America. Conservative cultural leaders called the new disease "The Gay Plague" and conjured images of a Biblical retribution for homosexuals. Despite negligible female homosexual infection rates and over 75 percent of the world's AIDS cases due to heterosexual activity, America's culture branded AIDS a gay disease. This is an example of how culture can actually alter reality and perception. If there is a firmly held belief in the culture (i.e., AIDS is a gay disease), then those in that culture will accept that belief; eventually that belief becomes reality. *Theory Break:* According to the Sapir-Whorf school of thought, language and culture actually give us categories to think of our world with (Whorf 1939, in Carroll 1961). Without these categories, we wouldn't be able to effectively talk about or even conceptualize certain ideas, because our culture hasn't provided us with the appropriate categories or tools. In other words, culture and language can also be a straitjacket on its members. Beliefs that the earth is flat, that the sun revolves around the earth, and that evil spirits will inhabit your body if you sneeze are all examples of culture overriding science and medicine of their time. For our urban culture, the language of AIDS as being a gay disease made the growing infection rate a problem that political leaders did not want to deal with, and a problem beyond the resources of any city's abilities. (For more information on the history of AIDS in America, watch the movie *And the Band Played On*, 2000).

In an effort to change the perception that AIDS is only a gay disease and the fight for a cure as being only a gay cause, the international fashion community came together to change culture and find a way to cure this disease that puts everyone at risk. There are two cities that have come to dominate international fashion, New York City and Paris. Other cities like Milan, Los Angeles, Tokyo, and London have designers and contribute to the fashion industry, but Paris and New York set the trends and have the industry headquarters. With many male designers openly gay, like Jean Paul Gaultier and Gianni Versace, the impact of AIDS was devastating to these fashion icons, and they decided to be at the forefront of a solution. In combination with movie stars like Elizabeth Taylor and music stars like Elton John, a campaign of AIDS awareness was begun with one small fashion accessory—a piece of red ribbon.

This may seem like an insignificant gesture, but in this way AIDS activists were able to use fashion to raise awareness about AIDS and start the most successful education and research foundation devoted to the disease. We should not be surprised at the success of gay activism and gay culture. After all, in fifty years, homosexuals have gone from being shunned deviants relegated to secret lives in the closet to openly gay businessmen and women, actors and actresses, and even a Congressman, Barney Frank, and openly gay Episcopal Bishop Gene Robinson.

PRODUCTION OF URBAN CULTURE THROUGH FASHION

Let's focus on how Paris and New York City became the urban fashion capitals of the world. Until the storming of the Bastille and the French Revolution of 1789, French fashion was similar to other fashion trends aimed at Europe's aristocracy, lots of silk, lace, waistcoats, and wigs designed to emphasize the difference between the wealthy aristocracy and the peasantry.

While a bit more effeminate in its approach to male fashion, Paris's aristocracy was ahead of other countries in all forms of fashion, and some might claim that Louis XVI did set fashion trends, being an especially vain man concerning his legs.

The French Revolution was the first nationwide attempt to break the classism and aristocracy of the feudal period, and changing the fashion codes of the time was part of their anti-aristocracy campaign. While the revolution wasn't completely successful at eliminating the class structure of France, for awhile it changed fashion 180 degrees. Suddenly, looking like an aristocrat was *bad* for a person's health and a more muted and conservative style of dress was the fashion. Black hats and waistcoats were the approved of fashion with the red, white, and light blue emblem of the revolution as the only ornamentation that could be safely worn by a Parisian.

We see a similar nonclassist style of dress worn by the organizers of the Paris Commune Demonstration in 1871. This was a fashion statement aimed at the government, which the Commune demonstrators felt had forgotten the common man of the first revolution. The dark pants and coarse white shirt of the working demonstrator became the symbolic dress of those urbanites who sympathized with the commune demonstrations.

As France entered the Industrial Revolution (1733–1850), wages paid to the proletariat[8] provided workers with surplus income that, combined with a growing middle class of merchants, managers, and service providers, ignites a renewed interest in fashion. Yet, instead of that interest in fashion being for the aristocracy, these new fashions are for the normal citizen. They were not designated to enforce the line between the wealthy and poor, but the fashionable and unfashionable. Invariably, the "fashionable" of France were in Paris, where new clothing styles were changing constantly. It became a component of Parisian culture to follow those new clothing trends. New designers in Paris were at war with the dowdy fashions of the Victorian era, and they attempted to rescue the average urbanite from a life of stiff black dresses and high necklines.

New York City's place as a fashion city is a story of immigration and urban dominance. Between 1880–1920, a large immigration wave hit the United States from Southern and Eastern Europe and with this wave came a high percentage of Jewish immigrants. Unlike many immigrants making it to the shores of the United States with no money, no education, and no job skills, many Jewish immigrants had some money, some education (often religious or rabbinical), and some job skills in finance, craftwork, or tailoring. The Jewish immigrant possessed these valuable tools of capital because of the historical urban segregation that Jews had endured in Europe for hundreds of years. The first urban segregated areas designed to keep one religious group from another were the Jewish ghettos of Europe. Hated by the religious Christian leadership for their refusal to convert, Jews were often made scapegoats for many social problems, and often given jobs that

---

[8]The working class

Christians thought were too base to be held by Christians, like money changing and tailoring. The Jewish community turned inward, faced with all this animosity, and developed an ethic of "community reliance," in which they would educated their own children, train themselves for the jobs available, and spend their money in their own community. This translated to increased opportunities for Jews with job skills and education, versus other immigrants landing in New York without these skills. In Jewish neighborhoods, craft businesses and tailoring/textile shops flourished by capitalizing on cheap immigrant labor, community support, and investment in Jewish-owned businesses.

As for New York City's fashion dominance, manufacturing overshadows design as the reason the city commands so much attention in the fashion industry. It was not unique, socially challenging designs from New York that focused world attention on its fashion scene, instead, it was the amount of textile production from New York City's garment district that dazzled the world. Formed by an influx of Jewish and Italian immigrants willing to work the slave wages of the day, the garment district of Manhattan had the unique distinction of immigrants taking advantage of other immigrants to produce textiles. Previously, the dominant ethnic group (whites of English ancestry) forced recent immigrants (Irish or Germans) into subordinate jobs and made substantial profits from their labor. While Jewish clothing makers in the garment district would sell to stores or clothing buyers of English descent, it is important to remember that the workers, clothes designers, tailors, and owners of the factories were all Jews from the garment district.

Today's New York City garment district has undergone some distinct changes in the past hundred years, but the more things change, the more they stay the same. Much of the garment industry has moved farther uptown from its origins on the Lower East Side. For the area known as the garment district, there has been encroachment by condominium projects and the expansion of other businesses from neighboring New York areas, like the financial and theater districts. Yet, clothes are still made and traded there and many of these textile businesses are still owned by Jewish families. What has remained the same in the garment district is that an immigrant labor group continues to sew by hand or machine the garments in this district. That group of workers has changed from Jewish immigrants of the 1880–1920s to the Mexican and Chinese immigrants of today.

Sadly, the poor pay and working conditions haven't improved much since the Jewish immigrants were working there, but today transnational corporations sell the designs and clothes they are making all over the world for great profit. There are places where clothes could be made cheaper than Manhattan, however, and the Jewish community's textile entrepreneurs realize that to maintain their market position they need to maintain their position in the urban environment. By being close to New York City's top designers like Ralph Lauren, Tommy Hilfiger, Bill Blass, and Donna Karan, and top retail clothes buyers like Macy's and Bloomingdale's, the garment district is more visible and can produce clothing items quicker than a garment maker in New Jersey, Mexico City, or Hong Kong. This is why the garment district has kept many of its historical owners, but changed the ethnicity of its workers. For New York City's clothesmakers, the urban component of fashion is often their proximity to new ideas in the fashion world, but initially it was New York City's ability to manufacture fashion styles quickly in the 1920s that made it dominant. *Theory break*: For Marxist theorists, the revolving ethnicity of the workers demonstrates the enduring nature of class oppression in urban culture. Despite the terrible conditions that Jewish workers encountered in the garment factories, once they became the factory owners the temptation to exploit a new immigrant group proved too strong.

Most of us see haute couture in the top fashion magazines today and laugh at the bizarre fashions. Since many of these avant-garde clothes are featured in the Parisian shows, Americans feel that Parisian styles are very outlandish and foreign. Yet, a quick look at the popularity of Hip Hop fashions in the past decade might seem just as bizarre, if one didn't understand the urban context of the fashion. Large, baggy pants and jackets come from the influence of prison clothing and gang clothing on urban youth culture. But with one quarter of African American men in prison or on parole or probation, this fashion style is particularly resonant to the urban African American community (Table 6.1).

Large, garish graphic designs on oversized shirts are reminiscent of spray-painted graffiti on buildings, and large gold chains seem to be an attempt to display wealth and position that is often beyond most innercity members. The urban environment of New York City influences the fashion trend, as Hip Hop clothing delivers something to its consumers that the Gap

Table 6.1   Percentage of Population Incarcerated

Inmates by Race*	
White:	95,077 (56.3%)
Black:	68,413 (40.5%)
Asian:	2,640 (1.5%)
Native American:	2,628 (1.6%)

Increase in Sentenced Prisoners (more than one year) in State/Federal System by Sex and Race 1985–1995†	
White Male	103%
White Female	194%
Black Male	143%
Black Female	204%

*Federal Bureau of Prisons 2003

†Bureau of Justice Statistics Bulletin 1997, June Edition, "Prisoners in 1996."

clothing store does not supply. Clearly, it is the inner city urban culture that is missing from the mall fashion of the Gap.

To Parisians, I am sure these fashions look preposterous, because Parisians don't understand the urban context of the clothes. New York City was the first city of Hip Hop fashion, due to its combination of rap innovation and textile manufacture. Today, leading Hip Hop designers Fubu and Sean John have their design headquarters in New York City to take advantage of the new urban culture that bubbles up from the streets of New York City.

Urban culture from New York City has found its way to middle America, as the largest market for urban Hip Hop wear turned out to be white suburbia—just like the market for rap music. Urban culture continues to form from the urban elements of race, class, and gender in the city, and once established, that urban culture can influence the rest of the nation and the world.

References

CARROLL, JOHN. 1961. *The Study of Language.* Harvard University Press: Cambridge, MA.

CASTELLS, MANUEL. 1983. *The City and the Grassroots Movement.* University of California Press: Berkeley, CA.

FLINT, S.J., L.W. ENQUIST, R.M. KRUG, V.R. RACANIELLO, AND A.M. SKALKA. 2000. *Principles of Virology.* ASM Press: Washington, DC.

HOBBES, THOMAS. 1651. *Leviathan.* Touchstone Books (1997): New York, NY.

KOLATA, GINA. 1999. *Flu: The Pandemic of 1918.* Touchstone Books: New York, NY.

KURTZ, LESTER. 1988. *The Nuclear Cage: A Sociology of the Arms Race.* Prentice Hall: Upper Saddle River, NJ.

LITTLE, CHARLES. 1989. *Deviance and Control: Theory, Research, and Social Policy.* Peacock: Itasca, IL.

MACIONIS, JOHN, AND VINCENT PARRILLO. 2001. *Cities and Urban Life.* Prentice Hall: Upper Saddle River, NJ.

MACHIAVELLI, NICCOLO. 1538. *The Prince.* Trans. Neil Thompson. Barnes and Noble (1999): New York, NY.

NOBLE, JOHN et al. 2002. *Brazil.* Lonely Planet Publishers: Melbourne, Australia.

SIMMEL, GEORG. 1908. *The Sociology of Georg Simmel.* Kurt Wolff (ed., 1950 edition). Free Press: Glencoe, IL.

SWIFT, JONATHAN. 1726. *Gulliver's Travels.* Penguin Books (2001): New York, NY. Originally Published Benjamin Motte, Jr. Publisher: London, England.

UNITED NATIONS. 2000. *Report on Population 2002.* UN Department of Social and Policy Information. UN Publications: New York, NY.

WARD, PETER. 1996. *Mexico City.* John Wiley and Sons: New York, NY.

CHAPTER SEVEN

Photography, Film, and Television

The first photograph was taken in 1826 by Joseph Niepce of a small village courtyard in France (University of Texas Ransom Center 2002). From this auspicious beginning, the reproducible image has had a long history with the city as subject matter and influence. At first, the city was just an interesting still life to take pictures of, but later the technology of the city influenced the art of photography and has influenced our perception of the city. Parisians had the first love affair with photography and a new device called a daguerreotype. This new way of capturing images swept Europe and then moved into the Americas as people from a broader class background could afford these pictures. Since its size and the chemical alchemy needed to produce the daguerreotypes was preventative for most rural areas, itinerant photographers roamed like minstrels from town to town to satisfy the demand for these prints. During this period, as the photographic art improved and gained popularity in America, the urban influence on photography was limited to the fact that cities possessed larger audiences for the sale of portrait photographs. Photographers could open shops in the retail district downtown and reach enough customers to survive.

Photography in America was following a progression of slow retail expansion in urban areas when in 1861 the Civil War actually made photography a rural art form. Matthew Brady (1823–1896) took the most shocking photos of the Civil War, often just minutes after a battle (Domingues 1999). Brady's photos stripped the romance from war. Gone were the heroics and grand ideals and all that was left were the bloated and rotting corpses of the thousands of Confederate and Union soldiers. With the pictures, public opinion began to change about the war that took American lives so freely, and that opinion was a rural one, because that was where most Americans lived in the nineteenth century.

A one-room tenement apartment in New York City, circa 1890, photographed by Jacob Riis for his book *How the Other Half Lives.* Stories of urban poverty and deprivation had regularly appeared in the press since Charles Dickens's time, but Riis's work was unique because of photographs like this one. The cramped living space and squalid conditions for these seven people was not uncommon in the slums of New York, but the middle and upper classes had only seen the outside of these buildings. Now, the reader was in the story and seeing the private world of urban poverty.

Jacob Riis (1849–1914) took a new occupation called photojournalism to a new level in an urban context with his exposure of poverty and squalor in New York City in *How the Other Half Lives* (1890). Pictures of the topic he was writing about captured his audience in a way that no printed exposé could manage. Several other journalists and many left-wing political parties had been crying to the public about the horrid conditions of the new groups of immigrants to the city, but until the public saw the wretched conditions of the back alleys and tenements of the slums firsthand through photos, no action was taken. This same sort of activism through pictures changed the meatpacking industry, where one photo of rats perched on rotting meat was worth ten thousand words.

Nellie Bly (1864–1922) was another of this new breed of sensationalist photojournalists. (The practice was sometimes referred to as yellow journalism.) While working for Joseph Pulitzer's *New York World* newspaper, Elizabeth Cochrane adopted the pen name "Nellie Bly" and wrote exposé articles about the terrible conditions of New York's insane asylums (by having herself committed to one), the Pullman workers strike on the nation's railroads, and crusading feminist figures like Emma Goldman. Her most memorable stunt as a journalist was to break the fictitious record of Jules Verne's character Phileas Fogg in *Around the World in Eighty Days* (Nash 2001). This brought her fame and increased Pulitzer's circulation. She was the first woman to have dolls, songs, cartoons, and poster ads made of herself commemorating her adventure in 1890. After marrying a wealthy industrialist in 1895, Nellie Bly was the first female industrialist to run not one, but two, million-dollar companies in 1905 after her husband's death. Believing in her crusades of the past, Nellie ran her businesses as social experiments with on-site health care, literacy studies, gymnasiums, and library programs for her workers.

After Riis's and Bly's photos, simple illustrations were no longer adequate to sell newspapers, and photos became the necessary element to ensure circulation success. Photographs of people from different walks of life and different ethnicities helped to make their lives and suffering more real to the dominant class that read the newspapers. In the photos, they became real people to anyone who read the stories, including members of the working class. Unions used photos in an attempt to halt the use of child labor in dangerous work settings. Crime photos made the danger of the city immediate, while photos of leaders made them seem like actual people, rather than mere figureheads. The photos in these newspaper articles made the urban problems of their time real, and in a sense, provoked people into action to engage the urban culture they were presented with and to change it.

Conflict theorists would be quick to remind us that after the power of photographs in newspaper articles was discovered, many elites crusaded against them, fearing that shocking photos of tenements or workplaces might erode their own elite power. So, the next urban cultural reaction to photography to be discussed is censorship. Three kinds of censorship affect urban photography and art: government censorship, business censorship, and public censorship. Government censorship, which can often be in collusion with powerful business and religious elites, first focused its attention on the "moral" turpitude that photography would represent. Sometimes referred to as "formal" censorship, since it is an official and formal act of the government, this is what most people think of when discussing censorship—the government banning a book or movie from public consumption. In the same way that one of the chief subjects of painting was the human form, so too photography allowed exact representations of the nude form. Immediately, the government censorship machine went to work eliminating or restricting access to nude photos or film in an effort to "protect the citizens and children." The idea was that any man viewing such salacious material would be moved to become a ravenous rapist and any child exposed to such images would be forever damaged and warped.

Two cases stand out in the history of this effort of government censorship of photography: Larry Flynt and Robert Mapplethorpe. Both cases stem from the same urban area's attempt to curtail access to nude photography. Larry Flynt began his crusade for access to nude photography as a strip club owner who advertised his club's female attractions in a small magazine to local readers in Cincinnati, Ohio. Soon, Flynt realized that he was able to make more money from the sale of the magazine than from his strip club. Predictably, government censors took him to court in a series of cases that defined the government's position on photographic pornography. In 1977, the Supreme Court said that the photographs in question were protected under the First Amendment.

> "Congress shall make no law respecting an establishment of religion, or prohibiting the free exercise thereof; or abridging the freedom of speech, or of the press; of the right of the people peaceably to assemble, and to petition the government for a redress of grievances."

Despite this ruling, however, local municipalities were still permitted to restrict and regulate access to the material on the basis of "community standards." With this vague ruling, communities felt they could regulate this "dangerous urban photographic culture," while publishers and photographers felt vindicated that they could pursue their photographic art and commerce.

This delicate balance was upset in 1990 by the Robert Mapplethorpe (1946–1989) exhibit in Cincinnati, Ohio. The photographer had died in 1989 and a showing of his private collection of photographs was being exhibited at the Contemporary Art Center. Local officials, responding to complaints, tried to censor the exhibit and the director of the center was arrested, tried, and acquitted of obscenity charges. The explicit, homoerotic images pushed the boundaries of most people's definition of good taste, but the court refused to validate the urban community's standard of obscenity. When we think of censorship, this is the image that most readily comes to mind, and its impact on the urban culture is to place official boundaries on specific types of culture for some to respect and others to break (Marien 2003).

Public censorship or "informal" censorship is the refusal to patronize an objectionable establishment or exhibition. Most often, small groups of what Howard Becker called moral entrepreneurs[1] organize an awareness campaign or demonstration. Often, these efforts at censorship are not successful, because for every group committed against the showing of a film or art exhibit, there is likely another group that is committed to it. Urban public censorship boycotts can be successful, as shown in the National Federation of Decency's boycott of 7-11 convenience stores for carrying *Playboy* magazine, in which the Southland Company, 7-11's parent company, opted to remove *Playboy* from its stands. Another example of a successful effort was the conservative Christian American Family Association theater boycott of the Martin Scorsese movie, *The Last Temptation of Christ*. The movie failed to meet earnings projections in 1988 at the box office and was quickly moved to video, where Blockbuster Video opted not to carry it in response

---

[1]Someone who is crusading to change a law or norm

to the protests. An example of a public censorship protest that has not been successful is the efforts by some conservative religious leaders and some feminists to stop or criminalize *all* pornography. Often, the only place such broad protests (i.e., all pornography) will work are in rural and semirural areas, where there are fewer people and fewer individuals willing to break with the dominant morality of the community. Obviously, in a larger metropolitan area, public censorship is difficult to maintain, since there are often as many people for a censored work as there are against it. But, as these examples show, if enough individuals bring pressure, public censorship can be successful.

Business censorship of culture can be the most insidious of all three types. This is when information or images are censored not because of official policy, but because of economic or business concerns. The economic or public relations of this information is often deemed dangerous and the businesses that represent the media bury or ignore the story. Not all businesses have the ability to manipulate the media, yet the subtle business perspective of our media is so pervasive that most of us miss it. Business censorship was responsible for Bill Maher's removal as host from the popular late-night television show, *Politically Incorrect* in November 2001. His removal was precipitated by very vocal critics who promised to boycott ABC advertisers after his statement that the terrorists of 9/11 were not cowards because they died in their attempt to attack the United States, as compared to the U.S. forces who attacked via long-distance weapons that didn't require risking the loss of American life. While many may take exception to his remarks, the use of business censorship essentially eliminated the debate.

Since there are so many different business concerns, and only a few media outlets, the level of this kind of censorship can be profound. For modern urban Americans, the idea that the information they receive is censored in any way seems preposterous, because there are so many television, newspaper, and radio news sources. But, a quick look at some of the huge conglomerates that own multiple newspapers, like the Gannett corporation, which owns ninety-nine separate U.S. newspapers in over forty urban areas, and the fact that the four major television networks news programs are owned by four powerful multinational corporations, make the idea of business censorship more plausible:

ABC—owned by Disney

CBS—owned by Viacom

NBC—owned by General Electric

FOX—owned by Rupert Murdoch's News Corporation

These media corporations in turn own stock and sit on the boards of many other large corporations. This interconnectedness of corporate leadership leads to a closed culture of corporate thinking on the issues of censoring challenging or threatening material. *Theory Break:* C. Wright Mills called this

The Power Elite (1956) in which interlocking directorates lead to a small number of very powerful men making the decisions for hundreds of companies. William C. Domhoff (2001) duplicated and revised Mills's analysis in 1980 and 2000 and found even more collusion at the top of the corporate world than Mills found in 1956. Combining this analysis with a critical look at media sources in general, Noam Chomsky developed the Propaganda Model of elite corporate interest and censorship of the popular news media. Expanding on this notion, the Peter Phillips Censorship Project published *Censorship 2000*, a book of the most censored and overlooked stories that the panel felt had been ignored in the previous year (they have published this book for each successive year). The common theme of many of these news stories identified by the censorship project was corporate misdeeds or wrongdoing that caused these stories to be eliminated by corporate censorship.

Certainly, the media blows the whistle on some corporate wrongdoings, but the amount of time that it takes and the trepidation the media exhibits when approaching such a project demonstrates the point. Media sources worry about the litigation a large corporation can bring, even if the story is correct, often killing the challenging story rather than risking litigation. As an example, we should examine the case of ABC's news story about the tobacco industry memos that demonstrated that thirteen tobacco companies manipulated the level of nicotine in cigarettes and that certain cartoon advertising was aimed at underage smokers. The pressure from big tobacco's lawyers was enough to illicit an on-air apology from ABC's Diane Sawyer and was enough to have the normally fearless CBS *60 Minutes* photojournalists bury a story they were contemplating about the tobacco industry [this event was the subject of the movie, *The Insider* (1999)].

The impact on urban culture of corporate censorship is to create a culture in which urbanites don't have enough clear information to make informed decisions about the issues that most often affect them in their urban environment. Corporations are able to manipulate the news and information to suit their needs, confusing or misleading the public on issues that are of concern like corporate influence in politics, environmental pollution, or plant closings and relocations. Just as an example of the effect on urban work culture, most U.S. workers don't feel that there is anything they can do about plant closings due to a probusiness slant in the media. Yet, European workers are guaranteed up to a year's advance warning of impending layoffs or plant closings. Probusiness media rarely bring this discrepancy up during coverage of the latest layoffs.

HOW PHOTOGRAPHS BUILT A CITY

For seven months out of the year, western New York State is as cold and bleak a place as the arctic winds and Great Lakes' snow can make it. Aside from Niagara Falls, there is little photogenic about the area except for perhaps the change of the autumn foliage, but photography as we know it was changed by a wiry urbanite from Rochester, New York. Despite the region's fierce weather, Rochester had grown as a flour-milling city and had taken advantage of the small waterfall in the downtown section for power, creating a wealthy city when a young George Eastman (1854–1932) arrived in 1860 (Bannon 2002). A driven entrepreneur, George Eastman didn't invent the little camera that the world would know as the "brownie," but he refined a process in 1888, in which the camera could be sent to Rochester for film developing and the company would mail your photos back to you. Thus, film and camera giant Kodak was born. The small camera and its versatile successors began a photography revolution, where common people would not only photograph themselves, but their homes, vacations, birthdays, and all the events of their lives. An explosion of photography occurred and it changed the city of Rochester.

The downtown skyscraper-style headquarters for Kodak is still one of the preeminent structures in the skyline of Rochester and has been enlarged numerous times to accommodate the growing legions of bureaucrats necessary to keep the company operating. Between the blue collar and skilled line jobs and the management salaries, Kodak's influence on Rochester's economy brought workers flocking to the inhospitable area. Those that found employment with Kodak could buy nice houses and build neighborhoods that rivaled any Northern city between 1920 and 1960. But, George Eastman wasn't content with that, he proliferated philanthropic efforts to make Rochester a world-class city of its time. A world-class university modeled after the Ivy League schools, the University of Rochester, actually predates Eastman, but it was his gifts that have carried it to the stature of today. A pet interest of Eastman's was music, and his donations made the Eastman School of Music one of the most well-respected centers for classical music instruction in the world. Parks, libraries, and auditoriums were all part of Eastman's gift to a grateful city, only made possible due to the unparalleled popularity of urban photography. In effect, the photographic process and the popularity of the Kodak camera made Rochester, New York, the city it is today.

TINSEL TOWN

Hollywood, California, exists as the land of movie dreams and movie companies because our culture has programmed all Americans to think of this Los Angeles suburb as the movie Mecca. In the early days of the nickelodeon, circa 1905–1907, moving pictures were made on both the east and west coasts of America. But the success of Max Sennett's Keystone cops and later his films with Charlie Chaplin made the Los Angeles area the focal point for moving pictures. Metro Goldwyn Meyer, Warner Brothers, Paramount, Universal, and United Artists began in the Hollywood area because of the need to be where the successful artists are producing their work. A

The smokestacks of the Kodak Park plant in Rochester, New York, have come to symbolize the economic and environmental domination this one company has over the entire urban culture of the city. Linked to respiratory problems, polluted soil, and toxins in the water, the output of the plant has become the flipside to the employment benefits, parks, and educational grants that Kodak has given to Rochester. In hard economic times, there is a tough choice that must be made between jobs and economic growth, and pollution and waste from urban manufacturing.

short film of the time most often took less than a month, because the public was demonstrating an insatiable appetite for movies.

So, how did this city that was located 3,000 miles from the population centers of the East Coast manage to become the movie capital of the world? Let's begin with location. At first glance, being away from the East Coast's population centers might be a detraction from the location of Hollywood. But, considering climate and the public's demand for movies, production of movies needed to be virtually constant, something that was only possible in a place with a temperate, sunny climate, unlike that of the East Coast cities, where movies could be shot year-round.

Southern California's climate was ideal, as were the many different terrains that could be used as backgrounds for Westerns, police chases, multiple urban scenes, and even mountain scenes in the Los Angeles area. Hollywood's own picturesque view of Los Angeles became important as a highly sought after living space for superstar actors like Douglas Fairbanks and Charlie Chaplin, even more than its value as just a movie production center. This unique distinction made living in the Hollywood Hills an urban address with a great deal of cultural meaning. With production and labor locating itself in the Los Angeles area, movie production became synonymous

MAX WEBER'S METHODOLOGY

Max Weber examined the cultural production of music in Europe and developed a methodological link between climate, class, status, urbanization, rationalization, and musical literacy in his famous book *Economy and Society* (1921, 1979). It was Weber's contention that European music and harmony developed in Northern Europe because the Roman Catholic bureaucracy invented a method of musical notation from its fastidious choral tradition. This tradition was consistent with what Weber identified as the rationalization process, a societal phenomenon in which the traditional power and authority of a social group (i.e., traditional power like a tribal king or chief) is replaced by a rational power and authority (i.e., the agreed-upon authority of society's laws and rules). As European society became more urbanized and divided by class, social capital like music appreciation, training, and literacy became more prevalent in the growing middle class. The middle class of Northern Europe wanted music in their homes because of the climate of Northern Europe, the instrument had to be brought into the home. Cold weather for most of the year brought music making inside in Northern Europe, and the desire for status made the piano the instrument to have for a middle-class family. Written music for the piano became almost as important as the instrument itself, and an explosion of classical, ragtime, and later, jazz music for the piano migrated to and from the New World. One of the key elements of Weber's methodology is incorporating lifestyle and climate to his analysis of music as a social phenomena. This is necessary methodology for our understanding of the film industry's need for a climate and lifestyle conducive to year-round film schedules. To grasp the complexity of a phenomenon like film production, a broad inclusive methodology that incorporates elements of social process like climate is necessary.

with Hollywood and Los Angeles by 1910–1920. Again, with the theater and radio production established in New York City, one might have assumed the movie industry would have located in New York because of the concentration of actors, producers, and investors in the city. However, with the need for a wider distribution network for film and an outdoor production schedule, the West Coast superceded the acting availability and financial control of New York City.

After the Great Depression, movie production in Hollywood was centered around the studio system of contract players and sound stages. While not all of Southern California was excited about "movie people" taking over Hollywood, the area was the headquarters for all of the big movie studios by the 1930s. Even if a movie was shot on location in the South Pacific or Paris, the movie idea and original production decisions from cast to costumes were made in the Hollywood studio system.

Moving pictures, prior to Hollywood's studio system, were small-budget, independent ventures. Ithaca, New York, was the site of many silent film productions before the Hollywood system developed, because it was close to the population centers of the East Coast and possessed some varied scenery. Actors and financiers from New York City would travel to Ithaca to make the movie and then would take it back to New York City for distribution. Many silent films were made in the midsized cities of the East and Midwest; in fact, it was the weather and film difficulties in Chicago that brought Hollywood its first big production. D.W. Griffith was filming a larger than usual production for the silent movie industry in 1908, *The Count of Monte Cristo*, and it had to be completed in Hollywood because of weather and other delays. This was the first major movie production that had been made in Southern California, but the movie director and producer were impressed with all that the area offered. Clearly, this city was considered to be the future of movie making when Griffith's experience in Hollywood was circulated among other movie makers.

Three years later the first movie studio in Hollywood was built, and by 1913 twenty moving picture companies were located in Hollywood, soon to include Cecil B. deMille, Samuel Goldwyn, D.W. Griffith, Louis B. Mayer, and Darryl Zanuck. Perhaps the ability to finish the largest-budget picture to date in 1908 emboldened Hollywood with the success for making moving pictures that, at that time, no other city possessed. And, with the increasing demand for movies, the industry needed an urban center to concentrate production to meet this demand. It should be emphasized that, in many ways, Hollywood made *no sense* as the center for a movie industry during the 1910s and 1920s. It did not possess the theater talent or vaudevillian talent of New York's stage community or the growing writing and production talent of New York's or Chicago's burgeoning radio networks. No finance industry to help with the cost of making films or an established distribution network from Hollywood to the rest of the country existed; only the Los Angeles area's growth and good weather were to its credit. For Hollywood, it only took one major movie production to raise the visibility of this unique urban environment. *Theory Break:* This example demonstrates how two different urban ecological principles can conflict with each other. The key function of New York City's entertainment industry, coupled with the agglomeration of the entertainment businesses of theater, acting, and radio, should have made it the center of the film industry. But, the physical environment of Hollywood was such a superior location that it drew the industry to the West Coast.

The studio system thrived in Hollywood's closed social world of contract actors and movie stars in the 1930s and 1940s. The city generated a "film scene" in which not only movies are made, but also auxiliary businesses for movie production thrive (like talent agents, managers, hair stylists, catering companies, costume designers) and an urban culture grows around the production of films. While Warner Brothers, Paramount, Metro Goldwyn Mayer, and Columbia continued to dominate the major motion picture business in Hollywood, the studio system's control over the actors and other aspects of movie making was diminished by independent initiatives in the film and television industry during the 1960s and 1980s. Yet again, even in these times of change in Hollywood, it is still this city that controls most of the United States's and the world's moving picture culture.

While foreign movies today like *Crouching Tiger, Hidden Dragon* (2000) and *Chocolat* (2000) win financial and critical acclaim, they still have to be distributed through the major film networks of Hollywood. These distribution networks are dominated by the motion picture industry, and films that are placed in these networks are just products for sale. The film industry has a great deal of power in selecting what films will make it into lucrative markets for potential success. Thus, the film industry directs foreign film production by communicating what is acceptable for the American market and what they will allow to be distributed. Hong Kong stands out as a city that through the 1980s and 1990s did not initially develop movies for the American market, but instead created an entire motion picture industry devoted to the 1.5 billion-strong Chinese-speaking audience. At first, the Hong Kong film industry made martial arts films, a genre made famous to American audiences by Hong Kong actor Bruce Lee. Contact with the U.S. market in the 1960s and 1970s demonstrated the potential for these movies in the West, but also exposed the Hong Kong filmmakers to directors, technology, and film genres of the West that they then adopted for their market. Two key Hollywood influences are the "police-action" genre of films (i.e., *The French Connection, Serpico*, etc.) and the films of action director Sam Peckinpah. Combining the existing film industry of martial arts filmmakers with the gritty police genre and Peckinpah's over-the-top action style of direction created a new kind of urban film culture.

As of 2001, the top-grossing movie of the summer was *Rush Hour 2*, starring Hong Kong action and martial arts star Jackie Chan and American comedian Chris Tucker. It has taken two decades and numerous broken bones[2] for Jackie Chan to "break into" the Hollywood motion picture industry, but he has been able to transcend the Hong Kong martial arts genre and

---

[2]Jackie Chan insists on performing his own stunts and has broken several major bones.

overcome his heavily accented delivery of English dialogue to join the mainstream. Several films that Chan made in Hong King for distribution in China have since become underground cult classics in America, like *Drunken Master* (1978) and *Police Story* (1985).

Hong Kong director John Woo has also enjoyed crossover success in America, directing John Travolta and Nicholas Cage in *Face/Off* (1997) and Jean-Claude Van Damme (a martial arts expert from Brussels) in *Hard Target* (1993). The ultra-action style of John Woo with over-the-top stunt sequences and slow motion action is an updated directorial technique from Sam Peckinpah that took film audiences by storm. To Hollywood, Woo's style was considered brand new and cutting edge. One of John Woo's acting protégés from Hong Kong is Chow Yun Fat, a tall, dark, Asian leading man who projected charisma and danger in *The Killer* (1989), one of Woo's films that became a cult classic in America. Chow Yun Fat's American film success began with a Hong Kong style action movie costarring Mira Sorvino, but filmed in L.A., called *The Replacement Killers* (1998). Like Jackie Chan, the nervousness in Hollywood regarding Chow Yun Fat's thick Asian accent delivering English dialogue turned out to be unsubstantiated. Film fans loved the Hong Kong style action sequences in *The Replacement Killers*, regardless of the urban backdrop (Hong Kong or Los Angeles) or the ethnicity of the actors. Audiences weren't troubled by this Asian leading man, and he landed his next role opposite Academy Award winner Jodie Foster in *Anna and the King* (1999). Chow Yun Fat followed that film with the Academy award winner for best foreign film, *Crouching Tiger, Hidden Dragon* (2000).

Hollywood expropriated the film style, directing, and actors from Hong Kong to fill the action void left by the studio's fascination with megabudget pictures of the 1990s. The Hong Kong film culture, which again many feel is a reformation of the 1970s American action and chase genre, reintroduced a quicker, flashier, yet cheaper film product to the Hollywood film system. Despite Hong Kong's hold on the 1.5 billion-person Chinese-speaking audience, the income generated from this audience is no match for the finance, marketing, advertising, and distribution dominance of the Hollywood motion picture machine. While we can argue that Hollywood has been influenced by and has responded to the cultural products of Hong Kong, conflict theorists would point out that the power and expropriation flows one way . . . from Hong Kong to Hollywood.

Theory Break: An example of how this expropriation works can be illustrated by noting that Nicholas Cage hasn't left the Los Angeles area to make Hong Kong produced films in Chinese, but he has acted in Hollywood film projects that have brought in Hong Kong directors. Money for these films still ends up in the hands of the Hollywood movie industry machine. This is classic urban appropriation, where the dominant city takes what it wants from the subordinate city.

Hollywood's film industry is so powerful that it has even co-opted the radio and print medium, beginning in the 1930s with the public's fascination with movie stars and their lives. The producers and actors of the film industry occupy a special place in the hearts of audiences that consume their films, and that obsession with the actor's lives began with Charlie Chaplin in the silent film era. Gossip columnists and media paparazzi have pushed to fill the void of information concerning film stars. Walter Winchell was one of the first of the newspaper gossip columnists to write about the stars of Hollywood and he quickly became part of the Hollywood film system. In 1936, he was the highest paid radio personality in the world with his weekly expose on the loves of the Hollywood elite and the nation's famous. To this day, despite numerous legal battles to thwart them, gossip newspapers and "tell-all" weeklies feature outrageous and sometimes libelous stories about the Hollywood stars and their lives. One type of culture (the film industry) produces an auxiliary type of culture (the gossip columnists, weekly tabloids, and talk shows). This is evidence of a "film scene" in Hollywood that doesn't exist anywhere else. *Theory Break:* Dominant cities are not just the outcome of a natural urban process, say conflict theorists. These cities are the centers of bourgeoisie finance and production, which subordinates smaller urban environments. Hollywood stars and films dominate the media consumption of smaller cities.

Television is another medium complicit in the hype surrounding Hollywood, including Aaron Spelling's high school soap opera that immortalized the very zip code of Hollywood's elite, *Beverly Hills 90210*. Shows like *Entertainment Tonight* and the E! network on cable continue to make Hollywood the focal point for the star's lives and movie making. The city of Hollywood has grown to fill the needs of the movie industry, the movie stars, and the paparazzi that cover both. It has also created auxiliary businesses and has given rise to the next major urban entertainment medium we discuss—television.

LIVE TELEVISION TO STUDIO CITY

Television deserves its own section of analysis regarding urban culture because of its journey from one coast to another and the creation of a section of Los Angeles devoted to television production. Live television began in 1939, beamed to what would be seen today as only a handful of television consoles from studios in New York City. Like many types of American urban culture, the culture of New York City set the stage for television culture, featuring variety shows and daytime dramas similar to the types of projects produced for radio. Depending on the technicians, writers, producers, actors, and municipal networks that supported radio, people in many cities thought television wouldn't last. The shows were in black and white, lacking the polish of radio shows because they were broadcast live, without the benefit of editing out mistakes. The television consoles themselves were very expensive at the time, costing about $300 for a 7-inch screen (roughly $3,300 in today's dollars) in 1946 (Genova 2002). Yet, the humor and drama of what the audience could see on television outweighed the polish and history of radio, and by 1959 there were 67,145,000 television sets and hundreds of television broadcast stations affiliated with the three networks (ABC, CBS, and NBC) (Genova 2002).

The movie industry in Hollywood dismissed the threat of the home television set and continued to pay the price for their oversight for fifty years. Clearly, the convenience of home television entertainment drove down film revenue beginning in the 1950s and encouraged the networks to make increasingly more expensive television programs. With the stock antenna, the color television of today in the urban area can only receive two more networks than a viewer could in 1960 (Fox and PBS). It may seem that there is little threat to films because there have only been two new networks in forty years. However, with cable or a satellite dish, hundreds of television channels are available to viewers willing to pay for the service, bringing endless movie and entertainment options right into the viewer's home. Even in the days of three networks, there was an incredible drive for more and more programming to fill the airwaves.

Initially, live television programs were only on in the evenings when advertisers and program executives felt that the family, home from work and school, would be watching. Considered "family programming," shows like those of Milton Berle and Ed Sullivan were often revisions of vaudeville acts from earlier in the century with lots of slapstick comedy and tame humor. Soon, programmers realized the value of aiming programs in the afternoon to the 1950–1960s housewife. As the chief grocery and clothing purchaser for the American family, many housewives wielded a great deal of economic power. While in many respects urban women had been disenfranchised by the government and culture of the 1950s by returning them after World War II to the traditional role of wife and mother, the television industry saw a captive audience of vast commercial potential.

As we know from previous chapters, most Americans were living in urban or suburban areas by the 1950s. (The suburbanization movement of 1945 was facilitated by the government building housing for returning military personnel.) Television programming in the 1950s and 1960s began to reflect the suburban lifestyle of America. Instead of vaudeville-style variety shows, new sitcoms and dramas situated in suburban America began to be featured. Although these programs were often full of gender and racial stereotypes (when races other than Caucasian were mentioned at all), programs like *Father Knows Best*, *Leave it to Beaver*, *Dennis the Menace*, *Gidget*, and *The Brady Bunch* were produced to try and reach the suburban audience. These shows weren't just reflections of suburban culture, they were television's "constructions" or ideals of what suburbia should be, rather than a documentary of what suburbia really was.

In the 1970s, some television programs aimed at the African American audience tried to depict a different urban reality than just the white suburbs. While *Good Times*, *Sanford and Son*, and *What's Happening* were criticized for their own cultural stereotypes of inner city African Americans, one could not help but notice that the version of the city portrayed in these comedies was markedly different than other shows. The decline of American cities in the

1960s and 1970s furthered the process of ghettoization and urban poverty by concentrating an urban minority underclass in the inner city. The culture of resistance and anger from these minority groups were often represented in these comedy shows that tried to reach the African and Latino American audiences. On later analysis, we can see a conflict between these two cultures not only in television's representation, but in reality as well.

TELEVISION AND URBAN WOMEN

Television's "accurate" portrayal of gender in America has been abysmal, but to understand what is objectionable about the *Donna Reed Show* and *Father Knows Best* depiction of airheaded, house-servant women, we must know a little history to set the stage. In the 1940s, women weren't traditional homemakers that couldn't drive a car or hold a job as the television shows of the 1960s suggest. "Rosie the Riveter" became an icon of the "We Can Do It" slogan movement, which prodded 1940s women into heavy industry jobs needed for the war effort.

Depicted as tough and capable, American culture embraced Rosie and working women as confident and necessary laborers. But, when business and government needed to retool and refine its social and employment model with the return of millions of servicemen, a concerted effort began to return women to their traditional roles as girlfriends, wives, and mothers. First, the tough, capable women who had often relocated to the urban factories to do the jobs and build the tanks that won the war were unceremoniously fired in 1945–46. Their jobs were given to returning soldiers, but no accommodation was made for the women in alternative job training or education. On the other hand, the servicemen, at this time, were given education through the GI bill or were placed in the recently vacated industry jobs.

The culture industry of television, radio, and film seemed to legitimatize this gender switch by selling the image of homemaker women and breadwinner men to America. In the late 1940s and throughout the 1950s, women were portrayed as only capable of being wives and mothers, their competency to make serious decisions, work, or even drive a car was the punch line for many jokes of the time. By the late 1950s, women were almost exclusively portrayed by the television and film industry as frivolous sex objects without any skills or as full-time homemakers. The reaction to this image by women of the 1960s was to mobilize grassroots groups from the suburbs to urban college campuses to reject the packaging of women as incapable, yet amusing comic relief. The sexual revolution and the Women's Movement of the late 1960s changed some of the negative and stereotypical images of women on television and even brought female leads in some television shows. Sadly, this cultural reaction to break the stereotype of women was continually thwarted by 1970s television programming, including shows like *Charlie's Angels*.

Rosie the Riveter was part of the U.S. government's propaganda campaign to revise gender roles in the 1940s in order to lure women into factory jobs for the war effort. Strong, confident, and capable, this image of the American woman was a new one that differed from the demure stereotype of women circulated in the popular culture of the time. Since the jobs they would be asked to do, however, were also new to most women, a new, tougher image had to be constructed. Rosie was a real person, not an artistic creation. Rosie Will Monroe actually worked as a riveter on B-24 airplanes before being asked to be in this poster as well as in a promotional film for the war effort at home.

The production of television programming had changed in the 1960s, becoming concentrated in the Los Angeles area after having moved from New York City. Space and location are important components of this move, as television soundstages became larger and location shoots became critical to 1960s and 1970s programming success. New York City's soundstages and the city's vertical organization were ill equipped to accommodate these needs. Like the film producers in Hollywood, television producers wanted to be near the horizontal organization of Los Angeles, where larger space and year-round location shooting were necessary for television's demanding new programming schedule.

With the popularity of cable television in the late 1970s and early 1980s, television channels seemed infinite. This presented television executives with a new problem—how to fill all those stations with programming twenty-four hours a day. The first pay cable channels in the 1970s featured Hollywood movies that the public could not get elsewhere (this is still the time before the wide availability of videocassette recorders). Eventually, as the pay channels and specialty cable channels that followed had to develop programming to fill the twenty-four-hour day, the industry turned to Los Angeles as "television city." Other specialty channels now included children's programming, more channels directed at stay-at-home wives and mothers, cable channels that aired older favorite television shows from previous seasons, and the channel that set in concrete the youth revolution on television—Music Television (MTV).

MUSIC TELEVISION

MTV was born on August 1, 1981, with a format of twenty-four-hour music videos, introduced by "VJs" or video jockeys.

Only a few cable stations carried the fledgling cable offering, but young cable viewers were excited by the music videos. "I want my MTV" was an ingenious strategy for MTV advertising and marketing; viewers who lived in areas not carrying MTV were directed to call up their local cable provider and *demand* the channel. Based in New York City, MTV broke with the convention of glitzy television programming, generally produced in Los Angeles by this time. In contrast, MTV was run on a shoestring budget and only had a few thrown-together stage sets for VJs to stand in front of while they introduced videos. With its offices and small studios in New York's Times Square, MTV's location had little to do with the success of the upstart cable channel. Yet, being in New York City, the national record labels did make limited use of the channel at first. Quickly, New York's fashion and other cultural trends began to seep into the small production studios of MTV, and New Wave (the first real musical trend that MTV participated in) was the beginning of the "style over substance" decade of the 1980s. Big hair and outrageous clothing connected New York's fashion industry to the music industry, and MTV was certainly the platform for much of the excess. New Wave music had to be marketed visually for the fashion innovations to be successful (the music itself was unlikely to sustain a new music movement), and MTV's television presence was crucial to its popularity. Thankfully, most of the fashion nonsense peaked with the mid-1980s Hair bands of Heavy Metal. These bands, Mötley Crüe,

Ratt, and Poison to name a few, were often from Los Angeles, where hair and makeup still managed to equate with macho Heavy Metal posturing in the music. The appeal and fashion sense of New Wave, Heavy Metal, and later Grunge was marketed to the nation's white suburbs through the MTV studios in New York and the record labels in Los Angeles.

In the late 1990s, MTV retired its fake sets and backdrops and began to feature Times Square in the heart of Manhattan as its backdrop. At this same time, an often angry blend of urban rap and urban rock was being pitted against the saccharine pop of teen idols. So, the battle began at MTV: On one side were urban rap/metal bands like Rage Against the Machine, Limp Bizkit, and Linkin Park; on the other side were the industry-manufactured boy bands *NSYNC and the Backstreet Boys as well as teen pop sensations like Britney Spears and Christina Aguilera. With a growing audience, MTV is not just a force in the lives of the privileged cable viewer, but is a force in other areas of popular culture beyond television: from fashion, hip-hop clothes, and the revival of low-slung "hip-hugger" jeans, to language (slang from videos has white suburban youth parroting hip-hop phrases), to attitudes (as anyone who has witnessed the sneering middle-class youth affecting urban Gangsta-isms at the mall can attest to) for all of America. Urban zip code or not, the *urban message* of MTV is being beamed into every hamlet and village with a cable company or satellite dish. In this way, the urban youth culture of New York City and Los Angeles's record industry is transmitted through television.

Today, cable television brings us what seems like endless entertainment. While American programs are still produced primarily in the Los Angeles area, including such hits as *Baywatch,* where the beach landscape of Los Angeles plays a vital role in the "plot" of the show, and *Friends,* where the city landscape of Manhattan has been recreated on a Los Angeles soundstage. Television is poised to transcend the cultural definitions of urban or rural for Americans. With the proliferation of cable stations and satellite dishes, television programming has a show devoted to almost any given topic, and whole networks devoted to specialized themes. Home and Garden, Playboy, Lifestyle (directed at women), Black Entertainment Television, Cartoon Network, Country Music Television, Telemundo (a Spanish-language channel), ESPN (sports), Animal Planet (pet and animal interests), CNN (24-hour news), TNN, and Nickelodeon (children's programming mixed with vintage television programs from the 1950s to 1970s) are all available to any cable viewer or dish owner. This plethora of programming was once reserved only for well-connected urbanites. *Theory Break:* Functionalists would point out that as the entertainment industry grew, the specialty programming for women and minorities grew to fill the appropriate niche market, and that the white-male-centered programming of early television was only the by-product of marketing research that found that this group was the largest TV purchasers in the country. Suburban themes and urban themes in television programming only represent an attempt to reach an audience, not a subconscious urban influence.

References

BANNON, THOMAS. 2002. "Timeline of Photography." **www.Eastman.org**.

DOMHOFF, WILLIAM. 2001. *Who Rules America?* McGraw-Hill: New York, NY.

DOMINGUES, JANINE. 1999. "Timeline of Matthew Brady." Temple University: Philadelphia. **www.temple.edu/photo/photographers/Brady**

GENOVA, TOM. 2002. "Television History." **www.tvhistory.tv/index**

MARIEN, MARY. 2003. *Photography: A Cultural History.* Prentice Hall: Upper Saddle River, NJ.

MILLS, C. WRIGHT. 1956. *The Power Elite.* Oxford Press: New York, NY.

NASH, ANDREW. 2001. "Nellie Bly." Puppycup Productions. **www.julesvernes.ca.nelliebly**

PHILLIPS, PETER. 2000. *Censored 2000: The Year's Top Twenty-Five Censored Stories.* Seven Stories Press: New York, NY.

HARRY RANSOM CENTER. 2002. "Photography and Film Collection." University of Texas: Austin, TX. **www.hemingway.hrc.utexas.edu/photofiles**

RIIS, JACOB. 1890. *How the Other Half Lives.* Charles Sanbers Sons: New York, NY.

WEBER, MAX. 1921. *Economy and Society: An Outline of Interpretive Sociology.* Claus Wittrich and Guenther Roth (eds) 1979. University of California Press: Berkeley, CA.

CHAPTER EIGHT

Government and State Culture Production and Social Movements

Up to this point we have concentrated on the culture that individuals and small groups have produced in the city, the effect the city has had on this culture, and the effect the culture has had on the city. In this chapter, we are going to focus on how government, what we sometimes call the state, can produce culture in the city and how social movements produce culture and change in the city.

We label any ordered social arrangement or grouping that can be found across human time or society and that satisfies some basic human need as a *social institution*. Examples of social institutions range from religion, politics, education, and the economy to the family and social movements. Government has evolved into one of our most powerful and organized social institutions, and it is most often dominated by the top of the social order (wealthy classes). Grassroots social movements, on the other hand, receive their power as a social institution from the actions of the people at the bottom of the social order (the everyday citizen).

Initially, some of us might be resistant to the idea that government makes culture. Critics might say that it is "the people" within government that makes culture, not government itself. Yet, any one of us that has been caught in line at the Department of Motor Vehicles, the Unemployment Office, the College Financial Aid Offices, or *God forbid* the Internal Revenue Service knows that these outposts of "government" exist in a separate culture beyond the manners and common sense of the rest of society. *Theory Break:* Max Weber (1921) described much of governmental bureaucratic culture as an end unto itself, where rational, impersonal rules are supposed to govern employee-customer relations. Sometimes, though, the rules of a government bureaucracy become more important than the goals of the government agency. For those of us that have suffered through an unemployment line or

165

a student aid interview, Weber's theory comes to life as the goals of the agency (i.e., getting unemployment benefits to the unemployed or obtaining financial aid for a college student) are subverted by bureaucratic ritual and process. Filling out forms and the systematic process of the bureaucracy become much more important in the bureaucratic culture than helping the unemployed or getting aid to students. This is a culture that grows and survives in government agencies, in particular, though large private organizations can also mimic this culture.

An example of how government produces culture outside of their own organizational walls, albeit in an unintentional way, is through zoning and segregation in our cities. Zoning and segregation are the words we use to describe how urban governments prescribe where housing and businesses can be located, and what groups can occupy these businesses and houses. After the Civil War, Jim Crow laws in the South and restrictive housing covenants in the North produced racial and ethnic ghettoes in America's cities that exist to this day. Forcing a minority group to live in a specific location and then isolating them socially by generating negative stereotypes of the group will *produce* an urban ethnic culture different than that of society's dominant group. Often this urban ethnic culture is made to be subordinate by the dominant group through this process of segregation and stereotyping. The uniqueness of the subordinate urban ethnic culture comes from segregation and zoning by the municipal government. For example, immigration enclaves like Chinatown or Little Italy are not replicas of their home cultures, but instead are urban adaptations to the segregated life of a new immigrant. Segregtion in the new urban environment provokes the immigrant group to change its culture in the enclave. *Theory Break:* Authors Wilson and Portes (1980) wrote about the uniqueness of the Cuban enclave in Miami as an example of how an urban ethnic enclave is produced by immigration and segregation.

As we have discussed earlier, many ethnic groups have suffered this special segregation and cultural isolation. Italian immigrants came to the East Coast cities of America, beginning in the 1880s, where they were unwelcome at first in the neighborhoods of previous immigrant groups. So, they developed a culture in the city that established restaurants and grocery stores for Italian tastes in the Italian neighborhoods. This Italian urban culture is at first considered suspect and dangerous by the dominant white group until, by a process of assimilation, the Italian group interacts and intermarries with the dominant group (Gordon 1964). Even today, Italian culture has been overidentified with organized crime in the nation's cities, while Irish organized crime and other ethnic group's organized crime influence has been largely ignored. The city's government produced these cultural oddities (grocery stores to mobsters) by segregation and zoning laws. The city, through its government, provides low-cost isolated slums for new immigrants until they can assimilate and move to better neighborhoods. During this process of assimilation, the dominant culture is able to pick and choose what elements of the ethnic urban enclave it may want to appropriate, i.e., food, festivals, music, or dress.

African Americans, who had traditionally lived in the South, came to northern cities between 1910 and 1920 in search of better jobs and wages than the southern rural sharecropping system would provide. Many did find better wages and conditions than in the South, but many blacks also found segregation and racist wages (blacks were paid half the wage of a white man during this period). There were attempts in this new set of urban enclaves to bring a shared culture from the rural South that African Americans were familiar with to the new urban experience of America's northern cities.

Segregation of African Americans also brought about concentrations of ethnic intellectuals and artists in these segregated neighborhoods and boroughs of these cities. Aware of their new urban experience, these intellectuals and artists began creating new culture for the African American community. Not just a culture of resistance, where old rural ways would be revived, but a new culture that spoke of the urban experience. In the Harlem section of Manhattan, New York, a concentration of artists and intellectuals produced an explosion of black art, music, business, political awareness, and literature that came about unintentionally through the government's segregation of African Americans in New York City. Despite the New York *Herald's* 1905 assertion that the African American influx into the area "is inexplicable," the occupation of the streets above 134th Street in Manhattan was predictable since other areas in New York City had strict rules forbidding sale or rent of property to blacks (New York *Herald* 1905). Harlem grew from this point as Manhattan's largest African American community, due to the urban restrictions on housing in other areas of the borough.

Asian urban immigrants are some of the most recent victims of ethnic community zoning and segregation. When coming to America's cities, Asian immigrants will often seek a "Chinatown," "Little Tokyo," or "Koreatown" in the hopes of finding someone who speaks their language and understands their culture. In one respect this segregation is voluntary, but only marginally so, because what the new Asian immigrant finds is low-wage work and substandard housing, often provided by Asian slumlords or underworld figures. If the immigrant is on a legal visa, they may still want to do business in this part of the city because of the comfort of a familiar culture. If new immigrants are here illegally or have overstayed their visa, then they feel they must submit to the exploitation of this Asian enclave to avoid detection. The municipal government contributes to this kind of "informal culture" in these ethnic enclaves by allowing these areas a certain level of autonomy, including the tacit acceptance of organized crime, slums, brothels, and illegal immigrants as long as any problems stay within "Chinatown." These ethnic villages in the city are almost like "reservations," in which the need to address poverty, crime, and education are "someone else's problem." Thus, this kind of government neglect and segregation can produce an urban culture of exploitation.

In this cycle of neglect and segregation, cities also manage to create another urban cultural phenomenon—fear. If author Gavin De Becker (1997) is correct and fear is a "gift" because it helps us maintain our safety and physical well-being, then the urban environment has become the mall where we

THE HARLEM RENAISSANCE

The Harlem Renaissance (1919–1938) featured writers like Langston Hughes, W.E.B. DuBois, and Zora Neale Hurston, musicians like Fletcher Henderson and Duke Ellington, painters like Aaron Douglas and true Renaissance men like Paul Robeson (scholar, activist, writer, best-selling singer, playwright, lawyer, professional athlete, and stage and screen actor) who embodied all of these Renaissance traits. African Americans did not just want to consume white culture, but demanded new kinds of culture that reflected their new urban lives. Due in large part to the actions of Marcus Garvey, the Pan-African movement, and the writings and organizing of W.E.B. DuBois (who helped create the NAACP), African Americans in New York City became self-aware as an urban population and came to appreciate the culture of their own social place in the city. Finding a few neighborhoods North of 134th Street in Harlem that would accept black families begins the concentration of African Americans in 1900, and by 1930 over 350,000 African Americans lived in Harlem. At this point of critical mass, black money and cultural taste can sustain black writers, artists, and musicians without depending on white audiences or white tastes. The Harlem community creates and maintains the Rennaissance in New York with little help from the white community in Manhattan.

The literature from the Harlem Renaissance featured African American characters living vibrant and complex lives filled with the experience of black Americans in the city. Sometimes these characters faced racism or classism of their day, as well as problems completely unique to African Americans, like Zora Neale Hurston's *Imitation of Life* (1933) about a light-skinned black woman's attempt to pass as white. Literary essays like Hurston's also turned into political polemics by writers and organizers like W.E.B. DuBois, who began to demand an end to the second class standing endured by African Americans. Paul Robeson's unparalleled acting talent as Othello on New York stages and as *Emperor Jones* (1933) in film helped portray blacks as equals, and Robeson's political organizing helped the early Negro Civil Rights movement. Unfortunately, the white backlash against revolutionary black literature and political organizing ruined the careers of both Robeson and Hurston.

The blues music and Dixieland jazz of the South underwent a dramatic change in Harlem, too; jazz masters like Fletcher Henderson, Lester Young, Coleman Hawkins, and Duke Ellington melded Ragtime, Blues, and Jazz into the Jazz music we have today. Their complex chord changes, composition, instrumentation, and improvisation signaled a new musical direction in music that even classical music responded to. Big band music, jump blues, boogie-woogie, be-bop, cool jazz, and rock and roll came from the innovations of the Harlem

Renaissance musical movement. The jazz musicians of the next generation came to New York City's Harlem to study under the great figures in jazz of the Harlem Renaissance. Musicians like Charlie Parker, Dizzy Gillespie, Miles Davis, Billie Holiday, and John Coltrane all traveled to New York City to play and study with the great musicians of this movement. The ethnocentric government policies of segregation produced this hothouse for African American creativity that lured musicians, writers, and artists from Kansas City, New Orleans, and Chicago to come and be a part of the Harlem Renaissance.

shop for this gift. Living in the city "conditions" us as urbanites to fear the older, run-down sections of our cities and towns, and to fear the lower classes, especially the minority lower classes. Cities are where skyscrapers and airports exist for those of us with a fear of heights and flying. Traffic, deviance, pollution, crime, disease, foreigners, homosexuals, and crowds exist in the city for all manner of other neuroses; cities contain many things we fear. Now being neurotic or paralyzed with fear is not normal for someone in the city, but some amount of fear is prudent in an unknown urban environment. Anxiety or caution might be thought of as the appropriate level of concern for the complex environments in which we find ourselves, while neurosis and phobias would be the unhealthy extreme reaction to the city. From either perspective, the city contributes to a culture of fear.

The culture of fear surrounding crime in the city is probably the most widespread and recognizable kind. Not only do cities have large, well-trained bureaucratic police forces to combat the citizen's fear of crime, but also private security, private investigators, and home security corporations. To combat this fear, the public has been bombarded with images of crime and violence in cities by the media through the news and specialized television programs like *COPS* and *America's Most Wanted*. Big cities, in particular, are often featured for their supposed high crime rates in the media, rather than their cultural or commercial successes. According to the Uniform Crime Report of 1998, large Metropolitan areas have the same total crime rate as midsized cities and a slightly lower property crime rate (Tables 8.1 and 8.2).

Violent crime was 1.9 points higher per 1,000 community members in large metropolitan areas, but one has to ask oneself, "Is that really the reason we fear cities? Because of our ability to perceive a 1.9 percent change?" This is not an attempt to diminish completely the idea that large urban areas are the location of major organized crime activities, gangs, drug distributors, prostitution, and other criminal enterprises less common to the rural citizen. But, clearly a culture of fear in the city has grown with the help of media exaggeration and the segregation of the races and classes to the point where suburbanites see criminals in every working-class area and in every minority face. *Theory Break:* Crime locates itself near large populations of victims and customers for much the same reason any business is attracted to large

Table 8.1   Crime Rate per 1,000 Inhabitants by City Size 1998

	Property	Violent	Total for the United States
Rural	18	2.3	19
City of 50,000–999,000	45	4.4	50
City of 1 million plus	43	6.3	50

Source: Department of Justice FBI Statistics 1999

Table 8.2   Crime Index Trends (January–June 2002)

Cities	Crime Index Total	Violent Crime	Property Crime
Over 1,000,000	+0.2	−1.9	+0.8
100,000–249,000	+2.8	−0.6	+3.2
under 10,000	−1.9	−5.0	−1.6

Source: Department of Justice, FBI Uniform Crime Report

urban areas, Central Place Theory.[1] Human ecologists feel that Central Place Theory explains why large cities can wield so much economic and political power.

The culture of fear surrounding crime has continued to grow in the United States at the same time the nation's crime rate has actually decreased. In this way, the culture of fear perpetuates a fear of crime that is disproportionate to the real threat of crime. With the large number of unknown people and random situations that confronts an urbanite, the city is a natural place for disproportionate fears. This is not to insinuate that a city is the only place for such fears, but cities are the location of many such fears. The social institutions of a city make the culture of fear more visible (police patrols and news reports) and easier to maintain (private security firms and home alarms) in a city. At the same time the government is trying to calm and assuage fear in its citizens, the government must maintain the police, issue crime reports, and allow local crime coverage, which in turn perpetrates a culture of fear.

Governments sometimes get directly involved in making culture in our city, and at times are the entity we turn to for producing certain kinds of culture. An example of this phenomenon is that as urban citizens, we judge cities by the range and quality of their cultural institutions, which are often maintained by government entities. Orchestras, symphonies, operas, and theaters are maintained and assisted by local municipal governments, often

---

[1]Central Place Theory—cities thrive because of their abundance of resources and services, combined with the tendency for businesses to agglomerate or concentrate. Often this concentration will occur in a specific place in the city, i.e., car dealerships in one area of the city, or businesses concentrating in one city, i.e., Hi-Tech in San Jose, CA.

with the help of state and federal grants. These kinds of "high art" cultures can't survive in the city without government help; the city needs to provide the symphony halls, opera houses, and theater stages for these art forms, because they cannot sustain themselves economically.[2] This brings us back to social class and its impact on the city and urban culture. *Theory Break*: Marxist theorists would point out that it is the entertainment tastes of the upper class that receive *all* levels of government subsidies. From the federal government's National Endowment for the Arts (NEA), which supplies grants for budding painters, civic symphonies, and metropolitan orchestras and operas, to municipal bond issues that fund local Shakespeare troupes and community symphonies. The kind of culture that is being subsidized in each of these examples is "high art,"[3] which is disproportionately consumed by wealthier American urbanites of European descent. Functional theorists would say that the music of Bach and Mozart needs to be saved for each generation to appreciate, regardless of class. Music theorists would concede that musically, classical composers were writing more complex and challenging music than we hear on today's pop radio.

How could the rich use the public tax dollars of every citizen to subsidize *their* taste in art and music? Easily, the rich urban dwellers of your city have the time and interest to sit on municipal and state arts commissions that decide funding for cultural events. They also run civic groups like the "Committee for the Municipal Opera" or the "Commission for Art in Public Spaces," which are also very powerful cultural groups and become de facto political groups. These groups have political and social power because they are composed of rich urban elites, who will clearly remember in the next election cycle to vote against a candidate that didn't fund their opera project or worse, raised funds for the opposing candidate. The lower and middle classes most often consume popular culture, not "high culture." These art forms can't rely on government support, but instead have to rely on capitalist sales. These art forms have no political power or social committees and are in no way connected to politics, except as nuisances. How many of us feel that Britney Spears or the Backstreet Boys are deserving of a federal grant for art? How many think they are a nuisance? Before answering, think of the many ethnic or indigenous art forms and local music that might be lost without an alternative to popular music sales, since they cannot sustain themselves through popular sales. While awarding pop music stars grants may not seem like a good idea, popular music could help all music by using its profits to sustain local arts projects.

Proponents of symphonies, orchestras, theaters, and operas maintain the importance of these art forms from an educational standpoint. These art forms represent history and high ideas that wouldn't normally be available

---

[2]Except for Broadway and other theater shows in New York City, most local theaters have to be subsidized. Otherwise, the money they generate would not be sufficient to sustain them.

[3]High Art is most often European in form and dates mainly from 1300–1900 C.E. for painting, music, art, or literature. Modern works that are heavily influenced by this period are also considered "high art."

to the "masses." Examples of this point of view are the concert and opera pieces composed by Wolfgang A. Mozart and Ludwig von Beethoven and the theater of Anton Chekhov and William Shakespeare. Professors and experts in the fine arts agree that these and other "high art" artists are examples of the epitome of composition, musicianship, theatrical expression, and literature. They deserve to be maintained, some say at all costs. The question then becomes if the high art forms embody the pinnacle of human achievement in culture, how much should the government be involved in sustaining these art forms? Should the urban public be compelled to pay for them? We must be cautious in our response, because in a world of shrinking government budgets, what we want to find in the arts will be taken from some other urban budget item (i.e., child care or homeless shelters), or result in the dreaded property, income, or sales tax increase.

As urbanites, we already demand that the government sponsor certain cultural events at public expense, because the government is the expected producer and generator of culture. On Presidents' Day, Martin Luther King Jr.'s Day, Memorial Day, Veterans Day, Labor Day, and Independence Day, we leave it up to the government to sponsor and organize events for these celebrations. Paying for these events can, at times, amount to a considerable chunk of public expense, especially for Fourth of July orchestras, fireworks, laser shows, and famous entertainers to perform in large metropolitan areas. Even when there are competing events in a city on July Fourth, the legitimate patriotic event is the one sponsored by the city, and we demand that these events be provided by our municipal government.

Theory Break: Functional theorists like Emile Durkheim point out that ritual ceremonies of political solidarity promote social cohesion. The density of the city makes social cohesion very important to maintain, so it is important for patriotic ceremonies to be performed at regular intervals for social cohesion to be maintained. Even when the city doesn't sponsor the event, the local government is expected to facilitate events like Halloween parties, Thanksgiving Day parades, and Saint Patrick's Day celebrations that require extra police, fire, EMS, and sanitation personnel. These celebrations are important for the city, as well for their potential to allow citizens to blow off steam, and provide "acceptable" group deviance—drinking, celebrating, and so forth.

At certain times, the government not only produces culture in the city, but can also *make* cities. For the United States, George Washington helped the fledgling country found its capital city in the Virginia swamp of the Potomac River to make a cultural statement to other governments. It was designed to host the new representative democracy and its elected president. Its road design drew the city's visitors to the capitol building and the White House as the central features of the nation's capital.

The city was created to make an impact on foreign visitors and dignitaries to the young nation: a nation that was not steeped in hundreds of years of medieval architecture and needed to be able to make a good visual impression. A young government needed a new image and employed the cultural "hardware" of carefully designed streets, neoclassical buildings,

The design of Washington, DC's streets and buildings is evident in this photo. The founding fathers intended to make the U.S. capital a grand city with imposing buildings. An urban culture of classical architecture and manufactured grandeur has served its function by impressing foreign visitors and U.S. citizens for over two hundred years. Made to rival the best of Europe's palaces and parliamentary buildings, this urban culture borrowed architectural elements from the European past and placed them in an American cityscape.

and even patriotic songs to manufacture a grand culture for the new nation, where before there was none.

Brazil chose to manufacture a capital city for itself in 1960 when the country needed to update its former colonial image. The Brazilian government carved Brasilia out of the jungle to be their capital. Modernistic architecture was combined with a city that was actually planned around the function of government. Brasilia succeeded in changing the colonized image of Brazil. Breaking with Brazil's two major metropolitan areas (Rio de Janeiro and São Paulo), the government put the nation's capital out of the immediate control of the elite classes of those cities, which was the first major cultural change that Brasilia achieved. The second cultural revelation that creating Brasilia accomplished was that the visual image of the nation's capital would not be of the poverty, street children, urban dilapidation, and crumbling infrastructure of Rio de Janeiro or São Paulo but a brand new, modern city. Has Brazil's adventure in the culture of "city making" paid off? Financially, Brasilia is completely dependent on the government to sustain itself. Business has not followed the government's lead into inland Brazil. Yet, with the internationalization of global commerce, Brazil is always a significant player when discussing the Third World or Latin America, because of its improved image on the world's stage. Exotic but not backward is Brazil's modern image, and some of that new image can be attributed to the nation's futuristic capital city. Previous to Brasilia's construction, the nation's image was one of untamed Amazonian jungle or of unleashed hedonism at Rio's annual Carnival.

Carnival in Rio de Janeiro and Mardi Gras in New Orleans are examples of how the city's attempt to make urban culture can become part of the city's character and economy. These cities are known for their cultural celebrations more than for any other single characteristic of the city. In Rio de Janeiro, the city comes to a complete stop for Carnival's samba parades as the streets are jammed with Carnival revelers and samba bands. Neighborhood social clubs work all year round to create floats, costumes, and marching bands, no matter how economically deprived the area. In fact, some of the poorest neighborhoods in Rio de Janeiro are responsible for some of the most elaborate parade floats and bands. These neighborhood clubs are essential to the city's urban culture and Carnival is the event that identifies Rio de Janeiro to the world.

Similarly, Mardi Gras in New Orleans has become the United States's biggest annual party and is the city's most visible cultural event. The parades were started by social clubs of wealthy elites in the city (called Krewes)

Here are a few of the many floats seen in a typical Mardi Gras parade. The *krewes* spend thousands of dollars on a float, decorating it and manning it themselves. Two parades are held two each day for more than a month before Lent, generating millions of dollars and tons of trash from the tourists that make Mardi Gras New Orleans's most important economic event. This colorful set of revelers is in the *Krewe* of Rex, traveling down St. Charles Avenue toward the historic French Quarter.

and would culminate the Tuesday (Fat Tuesday, or in French, Mardi Gras) before the start of Lent (Ash Wednesday). It isn't just culture that Mardi Gras's parades produce, it's also commerce. The single largest employment category in New Orleans is tourism at 28.5 percent, and spending from all sources during Mardi Gras in 2000 totaled $1,056,000,000 (Gotham 2002). Both Rio de Janeiro and New Orleans have become invested in these huge celebrations, devoting city services to produce the parade (police, road crews, sanitation) and city money to promote the events. There exists a symbiotic and beneficial relationship between the city, the municipal government that sponsor the events, and these cultural celebrations.

Hong Kong is a city that was also created by a government, but in this case a foreign government. Before 1842, Hong Kong was a small port village that was known as the pirate's den of the South China Sea, but that year the small village was ceded to British control after the Opium War (see box on page 177) and the signing of the Treaty of Nan King (www.hyperhistory.com). As a growing British naval port, Hong Kong grew as a fascinating mix of cultures, Chinese culture sublimated under British rule. Conflict and war between the Chinese and the British put Hong Kong again on the negotiating table and it was reacquired by the English for a ninety-nine-year lease in 1898. The British created the Hong Kong we know today from a small sea village, making it a tiny piece of British political and urban culture in China. But, this culture was always in conflict with the culture of Hong Kong's majority—the Chinese.

The Japanese invasion of Manchuria in 1931, and the resulting war with China in 1937, brought about a period of refugee influx to Hong Kong. At the beginning of World War II, a third of Hong Kong's 1.6 million people were Chinese refugees and most of these refugees slept in the street. Hong Kong has been a haven for refugees for over fifty years, first from the Sino-Japanese conflict and then from the Communist takeover of China in 1949, swelling the city to an estimated 2.2 million—at least half of which were refugees (www.hyperhistory.com). A significant component of Hong Kong's Chinese culture comes from refugees, first from the Japanese, then the Chinese Communists. The flood of Chinese refugees continued to subordinate their culture in Hong Kong to the wealthy, elite British.

Communist China was upset with the British presence and control of Hong Kong, placing the two governments in a Cold War diplomacy situation for the next forty-eight years. A tense relationship between the British of Hong Kong and the Communist government of China lasted until July 1, 1997, when the city was reestablished as part of the People's Republic of China, with a population of over six million residents. Yet, even in this tense exercise of reverting Hong Kong's sovereignty back to China, Hong Kong was a mix of British and Chinese cultures. It will remain as a Special Administrative Region (SAR) in China, with an unparalleled degree of autonomy to ease the fears of the former British subjects now under Communist control.

The Joint Declaration of 1984 between China and Great Britain maintains that the lifestyle and policies of Hong Kong will *not* be determined by the Chinese Communist Party, except in the areas of foreign policy and defense, and only for the next fifty years, after which Great Britain cedes all interest in Hong Kong to China (www.hyperhistory.com). A very British/ Chinese solution to the problem of two powerful countries at odds over a very important piece of urban real estate is to slowly ease power to save face. While control of the region is of concern to both governments, it has been the British who have been most focused on control of Hong Kong; and it has been the Chinese government that has been concerned the most with saving face during this exchange of power. *Theory Break:* Marxist theorists would point out that initially the British controlled Hong Kong because of their military strength in the nineteenth century, but with the change in military, political, and economic power in the region since 1949, China has asserted its dominance over the city.

As a "rented city" by the British for one hundred years, Hong Kong is one of Asia's leading economic lights. "Made in Hong Kong" has become a label associated with manufacturing, textiles, and electronics for the past thirty-five years in the Western world, as the flow of refugees into Hong Kong made it swell with cheap labor and investment capital from all over the world. Even the People's Republic of China partnered with Hong Kong's business sector on several projects in the 1980s in an effort to normalize relations. Today, among its impressive skyline of skyscrapers, Hong Kong is one of the world's top ten economies and is mainland Asia's leading financial center. The British founded a Western-style financial and business culture in Hong Kong that became as stable for investment firms (for industrial and manufacturing operations) as any other former British colony. Chinese labor and unique raw goods, like silk, made the British investment a success.

But again, we have to remind ourselves that this is a Chinese city, with a majority of Chinese people as its citizens, a Chinese cultural outlook, and even a partial Chinese city design. Hong Kong has planned streets and boulevards from its English past, but the streets, alleys, and corridors that its Chinese citizens live in grew more "organically." At the same time the elite culture of the occupying English brought tea time and crumpets to Hong Kong, the indigenous Chinese culture of the lower working classes maintained a cooperative survival-oriented culture with community-owned woks and rice preparation. It is this cooperative Chinese culture that has built the urban camps of Hong Kong with snaking extension cords and telephone lines stretching over miles of urban space, garden hoses for water, and open gutters for sewers, all built or stolen "cooperatively" from the urban environment. Hong Kong's harbor is very much a product of the indigenous Chinese culture, with whole families and businesses that live their lives on junks docked on the water.

It is a cooperative urban aquatic culture, where one's boat is one's house, yet it is also part of the "pedestrian street traffic" that others must use to get from place to place. Services from the city like phone and electricity are often "appropriated" by the floating community, much like the urban camps on dry land. Harbor dwellers have created an urban space that no one was using and built it into an extension of Hong Kong: a time-honored Chinese

HONG KONG AND CHINA

The Opium Wars (1839–1842) were precipitated by Western intervention into Chinese culture and politics. British merchants before 1830 find China almost completely self-sufficient agriculturally and financially, but with diligent pressure from the merchants, are able to build a significant opium trade from India into China, crippling the country's self-sufficiency. The Chinese commissioner for opium, Lin Tse-Hsu in 1838, seizes and confiscates British imported opium, because of the social harm it is inflicting on the Chinese people. The commissioner becomes a folk hero to the Chinese and is one of the few non-Communist Party figures revered by the current Chinese government. A lopsided war begins, pitting the more technically advanced British navy based in Hong Kong against the once great, but now faded, glory of China's military and naval forces. The British win this war and Hong Kong is ceded to the British in the Treaty of Nanking. Pressure from American and French importers with similar treaties as the British crushed the once self-sufficient Chinese economy, but it is the opium trade and the eventual growth of poppy plants in China and Southeast Asia that turns China into a producer of opium, as well as a consumer of the drug. The growth of the opium trade made port cities in China, like Shanghai and Hong Kong, very important places for the import and export of goods and for the injection of Western ideas into China.

Another rebellion after the end of the Opium Wars was the Taiping Rebellion, which had its roots in a clash between Chinese and Western cultures. Considered the bloodiest war of the nineteenth century, it is estimated that twenty million people died in this rebellion against the Manchu government by lower-class rebels in the Eastern urban provinces (www.hyperhistory.com). The rebels based part of their revolutionary doctrine on an odd blend of Western ideas. Christian personal ideals were combined with a Marxist belief in public ownership of land and a return to a self-reliant Chinese economy. In 1851, Hung Hsiu-chuan led the rebels to the capture of Nanking, which was the most important political city in China, besides the British-held and heavily fortified port of Hong Kong. The leadership of the Taiping Rebellion quarreled about power so much so after their victory that many of their reforms were left uncompleted. A Western-backed army invaded Nanking and overthrew the Taiping in 1864 due to the chaotic leadership of the Taiping interim government. The Manchu government was too weakened by the Taiping Rebellion of the north and the British control of Hong Kong in the south to ever rule China again effectively after this period. China's cities become more like city-states after the Opium Wars and Taiping Rebellion, with no strong national ruler to unify the cities or regional warlords and the heavy burden of the Western powers dominating their port cities.

This lack of effective leadership weakened China to foreign influence in trade and defense. Japan defeated China in a brief war in 1895 that resulted in even more Western and foreign control of the Chinese economy. By 1900, a group of martial arts zealots known as "The Boxers" attempted to throw *all* foreigners out of China, and with the help of the Chinese Dowager Empress, the Boxer rebels succeeded in dislodging the foreign powers from Peking, Nanking, and most of China. Shortly after the Boxer Rebellion, the Western powers organized an offensive to retake these territories, and despite the Boxers' belief that their martial arts mysticism would give them power over Western bullets, the Boxers were brutally crushed by the better-armed Western powers. The treaties that were signed in 1901 by the new Chinese government were even more punitive than before, dividing China up among the competing Western powers for trade and domination. Key to this division of China were the port cities of Shanghai (occupied by the UK, France, and the United States), Hong Kong (UK), Guangzhou (UK and France), and Qingdao (Germany). *Theory Break:* Some economic theorists are concerned that what occurred to China in 1900 might happen to some modern countries that lack the economic or political will to resist the West. Trade treaties like GATT might leave less-developed countries unable to defend themselves against Western finance institutions, international corporations, and political pressure that will turn the culture of their cities and countryside into a pool of cheap labor that is force-fed Western ideas.

The chaos of the Japanese invasion of the late 1930s in Manchuria and China broke the Western powers' hold on China, as the Allied Powers (UK, France, United States, and USSR) had to fight Germany, Italy, and Japan (the Axis Powers) on several fronts. This left China to take much of the brutal Japanese onslaught without help from the advanced Western military powers. The rape of Nanking in 1937 by the Japanese military is one of the worst urban tragedies in the twentieth century with 300,000 people killed and over 20,000 reported cases of rape (Rutherford and Bell 2002). Refugees from the Japanese onslaught fled into Hong Kong's harbor looking for the protection of the British Navy. Others fled into the mountains, where Mao Tse-dung and the Chinese Communist Party fought the Japanese from 1937–1945. At the close of the war, Mao's Communist forces fought the last remnants of the emperor's followers and the Chinese nationalist Chiang Kai Shek. In 1949, the Communists forced Chiang Kai Shek off the Chinese mainland to the island of Taiwan; so small, the capital city of Taibei and the nation of Taiwan are virtually the same, but Western recognition of its sovereignty legitimatized Chiang Kai Shek's government. Thus, in 1949, nationalist Chinese essentially created their own island-nation-city, but they are constantly weary of the Communist Chinese that officially regard Taiwan as a "rogue" province of the People's Republic of

China that has been misbehaving for the past fifty years. Encompassing some 3,691,487 square miles and taking in the territories of Mongolia and Tibet, China's Communist government has become the world's only major Communist government and the world's largest populace at 1.3 billion (Rutherford and Bell 2002). Those fleeing Mao's cultural revolution and Communist control over their lives have often fled to Hong Kong, though now its status as an SAR within the People's Republic of China has seen a small reduction in refugees fleeing China. The city continues to be a product of its complex past.

solution to Hong Kong's problems appropriate human resources for communal goals. *Theory Break*: Functionalists would applaud the inventiveness of the harbor culture in Hong Kong and point to the logical, rational solution of using boats as urban space in this limited environment. Marxists would counter that the elite's class domination of Hong Kong's living space forced the landless working class into the harbor. The "hybrid" of the two cultures in Hong Kong has led to financial empires and skyscrapers, while at the same time it is the haven of black markets and refugees.

The other city in China made by government authority is Beijing. Once the seat of the Chinese emperor's own special administrative and cultural city, ancient Peking was an urban environment created for the royal court with gates, buildings, plazas, and temples just for the emperor and royal courtiers. This was completely accomplished through royal authority and money, an urban culture created by government edict out of the horse troughs of a previously Mongolian trade city (Rutherford and Bell 2002). The normal citizen in Peking had to make way and serve the royal court without a say in how the government was run. It will not surprise us that the urban culture of this city was formed at the top for the elites of Peking with little consideration for the city's common citizen.

Control of Beijing, as it is called today, fell to the government of Mao Tse-dung in 1949, and immediately the Communist government began to change the urban culture of the city. A first radical step was to open the emperors' Forbidden City to the workers and peasants of Beijing. *Theory Break*: Marxists would point out that having a special area for the feudal lord in the city is one of the ultimate examples of classism, particularly when this area is off limits to the other classes. One might even say it is a slap in the face, considering it was the peasants of China that made the wealth of the emperor's kingdom. A contemporary example of this same type of cultural classism is the gated communities of the wealthy and privileged in our own modern cities. These gated communities are the "forbidden neighborhoods" of our modern cities, where the poor and working classes aren't allowed. A city's culture cannot help but be affected by the message that the guards and gates imply—"you are not worthy or welcome in this part of the urban space." For the peasants that overcame their fear to enter the newly liberated Forbidden City, a new face greeted them and a new culture was put in place of the Chinese royal dynasties—Mao's Communist Party.

When it took power, the Communist Party began to construct new buildings around a new central plaza called Tiananmen Square in a decidedly new architectural style. Large imposing buildings in the stern socialist motif were placed around the central plaza with new inviting names like the Great Hall of the People. It was important for the new Communist government to build new impressive structures that did not have anything to do with the royal feudal past of China, to in fact create a new Communist culture for China. This new part of the city must rival anything the Forbidden City offered if the new government was to have any legitimacy in the eyes of the people.

In 1989, a student protest for more democracy in the Chinese government took over the "people's" Communist city center Tiananmen Square. This protest was unique because the urban college students of Beijing had the eyes of the world watching their movements through nightly Western news broadcasts. A "statue of liberty" was built in the square by the students and proposals were issued by the students for more democratic participation in all Chinese politics. The city of Beijing saw these students as mostly harmless

An ordinary man with his shopping bags confronts the might of the Chinese military and a fully armed battle tank the day after the bloody crackdown in Tiananmen Square, June 5, 1989. In the West, the image of Beijing and the People's Revolution is now symbolized by this individual, who helped to create a new type of revolutionary culture by no longer accepting the absolute authority of the state. Sadly, the urban culture of the students' pro-democracy movement ultimately failed, despite the bravery of people like this man, and the authoritarianism of the Chinese government prevailed.

THE BUILDING THAT WAS A CITY

There are three buildings that are so big that when the governments that built them finished, they were regarded as cities unto themselves. The first is Vatican City, which is actually composed of three main edifices—Saint Peter's Basilica (originally built by Constantine in 319 C.E., but rebuilt by Pope Julius II and Pope Paul III between 1506–1626), Saint Peter's Square (designed by Bernini and completed in 1667), and the complex known as the Vatican Museums (the Sistine Chapel, the Raphael Rooms, the Borgia Apartment, the Vatican Library, and the Chapel of Nicholas V). These three building complexes might seem small to qualify as a city, but to Rome and to Roman Catholics, Vatican City is more important than any other urban area.

The Vatican is also the smallest "country" in the world, recognized as the capital of the Roman Catholic World. That alone would make Vatican City and the building we know as Saint Peter's Basilica an immensely important urban cultural focal point, but Vatican City also houses the single largest collection of Christian art in the world, making it one of the world's largest art museums as well. Michelangelo (1475–1564), Rafael (1483–1520), Leonardo (1452–1519), and Donatello (1386–1466) are but a few of the masters that the Vatican possesses in its immense collection.

The second "building that is a city" is the French palace at Versailles, begun in 1668 by King Louis XIV (1638–1715). Constructed as

The immense dimensions of the palace at Versailles cannot be contained in a photograph. Truly a building that is a city, the palace was a royal city built to hold the intrigue of an entire noble court and keep the urban drama of Paris away from the king. No poverty or squalor would be seen by the French nobility, only splendid gardens and pristine buildings fit for the aristocracy. A fitting showcase for the pomp of court life, Versailles was a manufactured urban culture that ended up being too far removed from Paris, where the coming revolution would exact a price for the extravagance of this aristocratic complex.

a way to keep bickering and potentially treasonous nobles close to the king for control and surveillance, Versailles and its gardens cover 2000 acres and housed 20,000 courtiers and staff of the royal court for one hundred years. The grandeur of the palace created a separate royal city for the French nobility apart from the festering discontent of Paris. Yet, this disconnected urban arrangement led to class war in Paris and eventually to the French Revolution, since the nobility wasn't aware of the peasant anger and organization in Paris. When Marie Antoinette was the queen of the palace in 1770–1789, she constructed a working peasant village on the palace grounds, where nobility would "play" peasant by feeding and milking animals on the peasant farm. Had Versailles's nobles been more conscious of the plight of the peasants, they wouldn't have wasted their remaining days "playing peasant."

The third building with the feel of a city is the Pentagon in Washington, DC. Built between 1941 and 1943 and covering some 6.5 million square feet, the largest office building in the world is actually five pentagonal buildings built one inside the other, connected by tunnels and intersecting hallways totaling 17.5 miles. Four zip codes and roughly 23,000 people make up the working space of the Pentagon, which is the urban center for the Department of Defense's four branches: Army, Navy, Marines, and Air Force (Green Guide 2001). Run like a small city, the Pentagon has its own police, fire, and transportation systems within the building. Damaged in the September 11, 2001, terrorist attacks, the Pentagon was briefly evacuated, but resumed operations the following day. Like a city, its function had to be maintained, despite tremendous grief.

idealists and even local troops refused to clear the students from the square when an initial crackdown was ordered. Governments that build cities and cultures can also be provoked to defend them, and the Communist leadership drew troops from another province to brutally repress the protesters in Tiananmen Square, when the protests had gone on long enough to threaten the party's control of the city. Now, the proud city of Communist China was known for the horrible images of armed troops hunting down and shooting unarmed students in Tiananmen Square. This repressive action by the Communist Party quickly changed the image of Beijing's culture. No longer was this the shining star in Communist China's constellation of cities, but instead a city that brutalized its own college citizens; this became Beijing's international cultural image.

In fact, one of the most poignant examples of courage under any circumstance and a shameful image for a "People's Revolution" is the picture of an ordinary Beijing citizen with his groceries standing in front of a line of Soviet designed tanks. The tanks were part of the Communist leadership's retaliation on the city of Beijing for the student's protests as martial law was declared, but in this moment of unparalleled courage, one man faced a multi-ton tank and the might of the Chinese military. Ground to a halt, the tanks were stuck as this ordinary citizen climbed on top and demanded to talk to the commander. Clearly, the previous culture of peasant revolution worked in Beijing, China, to create an urban culture of proletarian protest of college students and everyday citizens. So well, in fact, did this culture influence the urbanites of Beijing that this ordinary citizen wasn't going to take blind obedience from the new cadre of Mandarin overlords installed in the Great Hall of the People. The government of Mao's workers' revolution created a new socialist culture in the city that proposed that peasants should overthrow their oppressors; a message many Beijing residents aimed back at the new Communist party in Beijing. *Theory Break:* Functionalist theorists would point to this incident as an obvious failure of Communist ideology in the face of the natural progression of urbanites in any city. The new ideas and education afforded to the urban Chinese by virtue of their urban environment would come into conflict with the Utopian ideas of Mao's brand of Communism. Most Marxist theorists would say there isn't anything "Marxist" or "urban" about shooting unarmed college students; this is just unbridled power and cowardice.

At other times, governments can create urban culture, not through a plan, but by the absence of a plan. Robert Merton (1968) referred to this as a "latent function" of a social institution. *Theory Break:* Manifest functions are those elements that were intended by a social group, social institution, or social policy. In urban planning, an example of manifest function is the designing of roads and area zoning to provide for efficient transportation and livable neighborhoods. Latent functions are those unintended effects that occur when the manifest function is implemented. So, an urban plan is put into motion for rational, manifest benefits to the city, but latent functions of this plan can arise when, for instance, roads or exit ramps bypass working-class, minority areas leaving them dispossessed and decaying. Many Functionalists would argue that the barrio and ghetto design in our cities is not the result of an intended function, but a latent function. The dispossessed areas and structurally abandoned sections of the city weren't "planned" to be rundown and decaying, they became that way because of the unintended effects of industrialization and poverty. The racial groups in these neighborhoods produce most of the culture that we recognize as barrio or ghetto culture. However, the city's latent function of disrepair and decay for the inner city has set or contributed some parameters for that urban culture, i.e., high unemployment, racial segregation, and decaying housing.

An example of one of these parameters would be unemployment, so the citizens use informal economies[4] to survive as a cultural response to the

---

[4]Drug trade, profits from burglary or theft, fraud, barter, and trade of personal services (prostitution) often constitute the informal or black market economy.

MAO'S URBAN CULTURAL REVOLUTION

Mao's revolution was not without its cultural growing pains. Youth groups that waved a collection of Mao's sayings known as "little red books" started what is known as the Cultural Revolution during Mao's plan for China's cultural and economic modernization called "The Great Leap Forward." Intellectuals, Westerners, and Western Bourgeois ideals were considered suspect by the Cultural Revolutionaries, and all of these suspect things were concentrated in the cities. Urban areas were cleared of these "contaminants," and much of the city's impressionable youth were sent to the countryside to find the "real meaning" of a proletarian revolution. The previous Chinese culture of the Emperors and Western-installed leaders was marginalized and the ideology of China sustaining itself through the efforts of every worker was glorified. This was to be achieved by most Chinese citizens focusing their efforts on growing rice, while at the same time limiting each family to one child. Draconian enforcement of these policies produced a change in Chinese culture and in Chinese cities.

As Mao force-fed industrialization to China's backward subsistance agricultural economy, the cities became important work and education centers for those who had undergone Chinese re-education camps. Living in the city became a highly sought after commodity by all workers for its access to work, housing, and education. The government employed this desire to stay in the city to achieve compliance with its domestic and social policies. If a citizen had more than one child or was known to be participating in some subversive Western culture, then their urban apartment and job could be confiscated. Effectively, this translated to a rural prison sentence for many noncompliant Chinese citizens. This was an urban culture of intimidation used by Mao's Communist Party.

lack of sustainable employment. Barrio culture in San Antonio, Texas, for example, was shown to make innovative use of the informal economy in reducing low-birth-weight children and the complications from low-birth-weight infants. Using the health insurance of extended family members posing as fictitious nuclear family members, Hispanic families would use the informal economy to secure services for pregnant mothers and newborns. The dominant culture and the insurance company would call this fraud. The barrio culture, on the other hand, would call this survival, and the culture places extra responsibilities on all family members to contribute to a pregnant relative or newborn (Frisbie 1994). This is an urban cultural innovation to a latent feature of the urban environment, high unemployment, and low availability of health-care benefits.

A similar cultural reaction to unplanned pregnancies can be found in inner city African American culture, where the role of "grandmother" has taken on special meaning. When a father cannot be counted on for support (in 1998, 51 percent of African American children were being raised by their mothers alone, compared to 18.2 percent of white children), many young mothers turn to *their* mothers to help raise and support the new infant (Census 1998). Housing, food, and day care are part of this cultural role that is common in ghetto neighborhoods and the inner city. This familial position also comes with extra power and input over the care and raising of their grandchild; more so than most other grandparents enjoy. Grandmothers in these households are not just members of the extended family who come over for holidays, they are equals in the childcare decisions and are often *the* focal point for family organization.

From these two examples, one can see how urban culture has an impact on something as fundamental as familial structure. In fact, the reduction of extended family relationships and the growth of the strictly nuclear family model coincides with the suburbanization of American cities. Before suburbanization and the availability of housing outside ethnic neighborhoods in 1945, many European Americans relied on extended family for housing, employment connections, and childcare, too. With the increase in the distance between neighborhoods in the city, the extended family loses importance and the nuclear family becomes the preferred cultural model of the suburban family unit. These inner city (barrio, ghetto) cultural solutions came about through the latent function of urban decay and neglect. *Theory Break:* Marxists who study urban decay and the process by which ghettos and barrios are formed would argue with the use of the term "latent function." They would say that latent function implies a benign mistake, an unforeseeable "oops." Marxists and those that study race and ethnicity in cities would point to the long and purposeful history of municipal governments enacting racist and classist laws and ordinances that in effect warehoused the poor and minority urbanite. This warehousing was not latent, but intended by racist and classist urbanites.

CITIES AND SPORTS

If the government can create a city and if it can create culture, even when it lacks a specific plan, then no one should be surprised at the odd hybrid of culture that occurs when business and municipal governments combine their energies to create "sports culture." Very much an urban phenomena, sporting teams rely on a combination of corporate sponsorship, city pride, fan enthusiasm, and government services to make urban sporting teams happen. Football, basketball, baseball, and perhaps the most insidious, soccer, has taken over the lives and budgets of whole municipalities around the globe, in which the actions of the city's sports club has a near life or death hold over the city's citizens. But none of these teams are possible without the municipal government's involvement, because it is the local government that supplies the stadium venue and urban "legitimacy"[5] to the sports franchise.

The only major team to actually be owned by a city is the Green Bay Packers football team, but the stadium that *every* city government provides a sports team in their area is essential to the sports business success and is so expensive that it has to be built by the city. A stadium is such a large building project that it requires the public's approval. This approval is given through the passage of municipal bonds for the construction of the stadium. If you are familiar with bond issues in your city, that knowledge is probably due to the passage of school bonds to build a school district's elementary and high school building or perhaps the passage of municipal bonds to pave a new expressway.

Bonds for sporting teams, which despite relying on civic pride are in fact private capitalist ventures, are highly controversial. They are controversial because of the ambiguous "social good" that a sports stadium might accomplish versus the clear, social benefit of a school or hospital. Supporters point to the visibility and positive public relations that cities with a sports team enjoy, and they can point to analogous evidence of business and political opportunities that cities that possess sports teams receive, over similar-sized cities that don't possess them. An intangible superiority is attached to cities that can claim a sports franchise over cities that don't. The perceived superiority of Buffalo, New York (Buffalo Sabres hockey team and Buffalo Bills football team), over the nearby city of Rochester, New York, which only possesses minor league teams in baseball, hockey, lacrosse, arena football, and soccer, is an example of this intangible benefit. One might argue that Rochester's Kodak, Xerox, and Bausch and Lomb headquarters and production plants combined with its similar population size to Buffalo would make it "more important." Yet most Americans have heard of Buffalo because of its sports franchise but would be hard-pressed to locate Rochester on a map.

It's obvious that the possession of a sports franchise is important to many civic leaders and urban areas. Houston, Texas, lost their football franchise to Tennessee, and many civic leaders have pushed to reclaim a football team as quickly as possible for the stature that this peculiar cultural element provides a city. Many Houstonians couldn't believe that a city as large as theirs didn't have a major league football team for almost a decade, before the arrival of the Houston Texans. The possession of a sports team not only provides its citizens with a sense of urban superiority and civic pride, for many citizens the sports team becomes deeply ingrained in their personal lives. Not just an occasional recreation or hobby, for many urbanites their own lives and emotional states can rest on the performance of the city's

---

[5]Legitimacy occurs through the official or tacit approval of the municipal government of the sports team. Supplying the stadium is one aspect of legitimacy, others might be supporting the team through mentioning it in official municipal communities or PR literature and having local government officials speak or throw out the opening ball on game day.

sports team. Business owners count on some of this devotion to sell tickets, market merchandise, and pass bond issues, but there can be a darker side to this urban sports identification that we will examine further in the next chapter.

CULTURE DIVIDES A CITY

Berlin is a great example of a city destroyed by political culture, divided by governments, and reunited by the sheer will of the people who live in the city. After WWI and the Kaiser's defeat, Berlin became the seat of power for the new Allied-installed government after the Treaty of Versailles in 1919. An unstable economy and political battles between socialists, communists, and various nationalist parties allowed Adolf Hitler's National Socialist Party to gain control of the streets, voting booths, and armed forces of Germany. In an effort not to repeat the mistakes of WWI after the defeat of the Nazi's in WWII, the Allied Forces (USA, UK, and USSR) occupy Germany and pledge to rebuild it. A new foreign political culture comes to dominate Berlin as it is rebuilt after the war; this city becomes the urban symbol of the Cold War.

Very different governmental forces come to act on Berlin and Germany at this point as the Western powers want to rebuild Germany in their image after WWII and the Soviets (who point out the Nazi invasion and loss of millions of Soviet lives) insist on occupying their portion of East Germany in the socialist image. Berlin, as the capital, is located within East Germany, but is "occupied" by both Soviet and American forces. A tense culture grows within the city as East Germans uncomfortable with the hard-line socialist government of East Germany and the draconian use of East Germany's Secret Police try to escape to the West through Berlin. In 1948, a blockade of the city plunges Berlin into the middle of Cold War politics and brings the world close to war as Western forces refuse to allow the blockades of Berlin to succeed. A massive airlift campaign is launched to feed and sustain those Berlin citizens trapped in the Western-controlled section of the city. The airlift succeeds in May 1949 in breaking the barbed wire that previously separated East and West Berlin. It is replaced with a reinforced concrete wall and guard towers. Berlin's culture is divided by this wall and the governmental ideologies that fought over the Berlin wall. One of the few places that connected East and West Berlin was Check Point Charlie in the American Sector. Diplomats, spies, and refugees crossed this man-made hole in the wall, which would come to symbolize the tension between the city's two political masters.[6] For Westerners, the East was a bleak repressive place where they had to keep their citizens imprisoned to avoid their escape. West Berlin, for East Germans and the Soviet Union, was the bastion of a bankrupt consumer capitalist culture that allowed the rich to feed off the labor of the working class, and the discos and popular culture of West Berlin were another Western

---

[6]This guard point in the Berlin wall can now be seen at the Smithsonian Museum.

BORDER CITY CULTURE

Border cities are examples of urban cultures that are created by the interplay between two national governments and are often their own unique cultural entities, i.e., not similar to any other cities in either country. Not completely the culture of one nation or another, border cities operate as the conduit for people, goods, currency, and contraband to flow from one nation to another nation. Visitors can quickly spot the difference between the well-planned border cities of Canada along the northern U.S. border and the haphazard border cities of Mexico along the southern U.S. border. Niagara Falls is one of the most beautiful sights in North America, and Niagara Falls, New York, shares the waterfall with Niagara Falls, Ontario, Canada. Facilities and bridges link the two countries and the two cities, and while the Canadian side enjoys the better view and greater economic health, both cities share a "border culture." The New York side is a distribution point for Canadian goods entering the United States, but has stubbornly relinquished much of the high-priced tourist business to the Canadian side of Niagara Falls. Niagara Falls, Ontario, has several high-rise hotels that rely on the superior view of the falls, as well as the burgeoning casino hotels. The Canadian side is the definitive tourist destination, and while it is its own city, the tourist businesses are there to attract U.S. dollars. Sadly, New York's side of Niagara Falls was the destination point for almost 100 years of honeymooners and vacationers, but lack of continued investment and government initiative has left the U.S. side of the falls a broken remnant of its former self.

Other border cities in the United States sometimes share a name with their counterpart on the other side, as in Laredo, Texas, and Nuevo Laredo, Mexico. Unlike the well-planned attractive bridges and attractions of the U.S.-Canada border, the Laredos are definitely a tale of two *different* cities connected by border culture. While Laredo, Texas, has newer buildings and better streets, it is still part of the border economy that some sociologists refer to as the Fourth World.* Informal and sometimes illegal subdivisions called *colonias* exist on the U.S. side, where desperate Mexican nationals try to establish a home and residency (often while caring for U.S. citizens—their own young children born in the United States). Nuevo Laredo, Mexico, has come to serve the gray area between the two national cultures, offering cheap goods to Americans and acting as a staging area for cheap Mexican labor and those wanting to come across the border illegally.

Economic opportunities are only slightly better for U.S. citizens in a town where wages are low despite the growth of many U.S. retail outlets that cater to Mexican national buying power made easier by the North American Free Trade Agreement (NAFTA). Nuevo Laredo is a typical Mexican border town, where cigarettes, liquor, and pharmaceuticals are

---

*The Fourth World are areas within the First World, like inner cities, Appalachia, and border regions that more closely resemble conditions in the Third World.

hawked in small storefronts, and cheap labor makes retail and manu-facturing goods for the U.S. and Canadian markets. All along the Texas-Mexico border, U.S. factories called *maquiladoras* employ cheap Mexican labor on the Mexican side of the border for the U.S. and Cana-dian consumer market. There are two socioeconomic perspectives on the *maquiladora* industry and its impact on cities. *Theory Break:* One per-spective is from the Marxist school of thought and emphasizes the loss of jobs (particularly from the Northeast United States) and the aban-donment of the inner cities by manufacturing companies that locate their operations in Mexico. This deindustrialization of the United States hurts American cities and increases segregation and racial ten-sion, and the work that benefited the United States economy now goes to Mexico or overseas under current trade deals. The second or func-tionalist perspective would emphasize the increased job opportunities in Mexico and lower-priced goods availability in the United States.

The benefits to Mexico's cities are questionable as well; border factories demand electrical, water, and transportation services from the Mexican city, while employing mostly young women (because they will work cheaper and are more easily intimidated). There is more cur-rency circulating in these cities, that can't be debated, but it hasn't been enough to supply housing or social services to the growing shanty-towns that are the housing for some *maquiladora* workers. The cheap labor seems to have not benefited some Mexican cities, where workers struggle in the border culture to survive and the city is actually losing money delivering some services. The Functionalist perspective favors global trade, and while it acknowledges some short-term unemploy-ment difficulties in the First World, the greater gains of wages and technology for the developing world far outweighs these difficulties. Cheaper goods in the United States help consumers and wages (*maquiladora* owners are quick to point out that they pay their workers well over the national median hourly rate for Mexico) in Mexico even-tually create more markets for U.S. goods in Mexico.

Having the technology of the factories and the links to First World markets are also considered invaluable for the cities in Mexico to make the transition from developing city to a technologically developed city. The free trade zone that makes *maquiladoras* possible under NAFTA was definitely a planned and negotiated instrument, but the effects on the American Northeast and Mexican border cities was not. Northeastern cities of the United States suffered the loss of thousands of skilled manu-facturing jobs, due to American businesses relocating to the Mexican cities across the border. The unintended pollution from U.S. factories that are located in Mexico was unplanned, and yet the pollution from these factories have been suspected in birth defects in El Paso, Texas, asthma deaths and sickness from California to Texas, and the poisoning of the Rio Grande river. Border culture is often the result of lack of planning and un-intended consequences rather than the result of urban political planning.

threat to the Communist bloc (Poland, Czechoslovakia, Hungary, Yugoslavia, East Germany, the Baltics, and the USSR).

The East German government and the Berlin wall collapsed in 1989, and the city entered an even more tenuous period of urban culture as two different countries tried to unite. Berlin again becomes the urban focal point for this cultural tension. West Germans saw the price of unification as a drag on their economy to bring East Germany up to West Germany's level of economics, social service, and education. For East Germans, their culture was effectively declared substandard and West Germany becomes their political, economic, and cultural masters. Many East Berliners welcomed reunification and the dissolution of the repressive East German government and police, but did not welcome the perceived second-class status that came with reunification. To this day, East Berlin bears the architectural stigma of its socialist past and its citizens lag behind their Western counterparts in jobs and opportunities. Some have pointed to this lopsided power dynamic between East and West Germany as a contributing factor to the rise of Neo-Nazism in East Germany.

References

DE BECKER, GAVIN. 1997. *The Gift of Fear*. Little, Brown and Company: Boston, MA.

FRISBIE, PARKER. 1994. "Birth Weight and Infant Mortality in the Mexican Origin and Anglo Populations." *Social Science Quarterly*, 75, pp. 881–895.

GORDON, MILTON. 1964. *Assimilation in American Life*. Oxford University Press: New York, NY.

GOTHAM, KEVIN. 2002. "Marketing Mardi Gras: Commodification Spectacle and the Political Economy of Tourism in New Orleans." *Urban Studies*, vol. 39, no. 10, pp. 1735–1756.

GREEN GUIDE. 2001. *Washington, DC*. Michelin Press: Greenville, SC.

MERTON, ROBERT. 1968. *Social Theory and Social Structure*. Free Press: New York, NY.

NEW YORK HERALD. 1905. "Negro Explosion in Harlem." Hearst Press: New York, NY.

RUTHERFORD, SCOTT, AND BRIAN BELL. 2002. *China*. Apa Publications/Insight: London, England.

"TREATY OF NAN KING." www.hyperhistory.com/online_n2/history_n2/html

UNIFORM CRIME REPORT. 1995–2001. FBI Statistics.

U.S. BUREAU OF THE CENSUS. 1998. "Marital Status and Living Arrangement: March 1998." U.S. Government Printing Office: Washington, DC.

WEBER, MAX. 1921. *Economy and Society: An Outline of Interpretive Sociology*. Claus Wittrich and Guenther Roth (eds.) 1979. University of California Press: Berkeley, CA.

WILSON, KENNETH, AND ALEJANDRO PORTES. 1980. "Immigrant Enclaves: An Analysis of the Labor Market Experience of Cubans in Miami." *American Journal of Sociology*, vol. 86, no. 2.

CHAPTER NINE

Spontaneous Culture and Social Movements

SPORTS RIOTS

Most of us can picture in our minds what a riot is and what it looks like. A running chaos of violence, mayhem, looting, and general group lawlessness is our collective social memory of a riot, and certainly there are riots and social disturbances that resemble this picture. Yet, there are some riots and destructive cultures that don't resemble this model. To illustrate this point, we will begin our discussion with urban sports teams and the riots and destructive culture that can form fan celebrations. The dark side of urban professional sporting teams is the all too frequent fan celebrations turned into destructive riots that have plagued cities with professional sports teams. Often occurring in the United States after the city has won that year's national championship, supporters of the team will gather downtown to revel in their victory, and a common outcome of the celebration can be a riot.

For many of us, this process may seem counter to our expectations—if our team has won, why would we start a destructive urban riot? Logic would dictate that fans would be more inclined to be angry if their team lost, not if they have won. The singular mentality of a mob, and the suspension of social norms while acting with the mob during a riot, seems to occur for fans of sporting teams mainly when they have achieved some great victory. After the victory, the fans gather to celebrate with each other and drink alcohol; at a certain point of critical mass there is a large enough group of fans to both promote a feeling of strength and invincibility, *and* a feeling of anonymity. At this point of critical mass, one of two things might happen: (1) the fans might sing songs and drink more or (2) the celebration might turn uglier and the mob need some physical expression of their euphoria. This might start with fighting or smashing a window, but could quickly escalate to turning over cars and looting. Again, this whole episode, oddly enough, begins with fans feeling *good* and being full of civic pride in their team. The city is the motivation for their pride, and the city quickly becomes the arena in which a bizarre destruction derby begins between burning, looting fans (many with no previous criminal record) and civic authorities, police, and the rest of the city. Urbanites at home watch battles erupt on the news between police and fans over the city's sports team winning their championship and the news audience wonders at the fans' sudden desire to loot.

Theory Break: Sociologists have best described this mob mentality and how ordinary people can be sucked into "group behavior" they would normally never participate in. It begins with the individual losing his or her own identity temporarily, as they become part of the crowd or group. While in the group euphoric state, the individual doesn't question the actions of the group, which may be setting new norms (albeit temporary and only within the group experience) of violence and lawlessness. Under normal circumstances, these individuals would *never* commit crimes, but while in the group, they are experiencing "mob mentality." Emile Durkheim determined that the social group makes the norms for the individual to follow. Each successive group that one belongs to places the group's norm into conflict with the successive group. For sports riots, the new social group of the mob creates a new set of norms (violence, looting) for the individual, though the new norms are in conflict with the previous social norms.

As urban researchers we would have to classify a single incident of sports teams leading to urban riot as an oddity or curiosity. However, after riots in Chicago when the Bulls won the NBA Finals three times in the 1990s, Los Angeles when the Lakers won the NBA Championship in 2000, and numerous college football riots in recent years, we cannot consider these isolated incidents. We must consider the celebration riot as part of the urban culture of having a sports team. Some element of having an urban sports team leads to the celebration urban riot and the culture that facilitates it.

In Europe, soccer sports clubs are associated with city, corporate, and national identity, but have also come to represent the worst among thuggery and violence of sports fans. Soccer hooligans have ruined games, provoked violent melees in the stands, and have even resulted in deaths of innocent fans that have been crushed in stadium riots. English soccer fans have been singled out as the worst examples of hooliganism after riots resulting in deaths on the European mainland occurred during matches with English teams. Today, English soccer hooligans are detained and prevented from entering some European countries during soccer season, and for a period of time after the riots, English soccer teams were banned from competition completely.

Some correlation has been put forth by the media with the soccer clubs from working-class English cities having a higher proportion of hooligans than wealthier cities, but that is a superficial analysis. Most soccer teams in England and Europe have had trouble with their fans, regardless of the composition of the urban workforce. In a bizarre piece of sports culture, soccer fans that live in Germany (of all classes) will meet at a predetermined location to battle the opposing team's fans before the match, then end the riot at an agreed time to attend the game. Not that class doesn't have *any* impact on the consumption of urban sports culture. For working-class urbanites, the performance of the city's sports team seems to be more important to their urban identity and entertainment than to most of the middle or upper class. From this culture consumption, many urbanites derive a great deal of pleasure and pride in their city. Those fans with a more violent propensity express their pleasure and displeasure with their team and any opposing team or fans by assaults and riots. This expression can quickly become an expected part of the urban sports culture.

DESTRUCTION OF CULTURE AS CULTURE

A larger question is: Can the destruction of culture be a type of culture in and of itself? Is a riot or a fire or violence an act of culture? Sports and soccer teams are the manifestation of urban leaders (business and government) who support this type of culture. Violence and riots and their resulting culture of destruction are a latent function of a fringe element of fans. Yet, that destruction is a part of the culture of urban sports teams. An example of destructiveness as a work of culture from the most remote part of the world might be illustrative. In Tibet's Buddhist temples, monks work meticulously on intricate and beautiful sand paintings called mandalas. At the end of this artistic and time-consuming cultural process, when the sand painting is complete, the monks don't save or even photograph their creation, they just sweep it away. They destroy it. That act of destruction is part of the culture. Most Westerners couldn't conceive of spending days creating a piece of art just to destroy it, but to the monks, it is an essential act of their culture to destroy the mandala to demonstrate the temporary nature of life.

In the urban environment, the initial act of urbanization is one of organized destruction of the natural environment. We change the natural world (trees, grass, streams) to fit our world (buildings, roads, parking lots) and *through* that destruction a new cultural product is made. Our modern urban world is still like this, where we need to destroy what is in the urban environment, like a building or parking garage, to be able to create a new building or parking garage. For the deteriorating inner city and those that live there, they live in a constant state of urban destruction with the broken buildings and abandoned economies as their surroundings. Is this "living space among destruction" an act of culture? The response to the living conditions by the inhabitants of this destroyed environment is to destroy even more. Actions from graffiti to arson are a cultural reaction to the destroyed or decaying areas of the city by the citizens that live there. Riots have become familiar expressions of the decay and destruction of the inner city, and are examples of destructive culture.

Riots don't have to be associated with sporting events or inner cities; historically, politics, economics, and ethnic struggles have been the generators of many urban riots in the United States. The urban environment is fertile ground for riots, since a city contains the critical mass of people necessary for a riot and also contains the poverty, racial tension, political intrigue, and police abuses that feed many rioting mobs. A quick examination of American history uncovers numerous urban riots that are obviously part of the urban culture of destruction.

URBAN UPRISINGS AS URBAN POLITICAL ACTIVISM

Boston is a good city to begin with when discussing urban riots. The stage for more than a hundred urban uprisings and riots, Boston's first urban rebellions were based on the lack of available food in the early 1700s (Tager 2001). Harsh winters and a short growing season in New England left the city unable to feed its poorer residents during the colonial period, yet at the same time export goods demanded by English financiers were leaving for Europe. Tensions often grew into riots that had to be put down by armed constables of the British crown. *Theory Break*: Immanuel Wallerstein (1979) developed a theory in which the world's nations were evaluated using a mode of interconnected relations and global colonization, and a stratification of these nations developed (core, semiperiphery, periphery). Core nations have what we call "developed economies" and most of these nations have previous colonial histories either as colonizers or as colonized populations. These core nations dominate the rest of the globe, developing a hierarchy in which the world's labor is divided among the rich, core nations who direct the poor nation's (periphery) production.

EXAMPLES:	
CORE	United States, Germany, UK, France
SEMIPERIPHERY	South Korea, Mexico, Brazil, Saudi Arabia
PERIPHERY	Myanmar, Liberia, Peru, El Salvador

Like capitalists using working-class labor in the city, core nations use poor nations for their cheaper labor, but their exploitation does not develop firm ties between the peripheral nations and the core nations. The lack of these firm ties to the core nations translates into no technology and no real capitalist investment in the periphery nation. In between core nations and peripheral nations are semiperipheral nations; these countries have stronger ties to core nations and they perform some important functions for the core nations. For these more important labor functions, the semiperipheral nation does get more capital and technology investment.

Applying Wallerstein's Theory to the Boston colonial food riots, Britain was a core nation and the American colonies were their property, making the American colonies an example of a subservient semiperipheral nation. I argue that although the American colonies were often valuable to the British crown for the raw goods that they exported back to Europe, they were still British citizens, who were receiving the full extent of British technology and service of the British government, not just exploited workers. Boston was a "connection point" for the British domination of the American colonies and the New World, because it was the port for British political and military administration. America was the extraction point for the raw goods and food stuffs exported back to England and Europe. This cultural arrangement was crucial to the riot; it wasn't that there was no food in Boston, the citizen's anger came from the fact that what food existed was controlled by a few wealthy merchants and was destined to be exported to Europe or to feed British troops.

Boston colonists had a deep hatred for the British troops quartered in the city. Often belligerent or abusive of their police powers and a drain on the local economy (housing and food were demanded of local citizens), British troops became the source of Boston's most famous riot—The Boston Massacre. On March 5, 1770, a mob of young men and boys began to taunt a lone British guard at the city's Custom House; when other British troops arrived a fight ensued and the soldiers fired into the crowd. Four Bostonians were killed immediately and the fifth, Crispus Attucks, died four days later. Paul Revere's most famous engraving immortalized the event, but it was also a clear example of effective urban propaganda.

Facts rarely get in the way of incendiary propaganda and this painting by Revere is no exception. The British troops are pictured lined up as if organized to do premeditated battle with the unarmed crowd. This does not reflect the eyewitness accounts at the time, which state a brawl on both sides. Also, Crispus Attucks (the first black patriot of the Revolutionary Period) is pictured as a white man, the closest wounded figure to the British troops in the engraving. This event was a rallying point for Boston patriots and was culturally changed from a mob riot to a patriotic battle. The public's rage over British domination and the Boston Massacre grew a fertile crop of urban patriots or urban terrorists as the British would have labeled them. These patriots or terrorists would be the colonists dressed as Native Americans[1] for the Boston Tea Party and would be the Minutemen militia responding to Paul Revere's famous midnight ride.

Boston's predilection for urban riots continues into the nineteenth century with anti-Catholic uprisings over Irish immigration, abolitionist riots

---

[1]Dressing as a Native American was a cultural symbol for colonists, who viewed Native Americans as the ultimate symbol of living free.

over slavery, and draft riots during the Civil War (Tager 2001). The Civil War obviously did not fix racial tensions in Boston or the rest of the United States, and in the twentieth century ghetto neighborhood growth and busing riots reminded Bostonians of the urban inequalities of race and class (Tager 2001). *Theory Break*: Emile Durkheim's theory of social disturbance might surprise us. Social riots and uprisings can be *good* for society. A riot can let off steam and give temporary release to pent-up tension or anger in the urban population. Social disturbances also call attention to stress or trouble in the urban fabric of the city. Boston's race and religious riots might be best described in these Durkheimian terms. After establishing an urban culture of urban riots and public disturbances in colonial Boston, it becomes an accepted method of voicing grievance or displeasure.

Los Angeles, California

The most important urban riots of the twentieth century were in Los Angeles, California, and were due to a specific kind of urban culture. The Watts Riot of 1965 and the Rodney King riot of 1992 both have a connection to race relations and the actions of law enforcement. In the Watts riot of 1965, a young black man was arrested for driving "under the influence." On the night of August 11, a crowd gathered to taunt the police during the arrest. This escalated the tense situation, and it was made worse by a record heat wave in Los Angeles that summer that had people angry and out in the street. Police reinforcements used batons on the crowd and a riot ensued which lasted five days, cost 200 million dollars, required over 15,000 National Guardsmen to quell, and resulted in 34 deaths (Horne 1995). Our assumption that an urban riot lacks thought, goals, purpose, or culture is challenged by the Watts Riot of 1965. The crowd focused its anger on white business and the white police force, by and large leaving black-owned businesses and churches alone (Horne 1995). Clearly, through the mayhem and anger, there was some "agenda" to the Watts riot. This agenda was created through the cultural experience of the Los Angeles urban environment.

The riot in 1992 followed the emotional trial of several Los Angeles police officers charged with beating a black man, Rodney King. The beating had been caught on videotape by an observer. The African American community of the city, in particular, followed the trial closely, feeling that for once their claims of police mistreatment would be vindicated with the clear abuse of police power caught on tape. But, in a legal twist that would show the difference between inner city African American culture and the suburban white culture of Southern California, the trial was moved to Simi Valley in Orange County. The mainly white jury acquitted the officers of assault charges, despite the disturbing images from the videotape.

African American community members in the city's South Central area were incensed at the verdict, as were Mexican American community members. South Central's high concentration of minority members (both black and Hispanic), high rates of unemployment, and persistent poverty made this population particularly volatile. Yet, race and class do not fully explain the riot, since racism and poverty have been a constant component of this area for over thirty years. It was the specific cultural message that this community received from the trial verdict that made them riot. The justice system had made it clear that the minority community members didn't count and couldn't expect fair and equal treatment from police.

This was not a singular instance, but the culmination of several episodes that had preceded the Rodney King verdict to prime this population for an urban uprising, and which had contributed to an emotional culture of angry disappointment. Months prior to the Rodney King verdict, two Mexican American youths were shot in the back by two Los Angeles County sheriff deputies. Although the deputies were cleared of any wrongdoing in the shooting, many Mexican American community members were angry at the police and the judicial system. A Korean shopkeeper had also recently been given probation for shooting a young black girl in the back of the head in a dispute over a carton of juice that was caught on videotape. For many minority community members, the interpretation of this episode showed that a young black girl's life wasn't as valuable as the Korean shopkeeper's in the eyes of the court. Some scholars and journalists offered theories that it was the economic conditions that sparked the riots, but it wasn't until the area's minority members were essentially informed that they didn't matter to the judicial system or law enforcement that the culture of this area erupted in violence.

In fact, examining the actions of the rioting mob are an interesting method of analyzing riot culture. After the decision in the Rodney King trial was announced, a large group of African Americans confronted a group of policemen trying to make an arrest (similar to the Watts incident). A local news crew filmed the police cars fleeing the scene after the crowd turned violent, and with the retreat of the police, all social order broke down. For several days, crowds of angry minority rioters seemed to emanate from Florence and Normandy Streets in South Central Los Angeles. What is interesting is some of the behaviors of the urban crowds. While some rioters burned buildings and attacked white motorists, others took a more businesslike approach to the breakdown of social order. To illustrate these two different cultural approaches to the riot, approach number one finds that numerous people of different social classes and ethnic groups in the area participated in looting. Their actions said a lot about the poverty in the area including that the first place these looters sought out were grocery stores to steal food. Eventually, however, all types of stores were looted as people of all ages took advantage of this situation. In the second cultural approach, the crowds that were involved in most of the violence were young black or Hispanic men. This group of young male rioters raged at the injustice of their own situation; the Rodney King verdict was just an occasion to give voice to that anger. Initially, this crowd targeted white motorists on which to vent their anger about the verdict. The feeling of betrayal of the South Central community and the frustration about the Rodney King verdict expanded from the white judges and jurors in Simi Valley to all white people. Truck driver Reginald Denny's savage beating by one of these crowds of young men was caught on a local news broadcast of the growing riot.

The random nature of the violent rioters was about to change as the racial hatred and anger over the probation sentence of the Korean store owner boiled into a very *specific* agenda. That agenda was to "get even" with Korean immigrants in nearby Koreantown, and many angry rioters descended on these Korean-owned businesses to deliver a vendetta for the shopkeeper's light sentence. While some Korean owners bravely tried to defend themselves and their businesses, the rioting crowds were too much for them. For many of the rioters, the Korean businesses were prime targets for revenge beyond the shopkeeper's probation verdict. That revenge also would be for the Korean-owned mini-marts and liquor stores that are so prevalent in the South Central neighborhoods, which charge steep product markups on goods, but never hire local residents as employees.

Theory Break: Marxists call this economic arrangement "urban neocolonialism," where the money of the inner city's resident is taken through higher prices and nothing is given back to the community, like employment or development. Rioters had done the economic math of that business model long before the riot started, and they wanted to redress the money they felt was stolen from their community. To be fair to the Korean business owners, they felt that their high prices were their economic insurance from frequent theft and robbery attempts on their stores. And, not employing local residents was their prerogative, if they had family members who would work more cheaply. Certainly, this clash of cultures in the city contributed to this direct violence of one ethnic group on another.

Police inability to restore order and gunfire directed at the fire and EMS units prompted the use of the National Guard to quell the growing rioters angry over the Rodney King verdict. When the arrest records of this uprising[2] were examined, Hispanics were the majority of those arrested by the police, not blacks. The media coverage of the event kept asking why this happened, as if the poverty, miscarriage of justice in the King case, miscarriage of justice in the Korean shopkeepers case, segregation, unemployment, racism, and the suspicious shooting of the two Hispanic youths in Los Angeles County wasn't enough to incite the Hispanic community as well.

A culture of emotional anger had been growing in the South Central area of Los Angeles, and while African Americans' anger over the Rodney King verdict may have started the riot, Hispanic anger over the sheriff's shooting, combined with each of the previously mentioned social barriers, prompted this ethnic community to riot as well. Most of America wanted the riot to go away and many middle-class white commentators in the media discussed the "pathologies" of the rioters, as if there was something psychologically wrong with individuals engaging in this riot and that they were

---

[2]Many in the South Central area refer to the event as an uprising, not a riot. Clearly, this illustrates a different cultural perspective on urban history.

RACE RIOTS IN AMERICA

America has had a long, unfortunate history of race riots in its cities. One five-year period was particularly bad for race riots, a combative culture developed in America's cities to settle racial differences with violence. *Theory Break*: Whites, as the dominant racial group in society, were the most likely to start racial riots and disturbances, because they had little to fear from the police or judicial system from perpetrating racial violence. In July 1917, years of white-black tensions, which had produced numerous lynchings of blacks and a four million strong membership drive in the Ku Klux Klan, erupted in a day-long riot in East St. Louis, Illinois. Sparked by the use of black workers as strikebreakers, 39 blacks and 8 whites were killed as rioting *whites* burned black houses and chased thousands of blacks across the river to St. Louis, Missouri.

As if in response to this white urban riot, in August 1917 over a hundred black soldiers from the decorated 24th Infantry (who had served with distinction in the Spanish American War) marched on Houston, Texas, after a black soldier was killed and two black MPs were beaten by the local white sheriff's department. After laying siege to the city, 17 whites and 2 blacks were killed in the resultant fighting, the U.S. military regained control over the "rogue" unit, and 64 black soldiers were court-martialed (13 hanged, 51 given life imprisonment). A "Red Scare" gripped the nation in 1918–1919, in which Bolsheviks were thought to be fermenting revolution among "docile" urban blacks. Several riots and general unrest in the black urban sections of U.S. cities were blamed on Bolshevik agitators. Twenty-six race riots occurred in 1919 alone, including Washington, DC; Knoxville, Tennessee; Chicago, Illinois; and Omaha, Nebraska that all have a familiar story: some act of defense or perceived defiance by urban blacks results in angry, violent white mobs.

The riot in Tulsa, Oklahoma, occurred in 1921 and holds many of the racial stereotypes that resulted in previous riots, when Dick Rowland, a nineteen-year-old black man, was accused of assault by a seventeen-year-old white girl and jailed. The May 31, 1921 edition of the Tulsa *Tribune* claimed that Rowland had "torn the clothes off the girl," and a white mob gathered that night to dispense their own vigilante justice (Hirsch 2002). A concerned group of black men also organized and armed themselves, fearing a lynching. As in Houston, former black army veterans were among the group who gathered weapons to defend the jail. Unfortunately, the white mob had also armed and mobilized; when the white mob encountered stiff resistance from the African American community, they proceeded to burn the black section of Tulsa, called Greenwood, to the ground.

Blacks tried to defend their homes but were hopelessly outnumbered. When the National Guard arrived on June 1 to restore "order," they proceeded to disarm and arrest the black citizens, interning 6000 blacks in makeshift camps—roughly half of Tulsa's black population at the time (Hirsch 2002). Red Cross assessments of the damage list 300 dead (almost all black), 1,429 black-owned businesses burned or looted, and over 1,000 black Tulsans spent the winter in a tent city erected after the riot. No white citizen was ever arrested or charged with a crime; Sarah Page, the alleged victim who accused Rowland, refused to prosecute him and a later police investigation found that Rowland had just accidentally stumbled into her getting off an elevator. The press at the time concluded that the riot was *not* the fault of black Tulsans, who came to the jail armed to defend the accused boy. Recently, in 1996, black legislators in Oklahoma have started an investigation into the Tulsa incident, including the idea of reparations (Hirsch 2002). By 1922, lynching had declined from previous years, and the Deep South seemed to have sorted out their racial differences.

New Year's Eve, 1922, however, changed that perception in tiny Rosewood, Florida, when a white woman named Fannie Taylor was found by her family, beaten and crying, sputtering about being attacked by an unknown assailant on a rural road in the small, all-white town of Cedar Key, Florida. A similar instance of a white schoolteacher attacked and killed left three black men lynched in Perry, Florida, which was no more than twenty miles away from Rosewood, just three weeks prior. A mob grew to 30 white men in Cedar Key, when the local sheriff brought news of an escaped black convict named Jesse Hunter. Bloodhounds led the mob to the black village of Rosewood. One black man was lynched and another was nearly dragged to death, as the now 50-plus mob searched for Frances Taylor's attacker. By New Year's Day, 1923, dozens of blacks had been killed and the town had been burnt to the ground (D'Orso 1996). The white town of Cedar Key possessed the power of the dominant race, which is why after the riot the town of Rosewood effectively disappeared, while the white town remained with no police investigation or repercussion. Despite the rural nature of these two small villages, the urban dominance of the white village overcame the black village through the use of racial power and a culture of rioting that left whites empowered to respond to racial threats (real or imagined) with violence.

From an urban culture perspective, the interesting element about these urban riots is how they quickly became "nonevents." The racial politics and power of the dominant white race that controlled the urban media, law enforcement, courts, and the political process. White urban leaders even controlled what is "history" by eliminating these events in the community's collective memory by means of not including them in textbooks or refusing to purchase textbooks that included the mention of these race riots.

somehow "crazy." The actions of Hispanic and African American community members help us to show that the circumstances of this riot were formed socially, not as the result of the actions of a few mentally disturbed people.

The culture that became the "L.A. Riot" grew from the social circumstances of neighborhoods of South Central, and within these overlapping circumstances were distinct value judgments that led to the riot. Clearly, both the African American and Hispanic communities defined their social breaking point as the exclusion of their ethnic group from equal protection under the law and judiciary. Black and Hispanic community members joined the riot when they heard news of the Rodney King verdict, which many interpreted as a dissolution of the social contract by the courts and judiciary between minority citizens and the city as a whole. Consequently, many community members no longer felt bound by urban social norms and the rule of law. It wasn't just the presence of poverty and unemployment, otherwise whites and Asians that were poor and living in Los Angeles would have rioted too, or blacks would have started rioting in 1950 and never stopped. Neither was it simply a one-dimensional racially motivated riot. The touchstone event was a conflict with the police, and the first episodes of violence were against the police (rather than just random attacks on whites or Asians, which did occur later). Both ethnic communities (Hispanic and African American) seemed to be fed up with the idea of being treated like second-class citizens by the law in a city that they felt was as much theirs as it was the city of the police or white elites.

Before we move on to our discussion of urban social movements, we should be honest about the language we are using in discussing urban riots. Some readers might be shocked to learn that many residents call the L.A. Riot the "uprising" or the "rebellion" instead of accepting the media's terminology of "riot." It was chaotic, destructive, and violent, so it must be a riot. Why then do we refer to the campus takeovers, sit-ins, and meetings of the 1960s as "demonstrations," when many of them turned into violent, destructive, chaotic events? The "demonstration" at the Chicago Democratic National Convention of 1968 was a riot by anyone's terminology, yet we rarely hear it categorized as such. The reasons for this turn of phrase are debatable, but it must be pointed out that when middle-class, white, college youths violently break social conventions, we call the acts demonstrations, and when poor, minority youths do it, we call it a riot.

URBAN SOCIAL MOVEMENTS

If we remove the violence at the beginning of an urban uprising and substitute coherent demands for blind rage, we could have an urban social movement instead of a riot. Urban social movements have shaped our urban lives and culture by demonstrating for running water, paved streets, education, and welfare as social entitlements. Manuel Castells summarized some of the more important urban social movements of the past two hundred years in his book *The City and the Grassroots Movement* (*1983*). He found that the most important and successful urban social movements were not organized around their production of goods, as they are in union organizing, but around their consumption of goods and services, like water, power, education, libraries, and so forth. This is not to imply that labor power and labor organization is not an important urban issue; in fact, we will examine that a little later in this chapter. Success as an urban movement often has to go across many different social classes and occupations, which usually means having united demands—schools, streets, and running water are services that all communities can unite behind. Everyone wants these services, so they become united.

An example of an urban social movement organized around consumption is the Veracruz, Mexico, demonstration for housing in 1922. The citizens organized their demands around their collective consumption of housing or lack thereof, rather than trying to organize as labor groups that were demanding housing. If the group had tried to organize their demand for housing by labor unions, then different labor groups could be pitted against one another (street cleaners against school teachers). Many of the collective groups' demands were met by pressuring local government and businesses for housing. As part of Veracruz's urban culture, housing began to be seen as a right of citizens. After the revolution of 1910, this universal demand for housing was incorporated into the Mexican Constitution, as a right of Mexican citizens. While the ultimate success of this "right" can be called into question, because of the lack of tax appropriation for the construction of new housing by the Mexican government, the urban culture from the Veracruz demonstrations has resulted in the squatting and appropriation of government lands by homeless citizens. When the government can't provide the housing, citizens take over unused government land (usually in the city) and build their own housing (Castells 1983).

Having compulsory education for urbanites came about through a combination of labor and collective consumption in Glasgow, Scotland. Education was offered for factory workers and their children by the owners of factories as an incentive to move to Glasgow in the late 1980s, but quickly the other urbanites in the city began to organize to demand education for *all* children in the city. This may seem perfectly reasonable to the modern reader, but we must remind ourselves that up to this point in urban history, education at even the most basic level was reserved for the elite classes of society. To demand universal compulsory education for the whole city's working classes, rather than a small incentive program provided by one urban employer, was absurd. Yet, as the population organized itself in Glasgow and began to pressure the government and local employers, their demands for education were met for what we now call elementary school (free and compulsory) (Castells 1983).

Theory Break: The key for the success in Glasgow was that the urban social movement was organized around the collective consumption of education, rather than as separate groups of laborers or artisans trying to coordinate their demands. Often elites, who want to resist an urban social movement, will try to pit one interest group against another to derail the popular momentum enjoyed by the urban social movement. In Glasgow, citizens maintained this unity and successfully had the schools opened for all children in the city. After gaining this valuable new service, other cities were pressured by their citizens to begin providing schools and education as well. This demonstrates the success of an urban social movement centered around collective consumption of education as a service and maintained across many urban areas due to the shared belief in education held by the movement's participants.

Businesses also recognized that schools and education were a powerful motivating factor in attracting labor to factory locations. It even makes sense in a business model for providing education for employees, and this is part of the reason education has become a part of urban culture. For business to progress, the laborer must become more and more educated by some means to keep up with demands of the job. So much education is necessary for the worker in a modern industrial setting that it cannot be provided for solely in on-the-job training.

The education process (acquiring literary skills, math skills, verbal communication, reasoning skills, and exposure to the lecture method)[3] has to be started earlier than the worker's first day on the job. Preferably, when the worker is a child, workers are taught valuable skills that the business needs them to know, but hasn't the time to teach them on the job. Since we are all going to be workers, it makes sense for business to pay for education, as in the Glasgow case, because business needs this prior education for its workers. But, an interesting thing happened in Glasgow and has been happening ever since: business has turned the expense of paying for schools over to the urban laborer-citizen. Business shirked its local taxation to pay for schools by putting the burden onto the urbanite worker through property taxes. Now, through this taxation, urban citizens pay for their own job training.

Modern urban social movements have a new set of issues to deal with in the Information Age. The modern Western city and the kind of production the city engages in has changed in the Information Age. Modern Western cities are sites of information and administrative production, and since 1960 new informational technology development has changed the relationship of labor and management, as well as the products the city makes (Castells 1989). Inventions like the integrated circuit (1957) and the microprocessor (1971) have made productivity advances that have blurred the lines of worker and management. These inventions have also redefined what is an urban industrial product, which previously was an automobile or a toaster oven, but now can be a microchip or a financial report (Castells 1989). Computers have made drastic changes in the work of the urban white-collar worker in the Information Age. The kind of work that modern laborers perform and the work that managers perform has essentially become the same. Urban products have changed from manufactured goods to information.

---

[3] The lecture method of learning consists of a teacher reciting or teaching a lesson or skill to a class of students who passively write the information down without comment or participation.

THE LABOR MOVEMENT

The Labor Movement in the United States became a social movement on the night of May 4, 1886, when several thousand people gathered in the Haymarket area of Chicago to protest the deaths of two locked-out union organizers, killed by police. At the end of the meeting, 180 police arrived and ordered the crowd dispersed. A dynamite bomb was thrown into the ranks of police, killing one officer instantly and fatally wounding six more. Rioting ensued, and the police rounded up dozens of protestors and "political radicals" that the police had under surveillance after weeks of investigations and interrogations. The city's urban labor consciousness was aroused by the Haymarket Riot, and a combative culture in Chicago developed around the labor movement. In what some considered a show trial, eight anarchists were convicted of murder. Most of the public, including many in the working class, considered the defendant's political views dangerous and threatening in a time of increased immigration and urban tension over cultural issues. Many feel that the trial really was an indictment of anarchism and socialism, rather than a murder trial. Four defendants were sentenced to death and executed on November 11, 1887, a fifth hung himself, and three others were sentenced to life imprisonment or fifteen years hard labor (later they were pardoned by the governor of Illinois in 1893). Other labor strikes had occurred before this urban movement and riot, like the national railroad strike and union organization of 1877, but for Chicago, which was becoming a center for the new industrialization of America, this event was crucial.

For labor, the Haymarket uprising was crucial too, because it gave a rallying cry for union organizers like Mother (Mary Harris) Jones (1830–1930), who attempted to organize coal workers in the 1880s and 1890s. Labor needed these boosts to morale, because Haymarket and other labor/management battles had made it clear that the police and the courts were most often in the hands of wealthy industrialists and capitalists, whether in the city or in the country. When the police were unwilling to do the dirty work of the capitalists, private thugs were paid in the disguise of "private detectives," like the Knuckles Agency, and employed to bust the heads of union organizers. Cities and the emerging urban work culture of labor strife offered one benefit to the union cause; when they organized in a city, large numbers of workers were willing to fight back against oppression. As a footnote to history, the issue that started the union organizing that led to the Haymarket Riot was the eight-hour workday—an issue we take so for granted that it is hard to believe that so many lives had to be lost to secure it for us.

The next important urban social movement and labor movement event was the Triangle Shirtwaist Company fire on March 25, 1911, in Manhattan, New York. From the north floor of the Asch Building, employees leapt to their deaths to escape the flames because the doors to the factory were locked by management to thwart employee pilfering. When the flames were doused, 146 of 500 employees were dead, and the unions and New York City citizens were outraged. Unions organized themselves in 1911 around issues familiar to modern workers: subcontractors paying low wages, unsanitary working conditions (water and bathrooms not available), and unsafe working conditions (the need for fire and occupational safety). Textile and industrial workers joined unions and struggled to fix these bad working conditions, but despite the city's anger over the senseless tragedy at the Triangle Factory fire, the owners of the factory, Max Blanck and Isaac Harris, were acquitted of wrongdoing eight months after the fire (*New York Times*, March 2, 1911, and December 11, 1911; Cornell Institute of Labor Research 2001).

Labor unions reshaped urban work culture after these two events by organizing the urban workforce around the dangers of factory work and the realization that the police were in the pockets of the industrialists. The culture of labor unions turned violent at times to guard against the dirty tricks of the urban industrialists, and periodic alliances with organized crime figures has tainted some of the biggest unions, especially the Teamsters. However, lets examine the progress that was made on behalf of the urban workers by unions.

- The legal prohibition against child labor, a common practice up through the 1930s.
- The forty hour workweek
- The eight hour workday
- Overtime pay
- Worker's health and safety standards
- A minimum wage
- The right to organize into unions
- The right of collective bargaining
- Social Security
- Unemployment insurance

While these rights benefit every worker, both urban and rural, the labor battles and the labor conditions that the unions fought against first were in the cities.

In fact, information is the "raw" product of urban production, and after the information has been processed, it is also the "end" product (new information compiled from old information in a new format). The impact of this change in urban production on social movements is, first, to make organizing people and disseminating information through the Internet much easier. Second, the distinction between labor and management has been diminished by the kind of white-collar work urbanites perform. This lack of distinction will make social movements that center around consumption more successful as laborers and management will often be on the same side of an issue like housing or education.

Traditionally, labor and management have been pitted against each other in urban social movements. *Theory Break*: Marxian analysis of revolution actually depends on the conflict of workers (proletariat) and the owners (bourgeoisie) in the city for the full transformation of urban production from capitalism to socialism. The conflict between the two groups in city factories is supposed to become so great that an entire revolution develops out of the conflict. If the Information Age and the Information City actually reduce the distinction between labor and management, then one would expect less fuel for a social movement. There will of course be more social movements, not less, in the modern city, and the Information City in Western countries will play its part in a slightly different way than Marxists predicted.

Capitalism places the control of production (factories) and surpluses (profits) in the hands of capitalists, while statism (what many modern socialist or communist states today are labeled) puts the control of production and surpluses in the hands of those that control the government (Castells 1989). Information on the Internet will be beyond the control of the business or state and can link different classes and interest groups in urban social movements against capitalists or statists. It may come to pass that Marx's "working class revolution leading to a real utopian socialist state" comes not from the industrial proletariat against the bourgeois owners, but from the common goals of an Internet-linked white-collar workforce during an urban social movement.

RURAL SOCIAL MOVEMENTS

So, what exactly is the difference between rural and urban social movements? Urban social movements have an urban component to their message (i.e., urban housing), are often centered around a group's consumption of urban services (water, education, power), and the population that sustains the social movement is an urban population. Rural social movements, on the other hand, are different in that the movement is often centered around the means of production (land), rather than consumption, and the movement is composed of a primarily rural population. How is consumption and production different? For social movements, consumption means the use of some service, like demanding the provision of water to a new urban housing development.

Production is the actual making of a product or the process of making something, like the organization of land and labor to grow food.

Many rural social movements are centered around the control of land for agriculture. Mexico is a good place to explore the impact of rural versus urban social movements. The Mexican Constitution of 1921 was influenced by the rural issues that Emilio Zapata and his constituents in Chiapas, Mexico (one of the more remote and rural states in Mexico), fought for during the war, specifically, the control and apportionment of land in Mexico. As the rural fighters came to write a new constitution, their rural social movements and values influenced their provisions for "ejidal lands" that were not privately-owned but community-owned growing lands. They forbade the foreign ownership of Mexican lands and established the protectionist tariffs of Mexican agriculture to protect Mexican farmers from cheap foreign food. From this time, Mexican peasant agriculturalists established a culture of organizing co-ops, growing on community ejidal lands and maintaining social movements centered around subsistence farming.

On January 1, 1994, a group of peasants in the southern state of Chiapas came out of the jungle organized as a rural social movement and military force to protest the implementation of the North American Free Trade Agreement (NAFTA). Some of the Emilio Zapata Liberation Nacional (EZLN) army of peasants were only armed with shoe-polished broom handles made to resemble rifles, but the impending danger of this trade agreement to the price of agricultural goods, like corn for tortillas, caused these peasants to challenge the powerful and repressive Mexican military and federal police. Harkening back to the Constitution of 1921, the Zapatistas wanted the government to withdraw from NAFTA, which they said would bring foreign ownership of land and business, destroy the price of their crops with a flood of cheap corn from the United States, and erode the place of community or ejidal lands in the rural areas. For ten years, the EZLN has held the jungles of Chiapas and has engaged in an "on and off" negotiations with the governments of ex-president Ernesto Zedillo of the PRI political party and President Vicente Fox of the PAN political party to improve the rural conditions of their social movement. Again, the participants were rural and their interests were in agricultural and land reform, which classifies their actions as a rural social movement, rather than an urban one.

Urban social movements and riots have an urban message, affect an urban population, and come from the urban culture. Often, these urban social movements and riots become part of the urban culture in our cities. However, both rural and urban social movements are agents of change from the bottom up, rather than coming from the elite classes downward.

References

CASTELLS, MANUEL. 1983. *The City and the Grassroots Movement*. University of California Press: Berkeley, CA.

CASTELLS, MANUEL. 1989. *Informational City*. Blackwell Publishing: Cambridge, MA.

D'ORSO, MICHAEL. 1996. *Rosewood: Like Judgement Day*. Boulevard Publishers: New York, NY.

HIRSCH, JAMES. 2002. *Riot and Remembrance: The Tulsa Race War and Its Legacy*. Houghton Mifflin: New York, NY.

HORNE, GERALD. 1995. *Fire This Time: The Watts Uprising*. University of Virginia Press: Richmond, VA.

TAGER, JACK. 2001. *The Boston Riots*. Northeastern Press: Boston, MA.

WALLERSTEIN, IMMANUEL. 1979. *The Capitalist World Economy*. Cambridge University Press: New York, NY.

www.ilr.Cornell.edu.laborinstitute

CHAPTER TEN

The Bad City
Versus the Good City

DEVIANCE AND URBAN CULTURE

Breaking society's rules is not specific to the city. Five minutes after the first rule was created by a social group, someone in the group was thinking about breaking that rule. The heart of deviance, which is society's term for breaking or refusing to follow society's expectations, norms, or rules, is the inability of any society to have everyone agree on *all* the rules. Many types of deviance predate the concept of the city. Take, for instance, the form of social deviance we as sociologists call prostitution. Euphemistically called the "oldest profession," women have been forced into trading sex for valuables or money for thousands of years in male-dominated societies. The city makes prostitution easier to organize for both worker and consumer for a variety of reasons. That stratification of prostitutes (from streetwalkers to high-priced call girls) exists is evidence of a city's need for several types of sex workers; the different class and group members in the city will desire different price structures and different services from its sex workers. Only a city could organize enough of a fringe group of "consumers" for there to be a stratified diversity among prostitutes and services. The highest-paid call girl with Web sites and pay-per-view Web cams, to the women working in massage parlors, down to the lowest paid streetwalker are part of the stratified institution of prostitution, which needs a city for customers and a physical space to operate. *Theory Break*: Many deviance theories have attempted to explain the social phenomena of prostitution. Feminist theorists have postulated that prostitution is the result of the subordination of women in male-dominated societies; from an urban theory perspective we find male-dominated cities with female prostitutes occupying the dispossessed areas of the city. Walter Reckless (1926) called this area the Zone in Transition, where business of an adult nature (brothels, bars, gambling, flophouses) would thrive, because this zone was between the Central Business District and the Industrial ring, well out of sight of community leaders.

Other kinds of deviance like gambling, drugs, loan-sharking, and murder for hire have existed before cities. Cities make these forms of deviance more lucrative and easier to organize. A common thread with these forms of deviance has been organized crime, and that has developed an urban culture all its own. Organized crime also predates the development of the city. There are ancient tales of bands of robbers, who stole from caravans as a way of life, from Persia to China. But, the modern conception of organized crime is very much an *urban* invention that begins in the crowded slums of the cities of America's Northeast. It may surprise some readers that the first families of organized crime in America were the Irish in the 1840s, rather than the Italian or Sicilians, who didn't immigrate to the United States until 1880. In the beginning, organized crime only preyed on the members of their own ethnic group by extorting protection from law-abiding immigrants, who were too scared to call the police. Organized crime also offered illegal services, such as alcohol, prostitutes, firearms, and gambling, to an ever-growing clientele. The Irish in America found organized crime to be an easy way of life in the slums of the city, where payoffs were culturally acceptable, roving youth gangs frightened the populace into submission, and the new urban police forces were often made up of fellow Irishmen.

The culture we most often associate with organized crime is the Sicilian and Italian mafia. Preying on their own countrymen in the urban slums of New York, Philadelphia, and Boston before 1900, the Sicilian and Italian organized crime elements, known as the "Black Hand," were initially junior partners in the established organized crime rackets run by the Irish and Jewish mobsters. But as the Irish organized crime bosses moved to behind-the-scenes financing schemes and influence peddling, the Sicilian and Italian mafia groups muscled the Jewish mobsters out and created a violent and much more visible organized crime culture during Prohibition. After the deaths of the two most powerful Black Hand bosses was engineered by Charles "Lucky" Luciano in the 1920s, the New Italian Mafia merged the old world's "family centered" crime culture of rural Sicily with the new world's urban corporate culture. Luciano created a syndicate of five New York crime families, in which there was a managing board of directors with Luciano as CEO and chief arbitrator of any disputes. Such a powerful and successful structure, built on the culture of absolute silence (with the penalty being death), weathered the end of Prohibition and had diversified each crime family's, enterprises into prostitution, extortion, murder for hire, influence peddling, and gambling. The profits and customers for these organized crime businesses were in the burgeoning new cities of America.

HOW GAMBLING BUILT A CITY

It would be the control of gambling that would cause organized crime to build a city hundreds of miles from anywhere to further their own brand of urban culture and empire of crime. Las Vegas, Nevada, was a sleepy town in the middle of the desert in the 1940s with two curiosities; the first was being on the road to Hoover Dam, and the second was the legislative oddity of having legalized gambling. Several small cities had legalized gambling to draw money and tourists from the long, lonely highway that courses through the state, and gambling was just that, a novelty for the passersby. Benjamin "Bugsy" Segal, however, saw potential in legalized gambling in the 1950s and took millions of Mafia dollars to build the Flamingo Hotel and Casino in the desert. Spacious rooms, card games, national entertainment acts, and luxury services distinguished the Flamingo Hotel from the other roadside saloons with slot machines in the desert.

With the creation of the Flamingo Hotel came the organized crime culture that had been honed in New York's Mafia families, which was a decidedly urban culture in a small isolated town. It was a brand new way to do crime, by using a corporate model, organized crime was no longer an individual endeavor but a planned, group activity, and this urban crime culture had spread to every major city in America. No previous crime culture had ever been able to spread like the Mafia's crime culture had or been able to *build* a city before. Crime culture flourished in Las Vegas, making millions of dollars for illegal interests back in New York, but also making millions of dollars for the city of Las Vegas and the state of Nevada. Sadly, this culture also destroyed many lives through the violence and retribution of the Mafia crime culture (including ending the life of "Bugsy" Segal), but also through the habitual gambling of some of the casinos' patrons, who could not manage their gambling as an occasional diversion. Gambling and the Mob removed this brand of urban culture from the confines of some unsightly area of a city in Reckless's Zone in Transition. With gambling's legalization in Nevada and the arrival of large sums of money from the New York crime syndicates, Las Vegas begins to resemble the Key Function and Central Place theories of urban ecology. The key function that Las Vegas begins to perform as an urban environment is as the main city in America for gambling of all types (cards, dice, slot machines, horse races, sporting events), because it is legal in Nevada. The Mafia culture has infiltrated all the major institutions in the city (hotels, casinos, banks, and law enforcement) and feels safe in concentrating these operations in this city. Las Vegas' Central Place in the State of Nevada and its central location in the West (making it ideal to coordinate operations from Washington to California on the West Coast) also contributes to this urban environment's importance as a gambling center (particularly during the Sun Belt migration of the late 1960s and 1970s).

After years of organized crime influence in Las Vegas and in the gaming industry, the state of Nevada sustained many victories in ridding the hotels and casinos of known crime figures in the late 1970s and early 1980s. Many thought that Las Vegas wouldn't survive without the mobster's money, but a new "syndicate" came to control the hotels and gaming tables, real corporations. Today's Las Vegas is awash in new hotels like the Excalibur, offering a medieval theme with jousting matches and castles to vacation gamblers, while Treasure Island features pirates, a nightly boat fight,

The neon lights of Las Vegas's downtown casinos symbolize how important the urban culture of gambling is to this city. Without that revenue, none of what we think of as modern Las Vegas would be there; truly this city was built by gambling. A type of adult carnival exists in Las Vegas, with flashing lights, amusements of all varieties, thrill rides, and even a seedy, behind-the-scenes culture of vice.

and Caribbean flare for tourists, the impressive laser-lit pyramid of the MGM Grand has a sphinx, and New York, New York recreates the Statue of Liberty and the New York City skyline. These hotels are owned by consortiums of businesses and transnational corporations. Beginning with the Mirage Hotel and Casino in the 1980s, it became clear that multinational corporations could outbid any of the old hotels and for that matter the Mafia for feature acts, employees, or customers. This was the beginning of the corporate takeover of the "Mob" city, but it must be acknowledged that it was the urban crime culture of New York City that initially came and built Las Vegas into the major gambling and entertainment center it is today. What mafia culture and money did to Las Vegas was promote gambling as a "tourist destination" for those who wanted to gamble, see nationally-known entertainment acts, and experience adult-oriented diversions. In effect, casinos, hotels, and the city government sold and marketed a vision of the city as an adult oasis in the desert. By the time the corporations arrived in the business of hotels and casinos, the city (both municipal government and the people) had decided to invest in infrastructure that would promote and continue tourism as a major industry and culture of the city (Eisenberg 2000). Selling an image of a city or marketing that city to potential tourists to revitalize a city becomes a new form of political economy, in which the gambling casinos, workers, auxiliary businesses, and utilities have a new postmodern view of their city (Gottdener 1997). This new view recognizes urban space and culture as new types of production and consumption for city goods and services that tourists will pay to experience. Advertising the unique urban culture of Las Vegas is the way to lure the tourists to the desert city.

WHITE-COLLAR CRIME

Another category of crime that requires a city in order to thrive is white-collar crime. Costing 200 billion dollars a year in the United States,[1] white-collar crime is often unseen by most Americans except for a few high-profile cases, like Ivan Boesky or Michael Milliken. The truth is white-collar crime is around us all the time in the banks, insurance companies, financial institutions, real estate agencies, brokerage houses, and office parks of our cities. As readers of this book, i.e., college-educated citizens, you stand a better chance of being a victim of white-collar crime than being a victim of street crime. There is a good chance that close members of your family have already been the victims of this type of crime.

How can someone assert such a wild claim that you or your family has been the victim of white-collar crime? Statistically, this can be said because of the large volume of insider stock trades or fraudulent stock activity[2] that occurs where the victims are rarely aware of the malfeasance that has occurred; many of these victims are known to law enforcement, even if they don't know that they are victims. This is particularly true because most Americans have some part of their savings or retirement invested in stocks or mutual funds, whose real value might be manipulated without their knowledge. The overcharge of goods at the grocery stores, the bogus name brand goods we think are real, and the unseen mechanisms of price gouging in the insurance, banking, and real estate fields mean that it is probable that we have *all* been victimized by at least one type of white-collar crime in our lives. Most of us will rarely know of an overcharge or systematic theft of a small amount of money at our banks, insurance agency, or grocery stores. Many white-collar criminals and white-collar crime businesses count on the theft of an insignificant amount of money from a large number of people to make

---

[1]Chambliss, William, 2001. *Power, Politics, and Crime*

[2]Stock activity that is generated by a few individuals to artificially raise or lower the value of stock issues

their crimes work. For example, many customers will probably overlook an overcharge of a fee at a bank or on a phone bill, or a service charge on a credit card, because the amount may total less than a dollar on a single month's bill. Multiply that by twelve months and thousands of customers and the diabolical brilliance of some white-collar crime schemes becomes apparent.

White-collar crime thrives on the financial and real estate businesses that are found in the city and that can actually become ingrained in the urban or business culture of the city. Think about how many used car salesmen or insurance agents that you trust. Why is the number so small? It is doubtful that we don't trust these people on a person-by-person basis, but instead because of the type of potentially fraudulent business practices that we associate with them. *Theory Break*: White-collar crime depends on the busy transactions and impersonal environment of an urban financial center to mask the movements of its perpetrators. Louis Wirth (1938) speculated that the city produces in its dwellers numerous relationships of limited depth that make the impersonal urban environment ripe for white-collar crime. From overcharges to fraudulent land deals, the city isn't just the cover for white-collar crimes, it is the opportunity and motive as well. To successfully attempt a white-collar crime scheme, one needs a large enough pool of victims (i.e., customers of banks, businesses, real estate agencies), as well as enough people to be potential investors whose impersonal interactions provide the cover for the crime.

The city is even said to be a motive for white-collar crime, whose perpetrators are often middle class or even wealthy, because these criminals often commit their crimes to maintain or increase their lifestyle of conspicuous signs of wealth. "Keeping up with the Joneses" is a pressure that many middle-class families feel, in which the drive to have visible and outward symbols of wealth (a luxury car, name brand clothing, expensive housing) cause families to drive up credit card debt and even engage in illegal activity. *Theory Break*: Marxists like Antonio Gramsci (1985) would say that capitalist desires of symbolic wealth are part of urban culture and that wishing to obtain these symbols would provoke middle-class or wealthy people to engage in white-collar crime. With little to fear from police scrutiny, the wealthy have set up an urban environment that promotes and cloaks white-collar crime.

One of the more frequent white-collar crimes in the city is real estate fraud. This can be selling property that doesn't belong to you, isn't what you claim it is (swamp land sold as beach front), or outright fabrication of land and title that does not exist. *Theory Break*: Authors Logan and Molotch (1987) assert that in a capitalist city, land's importance shifts from its use value (what land could be used for as housing, parks, hospitals, schools) to exchange value (the economic value the land can be sold for or used as collateral for loans); this value often has nothing to do with what the land will be used for. Since land is just another category of exchange like money, credit cards, stocks, bonds, or personal checks, then it becomes vulnerable to all the kinds of white-collar crime that affects these other instruments of capitalistic exchange. In cities, the inability for the citizens or public to use valuable land for its use value because the land is being manipulated for its exchange value constitutes for Marxists another kind of potential "crime" perpetrated by capitalist land owners against the landless poor in the city. An interesting perspective that Marxists have on the study of deviance and crime is that actions of resistance by the poor are often labeled as "crimes" by the rich (things like taking food or money because one is poor or unemployed), while actions of oppression by the wealthy are rarely labeled as crimes (examples are pollution, union busting, price fixing, or land manipulation).

URBAN DEVIANCE

Deviance doesn't always mean criminality, it can be just a violation of society's norms. Cities inadvertently facilitate deviance by supplying like-minded people to be deviant with and to act as an audience for deviance. Most of us don't think of sex as being cultural or having an urban component, but "deviant sex" can certainly be part of urban culture and in some ways is part of the urban landscape of all American cities. There are many kinds of organized deviant sex groups in almost every large to mid-sized city in America, from exotic dance clubs, bondage or dungeon clubs, massage parlors, sadomasochism clubs, to swingers clubs. For our example of deviant urban culture, we will discuss a growing element of urban and suburban deviant culture: swingers clubs.

Referred to as group sex, open marriage, or wife swapping clubs in the 1960s and 1970s, swingers clubs emerged in the 1990s to serve a growing segment of the married population who wanted to explore alternative relationships in marriage. But, before we get ahead of ourselves, we should examine what "swinging" is exactly. Most often, swingers are married couples who desire to go beyond the traditional confines of marriage by bringing other people into their sexual lives, either individuals or other couples. Those who participate in this subculture refer to it as "The Lifestyle," and explain to outsiders that they do not feel their extramarital activity would be classified as adultery, because they participate in these extrasexual relationships with the full knowledge and support of their spouses. Regardless of anyone's personal feelings on the validity of this belief, this sexual subculture is inextricably tied to modern urban culture. While infidelity may be tied to the institution of marriage from the Oval Office to the smallest rural village, it takes a large number of participants with a like-minded view of marriage to start a swing or lifestyle club. The urban environment doesn't, however, make organizing a group of swingers into a club easy. Most cities have civic leaders that would be actively opposed to such sexual deviance clubs being in their midst. In a large enough city, however, the chance to associate with other swingers will be sufficiently attractive to risk the sanction of the police or community. Put simply, it is easier to blend in and hide deviance in a larger city than in a small town, where everyone knows what everyone else is up to. Moral leaders simply cannot keep tabs on every part of the city, so swing clubs are able to grow, especially if they are located away from residential areas and the prying eyes of interested citizens. Louis Wirth (1938) referred to this anonymity and tolerance of urban citizens as part of the urban way of life. Not that urbanites are immoral, but that the culture of urban living teaches a kind of tacit tolerance of people, ethnicities, customs, or lifestyles that are different than your own. Cities have church and civic leaders that are offended by such sexual clubs; however, the anonymity and lack of comprehensive surveillance of the urban culture makes finding and enforcing sexual norms more difficult.

So, how do deviant sex clubs get members in the city? Clearly, they cannot take an ad out in the newspaper, because that would raise the attention of unwanted moral and law enforcement groups. Like most groups that wish to evade public notice, swingers have taken advantage of the enormity and anonymity of the city and the Internet. The bustling online Internet culture often will link swingers that live mere miles from each other, but who would never have met in the course of everyday city interactions had they not sought out other swingers online. But, if the major culture is online and most clubs intentionally locate themselves outside of city limits to avoid municipal rules, then how is this an "urban phenomenon"? Because it is *absolutely* dependent on the city for the couples that wish to participate in this deviant lifestyle.[3] Even if, to maintain anonymity, couples choose to communicate over the Internet,[4] or they choose to meet at a location just beyond city limits to avoid detection, the membership and culture of these clubs is definitely urban. They dance to urban music at the clubs, they dress in outrageous clothing of a sexually provocative nature, and even when the club is located in a rural area, the participants are generally from the nearby cities and have little in common with the rural dwellers of the area. *Theory Break*: Urban ecology's theory of Central Place states that a successful urban area will hold a preferential place in the environment to access resources. Once established, the city will often come to dominate the region around it by controlling resources and directing production and distribution through a hierarchical arrangement of cities in the region, what ecologists called Key Function. In the case of deviant lifestyle clubs, the city's population can infiltrate the marginal areas between the city's Lifeworld and the rural Lifeworld and make a place for the deviance to occur by sheer organization and numbers. The city is the location where all of society's norms and institutions come together and create new social paradigms by their interaction. Mumford (1961) said that the city's nature promoted interaction and fusion, so for deviance, the variety of social and sexual norms in the city combined to make an overall tolerance in the city's Lifeworld.

In an effort to dispel the myth that the participants in this lifestyle are just a fringe minority, a sample of the one hundred largest cities in America was taken. Not only was a club found in each city, but multiple clubs were located via Internet for almost every city of 300,000 or more inhabitants. To

---

[3]For clarity, I will reiterate that deviant does not necessarily mean criminal or wrong, just a departure or deviation from social norms and societal expectations.

[4]Computer ownership and Internet access are highly correlated with suburban populations.

draw a parallel between lifestyle clubs and another type of urban cultural consumption, that number would make participation in this alternative lifestyle as popular as participation in live country-and-western music bars. Generally, one country-and-western music bar was also found in each of these cities, with more being in larger cities. Swing clubs are not open every night, and generally, not even every weekend, since many depend on renting space in other venues to hold their events, but the number of people committed to a swinging lifestyle at least once a month and the number of people committed to listening to country music monthly is a good comparison. The difference between the cultural consumption of both groups is the amount of *visibility in the urban environment* that the city's culture is willing to afford them. Country music has gone through several periods of waxing and waning popularity, but in most cities it is not considered to be a threat to the moral or civic order of the city to have a country-and-western bar. Operating a club whose purpose is sexual contact between people, who aren't married to each other, would be considered a threat to civic order.

It is not violence but moral turpitude that concerns urban leaders about swing clubs, and several municipalities have taken steps to eliminate their existence. *Theory Break*: This is an example of what structural Marxists call the elite capitalists' domination of the government as a social institution. In an effort to control the lower classes, the elite class uses the government to thwart urban culture that might be threatening to the cultural and social norms that keep the elite in their privileged places. We, as fellow urban dwellers, do not even know of this lifestyle choice, because urban leaders and the police keep swing clubs underground. We know of local country music bars because of the ease of advertising (on the other hand, radio stations, television, and many print sources will not publish advertising relating to adult businesses) and because of the recognition of the bar's sign in front of the club. Swing clubs are denied even these simple methods of urban acknowledgement because of the urban leadership's desire to halt the population's access to swing culture. Deviance as an urban culture recognizes its marginal status in our cities and often adopts a pattern of low visibility to avoid legal reaction. At the same time, deviance needs the city to thrive, so it will always be a part of city culture.

POLICE CRISIS CULTURE

Law enforcement, the weapon that a cities' leadership turns on a cities' deviants, has its own type of urban culture. We have had specialized rule enforcers in some of our first ancient settlements, often as part of the religious or military's institutional function. Early cities began to make specialized rules that only pertained to the urban environment and the urban citizen, and a specialized garrison of urban rule enforcers was developed to administer these specialized rules. These were rules like your house can only be one story tall, or if you aren't of noble birth, you aren't allowed to wear certain garments or colors, or within the city walls you must observe curfew hours—all examples of municipal rules that would be enforced by the new municipal law enforcer. In China of 1600 B.C.E., the new urban rule enforcers would designate who could live within the city walls, because only nobility, administrators, and religious elites were allowed inside the decorated walls of the main urban centers. Commoners had to construct their housing outside these decorated walls, forming another ring to the growing Chinese cities. Pre-Columbian America had similar rules to their cities in 1500 B.C.E. Mayan tribes in Central America and the Incan empire of South America constructed elaborate ceremonial cities with pyramids, temples, palaces, and even observatories at their centers. Urban rule enforcers defined for the artisan-craftsman class a segregated area to live in, just beyond the religious- and noble-class housing, including rules that their homes not compete in size or decoration with the privileged classes. Beyond that ring were peasants and farmers, whose access to the ceremonial city center was defined by the religious and noble class and enforced by the new urban enforcers (often as not, the military). *Theory Break*: Sjoberg (1965) noted the unique design of the ancient city, but he didn't elaborate on the special class that would enforce the new municipal laws and norms of the ancient city. Marx (1859) would have pointed out that it was the elite classes who defined the laws and norms for other urbanites. Mumford (1961) demonstrated how in Rome of 264 B.C.E. the administration of urban rules had become such a part of Roman culture that gladiatorial contests were arranged for the punishment of Rome's criminals and rule-breakers. The urban mob of Rome considered it entertainment, and for the next 500 years the gladiator spectacle was part of Rome's urban rule-enforcement culture.

Today, law enforcement represents a distinct culture within our city, a crisis culture. We expect our police force to handle not only the rules of our municipalities, but also to deal with the constant crisis that our society is in—homelessness, domestic abuse, gangs, rape, organized crime, natural disasters, mental illness, and civil unrest. Culturally, the police have developed a view of "us" and "them" to cope with the stress of their job, and to cope with the fact that they have to deal with the worst elements of our urban society. The process of how this culture developed is connected to how law enforcement has grown in the past one hundred years. Modern policing in the United States started before the turn of the century in our nation's largest cities, but it was a cultural change from the informal method of policing[5] to a modern, professional bureaucratic form of policing. Law enforcement changed from neighborhood cops walking a local beat in the 1900s to a multisector strategy of police presence with police patrol stations in various sectors of the city in the 1980s. Sectors are larger then neighborhoods and can incorporate several square miles and many neighborhoods. *Theory Break*: Homer Hoyt (1939) pioneered sector analysis by augmenting Burgess's ring model of the city by using pie pieces or triangular segments

---

[5]The informal method of law enforcement was closer to barroom bouncers than the professional police force of today. The biggest local guy was often the policeman; he knew the "troublemakers" and his use of force kept the peace.

instead of rings (Figure 10.1). The value of these triangle segments is that often certain sectors in the city, like industrial sectors or high crime sectors, start near the city center in an area of high density and then they spread out resembling the base of a triangle.

There is a debate over Hoyt's model, in that it is more specific and fragmented than Burgess's rings, but that it loses some of the theoretical and predictive value of Burgess's model. Our discussion of the sector model is related to urban law enforcement. At the turn of the twentieth century, police departments in our nation's biggest cities placed substations and directed patrols in the sector model to divide the city for patrolling. This was an effort to take advantage of new technologies available to the police like radio dispatched patrol cars, computers in patrol cars connected to offenders' databases, high-tech surveillance equipment, and air patrol units, in an effort to be more efficient as our urban societies asked more and more of the police.

Ironically, at the turn of the twenty-first century, many of our largest cities are returning to the neighborhood police model of the late 1800s. After years of police functions being conceptualized to handle the myriad of crises in the urban environment, the increase in crime in the late 1980s to the early 1990s forced the police to refocus on crime prevention as a major function of the police. The answer the public favored and pushed to fight crime was the neighborhood policing model. Under the new label of "community policing," the solution they were seeking was similar to the neighborhood police

Figure 10.1 Shifts in the Location of Fashionable Residential Areas in Three American Cities, 1900–1936. Fashionable areas are indicated by shading.
Source: Adapted from Homer Hoyt, *The Structure and Growth of Residential Neighborhoods in American Cities* (Washington, DC: Federal Housing Administration, 1939), p. 115, figure 40.

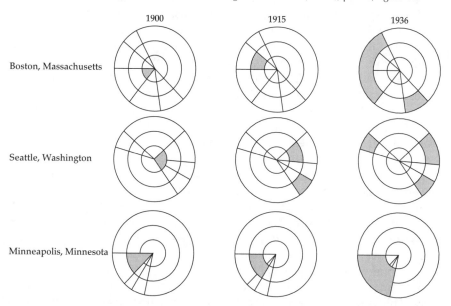

model of the nineteenth century. Having a cop walk a beat makes people feel safer, and the public felt that more cops on foot, versus in the car on sector patrol, reduces crime. Some studies have been done to refute the idea that increasing police presence reduces crime, but as the public saw violent crime as a crisis, the public demanded police intervention (Kelling 1988 and Sherman 1990). From 1995 to 2001, crime did decrease in America, and community policing was credited with partially aiding this reduction; other critics claimed that economic growth, not community policing, reduced crime during this time period.

The internal urban culture that police departments have developed to cope with our urban crisis is one of "us versus them." Because of stress, this culture has developed to combat the constant reality of dealing with the worst elements of our urban societies at a time when the public is also demanding perfect professionalism from the police as well. After all, the police are only called when something is going wrong in our lives. So, an insular culture grows to defend the mental lives of the police (us) against the community (them). Most of urban America would be surprised to find out that anyone who is not a police officer is a "them," not just criminals. To maintain this culture of crisis intervention, a code of silence is enforced so that police will often fail to inform on the criminal or unethical conduct of their fellow officers to maintain camaraderie and morale. This "code of silence" culture develops to allow police officers to share experiences with each other, behind the curtain of silence, because the society as a whole will not understand. Admitting mistakes, bribes, or abuses to a nonpolice citizen might result in investigations, loss of employment, and even imprisonment, so the code of silence is firm.

While elements of "us versus them" culture exists in many urban and rural law enforcement agencies, it is the professional, urban police force that was first assigned to deal with our urban crisis. At the same time, the urban police force developed its own reaction to cope with the mounting urban crisis. When this reaction culture becomes too insular and the stress too much for the individual officer to cope with, pathologies become evident in the officer and, when the culture is widespread, within the whole urban police force. The police officers are unable to distinguish between criminals and average citizens having a bad day, or are incapable of distancing themselves from the terrible crisis images they witness during the day. Even worse is the police officer that excuses or engages in criminal activity personally. From these cultural pathologies come police assaults, corruption, and police crime.

To thwart the worst elements of deviance and criminality in an urban law enforcement culture, a special unit exists in every major urban police departments in the United States—Internal Affairs. Designed to break through the culture of silence in the police force, the officers of Internal Affairs are thought to be turncoats by other police personnel and are often the most hated members of the force. Internal Affairs investigators often find their efforts hampered by the code of silence, because the witness to police deviance is often another police officer who has been educated in the culture of silence. This is part of a deviant urban culture grown in law enforcement and one that actually requires other police officers to combat it. For rural police departments, an Internal Affairs department would be a luxury that they could not afford, so they have fewer independent checks and balances on their officers (fewer journalists and fewer alternate law enforcement agencies, like the FBI or state troopers). The culture of silence in law enforcement is more prevalent in cities, and the counterculture of Internal Affairs to police deviance is also an urban phenomenon.

The internal battle between the culture of silence that permits police deviance and criminality and the response culture of the Internal Affairs department has been successfully played out in a number of cities and continues to struggle in several more. For most of modern memory, New Orleans' police force has been the subject of public ridicule and fear as charges of police shakedowns of businesses, bribery of officials, and the arrest of several officers in the mid-1990s on murder, racketeering, and drug running has hit the front pages of the *Times-Picayune*. Officials in state government, some indicted later themselves on separate charges, and NOPD's Internal Affairs department tried to root out corruption, but with the lowest paid urban police force in the nation (at one point starting pay was between $18,000–$22,000 for one of the nation's most dangerous cities) they were fighting apathy, corruption, *and* the code of silence. In 1998, Police Chief Pennington took over the troubled department and secured better pay and more thorough screening of new officers. While taking many years to combat the entrenched image of the NOPD as a rogue police culture, more New Orleanians feel that progress in combating deviant police culture has been made. *Theory Break*: Marxist theory would place the blame of this rogue culture on the lack of pay in this city; a professional police officer in New Orleans is most often from a working-class background and would require a sizeable income to be the "muscle" that enforced the rich, elite classes' rules.

Another city that has had to struggle with its urban police culture is New York City. One of the nation's oldest police forces, NYPD is also the nation's largest police force, with 30,000 police officers engaged in law enforcement in some capacity. The subject of two major periods of investigations for corruption and illegal activities, the NYPD has had years of investigation thwarted by the "blue curtain" of secrecy. In the 1960s–70s Mayor Lindsay appointed City Judge Knapp to investigate corruption and illegal activities of the New York Police and the level of deviance and crime surprised the city. From payoffs to ignore the city's codes and rules to conspiring in the drug trade and money laundering, the commissioner's report was such a national outrage its subject matter, including the difficulty in breaking the code of silence, was the inspiration for the Al Pacino movie *Serpico*. Sadly, the Knapp commission did not lay to rest the issue of NYPD's police culture of deviance, and in 1993 the Mollen Commission was enacted to investigate further complaints of police misconduct. While finding less prevalent and less widespread corruption, the Mollen Commission again found officers committing criminal acts and the police culture of silence covering it up. More recently the spectre of racism with NYPD's police culture was raised in several questionable shootings and the assault case of Amadou Diallo.

Another specific type of urban police culture was born in the most extreme of urban crises—a mass murder. In Austin, Texas, on August 1, 1966, Charles Whitman barricaded himself with an arsenal of rifles, shotguns, handguns, and ammunition on the observation deck of the twenty-story main tower of the University of Texas. On that terrible day, Whitman killed fourteen people, including the brutal shooting of a pregnant woman's unborn child, and wounded thirty-one others from his fortresslike sniper nest on the tower's top floor. While he was using rain gutters as his gun hole, the police and their short-range weapons were useless against Whitman, who was shooting more powerful rifles from a greater range. Eventually, an officer and an armed civilian used underground tunnels to gain entry to the tower, and the officer shot Whitman, who refused to surrender.

From this incident, it was clear that police departments were unable to handle this particular kind of crisis culture—a superiorly armed, barricaded assailant who wasn't intimidated by conventional police weapons and tactics. As a reaction to this extreme crisis, police all over the United States created SWAT (Special Weapons and Tactics) units to deploy military tactics and use special weapons against these types of unique urban crises. The type of crimes that require a SWAT unit response grew out of the increasing urbanization of America's society. Capone and Dillinger terrorized the nation's cities with bank robberies, machine guns, hand grenades, and shoot-outs with the police in the 1920s and 1930s. Cities were overwhelmed and demanded a federal response from the FBI, but today's cities realize that the millions of mobile citizens in their midst necessitate a local reaction to extreme crisis. While these units might be sent to suburban or rural areas, the motivation to create such a unique police unit came from urban crisis and the culture of dealing with urban crisis.

Specialized police culture, like SWAT teams, arising from local rather than federal power, would be seen by some political observers as an example of the devolution trend from federal power and authority to local power and authority. This trend has been advocated by conservative political pundits and politicians since the Reagan era, with the value of this approach stemming from the immediate contact citizens can have with their local representatives, versus the removed position of Federal representatives and agencies. *Theory Break*: Thus, like Mollenkompf (1983) demonstrated with federal policies, government intervention can have a dramatic impact on the urban environment and urban culture. For Mollenkompf, it was federal funding and urban renewal effects on cities; in the case of police culture, local governmental policies (rather than federal policies) responded to the threat of urban crisis—creating SWAT units.

RESCUE CRISIS CULTURE

Fire departments and Emergency Ambulance and Medical Services also have crisis cultures in our cities. The decisions and actions that these workers make have immediate life or death consequences, which puts tremendous pressure and stress on them. Again, the growth of fire, ambulance, and emergency room services were part of the first development of cities and urban bureaucracies, much like the growth of law enforcement. These services are planned and allocated by urban planners in the modern city, because of their importance in dealing with urban health and safety crisis. Fire and ambulance services are usually plotted in a sector model (see Homer Hoyt 1939), much like police substations, but more plentiful than police stations due to the crucial nature of response times; while hospital emergency rooms are usually more centralized due to the extreme costs of building a hospital and the density of urban centers that hospitals serve.

Let's examine the urban crisis culture of the fire department in our cities. Most of America's total square mileage is actually covered by volunteer fire departments, where average, local citizens donate their own time to operate the fire trucks that counties or municipalities buy for them to use. These cities or counties are unable to afford a full-time professional fire department, so they purchase the equipment and depend on a small bureaucratic contingent of fire professionals to coordinate the activities of the volunteers. *Theory Break*: Marxist theorists would say that volunteer fire departments are examples of working-class cooperative culture that exists to save small to midsized communities and that succeeds. Community theorists, who stress that modern urbanites live in communities of identity rather than in suburbs or cities, would say that volunteer fire departments are examples of people living in and taking responsibility for their community. But in our large, modern cities we have professional, full-time firefighters that not only keep our structures and homes from burning, but also respond to all categories of health and safety crisis.

Beginning in our large Northeastern cities first in the 1880s, professional firemen[6] were housed in fire stations that became part of the urban and suburban landscape. With large arch doors for the fire trucks and the inevitable brass pole that linked the firemen's upstairs living quarters with the truck on the ground floor, these buildings became essential fixtures in neighborhoods like streets, parks, and schoolhouses. Our urban culture has valued firemen as an essential part of city living, and fire departments are one of the few things that work about that much maligned social institute—government. Perhaps it is this positive attitude from their fellow urbanites of the essential job that they perform that makes the crisis culture of firefighters so different from that of the police. Not to insinuate that we don't value police and law enforcement, but it is the function of the police to arrest and punish society, where firefighters are viewed as a group that is helpful, nonpunitive, and saves lives in our society. Firefighters have a difficult job and they often have to deal with similar crises as police, but their crisis culture seems to have developed less distance from the people they serve. Firefighters have

---

[6]Most fire departments had prohibitions against women that are only now being dismantled.

some of the lowest job turnover rates among any of the crisis culture jobs. Simmel (1905), Wirth (1938), and Gans (1962) would point out that the tolerant and disengaged urban personality would resent the punishment and interference role of the police and embrace the positive and beneficial role of firefighters.

It is important for us to remember that firefighters and police officers are essentially municipal civil servants; they are paid by the city just like the city clerk or garbage collector. While they may have more power to arrest or kick down front doors, they are just doing a job, and it is a job that they don't get paid a great deal for when we examine the time these people put into their jobs. Another difference in the crisis culture of firefighters, as opposed to the police, is the social and psychological reward for a day's work. Firefighters may save a life, a house, or even a cat from a tree, and this is an immediate, tangible, positive reward. Police have to deal with arrests or domestic disputes that take weeks or months to adjudicate, and this is often seen as less positive and less rewarding. The stress level might be similar, but the social rewards and crisis culture response to these important urban jobs are quite different between fire and police service.

URBAN TERROR

On the morning of Tuesday, September 11, 2001, four domestic commercial jets were hijacked. Two of those planes were rammed into the World Trade Center towers in downtown Manhattan at 8:45 and 9:03, Eastern Standard Time. A third plane hit the Pentagon in Washington, DC at 9:43 A.M., crashing into the Army Operations section of the world's largest office building, slicing into four of the five rings that compose the building. This target was chosen after their primary target, the White House, could not be located from the altitude they were flying at. A fourth jetliner crashed into a field in Western Pennsylvania at 10:10 A.M. after brave passengers, informed by their families via cell phone about the World Trade Center crashes, rushed the hijackers in the cockpit in an effort to stop them using that plane as a weapon.

The hijackers, armed only with knives and box cutters, were trained at civilian "learn to fly" academies in Florida under the guise of learning to be private pilots. Identified later as being linked to Saudi-born terrorist Osama bin Laden, the hijackers on three of the planes went relatively unopposed by flight crew and pilots, because, until this tragic event, most hijackings were not about loss of life but about diverting the plane successfully to another destination. Sadly, these men were bent on using these planes and their innocent passengers as flying missiles. The hijackers' targets were two of the nations most visible urban symbols of the United States' financial might and New York's skyscraper culture, the World Trade Center towers.

At the time of their construction, the towers were the tallest buildings in the world and a symbol of the international economic power of not only

Symbolic targets of the United States and Western culture, the twin towers of the World Trade Center were attacked because of what they represented to Americans and the world. Signifying commerce and economic prosperity to the West, the towers represent Western colonialism and domination to some in the Middle East. Destroying these targets was a way to strike at the United States without having to expose terrorist organizations on September 11, 2001 to America's immediate military reprisal.

the United States but the rest of the Western, capitalist world. The Pentagon was the headquarters of the American military. In New York City, an estimated 2,797 people died in the attack, while Washington's death toll was 188, including the passengers on the plane that hit the Pentagon. When combined with the crews and passengers of all the hijacked planes, this attack was the deadliest and most visible act of terrorism ever. The terrorists were clearly focused on the symbolic destruction of the buildings, but also desired the loss of life as well. As symbols of American urban culture, the terrorists' plans were clear in the targeting of the World Trade Center, the White House, and the Pentagon; since a small band of terrorists had no hope of confronting the military might of the United States, then the destruction of the United States' symbols and the installation of fear in its urban citizens would suffice. A war against symbols and the destruction of urban buildings as terrorism is beyond any of the classical urban social theories we have discussed. No predictable ecological growth model explains it, nor does the political economy theories of Marx and Engels shed any light, since these are not the working proletariat rising up against the capitalist oppressor for a socialist revolution. These terrorists came from wealthy Middle Eastern families and were bound together by Islamic fundamentalist zeal and hatred for the United States.

Immanuel Wallerstein's (1974) World Systems Theory might provide some insight into the motives of this new terrorist threat. *Theory Break*: He said the world is divided into "have" and "have-not" countries essentially and that the wars we fought were not patriotic endeavors to defeat fascists or communists, but were in fact battles of a have country (the United States) against have-not countries (the growing imperialist threat from Germany and Japan in the 1940s, China and North Korea in the 1950s, Cuba and Vietnam in the 1960s). The Middle Eastern countries have split between those that have oil (Saudi Arabia, Kuwait, Qatar), which have aligned themselves with the Core nations of the United States, Great Britain, France, and others, and those Middle Eastern nations that oppose the West on religious grounds (Afghanistan, Somalia, Libya) or ideological grounds (Syria, Iraq) who don't share in the oil wealth of the other Middle Eastern countries. Islamic Fundamentalism is present in all these countries (though it must be stated that it is a small fraction of the religion of Islam, which is a peaceful religion with many of the same moral and religious tenets as the Judeo-Christian tradition), but it has consumed the political destiny of the have-not countries in the Middle East with no oil. For these extremists and terrorists, the large urban areas of the United States that represent the godlessness and cultural corruption of the West (New York City and Washington, DC); attacking these urban symbols was attacking the culture, government, and people of the West.

Why this attack would matter to Americans and Westerners can be found in the work of Gans (1962) and Firey (1945). *Theory Break*: Herbert Gans' research discovered that there was a cultural and psychological link to his urban neighborhood that wasn't because it fulfilled some efficient ecological purpose but because it embodied the social networks of his ethnic and class upbringing. New Yorkers probably never thought of the "value" or "meaning" of the WTC towers before 9/11, but they became part of the skyline and cultural identity of New Yorkers. Walter Firey's (1945) work established that urbanites develop symbolic and sentimental attachments to urban places that actually defy economic efficiency and ecological reasoning. For New Yorkers, Washingtonians, and all Americans we have developed attachments to the WTC towers, the White House, and the Pentagon even if we have never visited these urban cultural wonders. They represent symbolic values and sentimental attachments, not only to these cities, but to all Americans.

As another example of urban terrorism, we can examine the campaign of political and urban terror waged by the Irish Republican Army against the British government in Northern Ireland. After a seemingly never-ending campaign of British occupation in Ireland dating back to the fifteenth century, a civil war erupted, led by the mainly Catholic Irish Republican Army in 1916 against the occupying British army. Rarely was this war a conventional affair where two armies could meet each other on the battlefields. Instead it was a war of assassinations, bombings, and attrition, designed to wear the superior British Army down and, more importantly, chip away at the support for the war on England's soil. Eamon de Velara won a victory of sorts as the President of the Irish Republic, and it resulted in the partitioning of Ireland's Northernmost region, Ulster, into what is now known as Northern Ireland. Northern Ireland is held by British troops in collusion with Protestant Paramilitary groups, but the rest of the island, which is known as the Republic of Ireland is a sovereign state. Here again, a "have-not" country (Ireland) wages a terrorist war against a "have" country (England).

A Catholic majority populates the Republic of Ireland, but in Northern Ireland, Catholics are an oppressed minority and the IRA and Sinn Fein, the political faction of the IRA, are the only tools to fight the Protestant majority in Ulster. Terror and attrition had won part of this war, but for the last eighty years, bombings, kidnappings, assassinations, and armed violence have been a way of life in Northern Ireland's largest cities. Most of the conflict has centered around the large shipping and industrial city of Belfast in Northern Ireland, where poor Catholics live in ghettos, which are patrolled by hated British soldiers, and Catholics are often only able to obtain the most servile positions in employment. At the same time, Protestants who identify strongly with the British army and government are in the elite positions of business, government, and law enforcement. It became clear to the IRA that striking military troops in Ulster wasn't going to be effective against the large and well-supplied British military, so they decided to bring their terrorist campaign to the city populations of Northern Ireland and England itself. Symbolism would play a key role in their new activities, as the IRA assassinated a member of the English royal family, Lord Mountbatten, in 1979 by blowing up the boat he was on. This was a strike at the heart of the most hated English symbol—a useless and rich nobility[7] that has little to do with the actual operations of the British government, but represented the aristocratic, colonial past—a past in which the English landlord starved the Irish landless peasants off their ancestral land with ruthless taxation and sharecropping rental policy.

Combining the urban analysis of Firey (1945), Marx (1859), and the revolutionary tactics of Ernesto "Che" Guevara (1968) should illuminate the goals of the IRA. The symbolic attacks on the aristocracy were clearly attempts to show the real difference between an English urban population that supported the outdated lifestyle of their aristocracy as a part of a nostalgic past and an Irish-Catholic country with a partitioned section of Northern cities that hated *all* that the English aristocracy represented (oppression by occupation and domination). The urban component of this conflict can't be overlooked; the street battles, car bombs, occupation force, and marching season riots are all parts of the Northern Irish urban experience. The genesis of this terroristic hatred can be understood as part of the class warfare predicted

---

[7]As a family, the English royal family is worth billions of dollars, possesses numerous castles and estates, and pays *NO* taxes.

by Marx (1859). Catholic animosity may swell in rural Ulster, but it is the cities where it erupts into violence because of the wretched condition of the overwhelmingly Catholic working class. Combine the working-class revolutionary culture of the Catholic IRA with the symbolic English nobility's occupation of Ireland's Northern cities and the terrorist attacks make a kind of "revolutionary sense." For an urban terrorist organization with Marxist roots, the IRA is literally the poster child for Che Guevara's theories of how to wage a Marxist guerilla war. *Theory Break*: Che said that a guerilla force must turn its deficits into assets; so, for the IRA's urban terrorists, their lack of size makes them elusive and quick, their enemy slow and ponderous. A culture of oppression and occupation becomes a society of secrecy and retribution.

While symbolic, these attacks and bombings did not effect real political change in the British public, so the IRA changed its tactics to really bring their urban terror campaign to the British people. Adopting a more English urban focus, the IRA placed bombs in front of ministry offices, in train stations, on ferries, and at bus depots in the London area. This was meant to scare and disrupt the city's population and it succeeded in producing a culture of urban terror that reached all of Great Britain. "Civilized terrorism" became an IRA policy as the city's police were called with acknowledged code words to evacuate bomb sites to diminish loss of life, while maintaining the terror campaign. The reason for this odd approach to terrorism was to scare the British urban public, while still keeping them from hating the Irish. Urban targets to frighten and unnerve the British have had some notable instances of reaching the British public, the most visible probably being the bombing of the Canary Wharf office towers in London. This mega-office complex was a symbol of the new London planned under Margaret Thatcher's conservative government and a symbol of capitalism's promise for England. As an urban symbolic target, the Canary Wharf bombing shook the financial institutions of London and succeeding in showing the impotence of the British Home Office of Security. Because Marxism is an important influence on the IRA's formation, the attack gave the IRA the ability to deal England a double blow—economically and symbolically.

Other terrorist organizations were learning a similar set of lessons about conducting urban terror campaigns. The Palestine Liberation Organization, formed to oppose the state of Israel and their occupation of former Palestinian lands, took its local campaigns of bombings and hijackings to Munich and the Olympic Games of 1972. After taking Israeli team members hostage in the Olympic Village, the terrorists managed to send their message of Palestinian grievance to the top of the world's agenda. Yet, even as their agenda was being realized, when a rescue attempt by German commandos failed and the terrorists and hostages were killed, the overall world sympathy went against their cause. The world decided that the Olympic City was *not* an acceptable platform for political issues, and that terrorism at the Olympics would be punished with ostracism from the world community. PLO activists and other terrorist groups began to realize that to gain in political acceptance after an urban terror campaign, some norms concerning the loss of life must be observed.

To gain political stature in the international community, Yasir Arafat, the leader of the Palestinian Authority, which has control of the Palestinian areas of Israel, has since the 1972 incident renounced terrorism. New terror groups like Hamas in Palestine have surfaced to carry on terror bombings in Israel's cities with recent bombing innovations such as suicide bombers strapped with dynamite. Striking fear in the urban citizens of Israel had been able to drive the political apparatus of the country to the negotiating table by the mid-1990s, but too much bombing of Jerusalem civilians threw the Israeli citizens to the political "right" and provoked the government to exercise a heavy hand with suspected terrorists. Again, the symbolic significance of Jerusalem made it an unacceptable urban space for terror bombing, because of the religious importance it holds for Jews, Christians, and Muslims. A new campaign of suicide bombings by Hamas beginning in 2001 has caused Israeli crackdowns in the Palestinian areas of Jerusalem and the other Palestinian territories. Intended to destabilize Arafat, it has only made him stronger in the eyes of the Palestinians and has reinforced the tactic of urban terrorism.

Terrorism in Italy was a conflict of ideas centered, not in random, faceless bombings, but in personal attacks and abductions. The Red Brigade in Italy of the 1970s and 1980s were Marxist idealists who were angry that after the defeat of fascism in Italy post-WWII (a defeat that many communists and socialists helped to bring about) the Italian communist party had either been corrupted or dealt out of the political landscape. Composed of radical, often middle class, Italian college students, the Red Brigade realized bombings often hurt the urban working class they were pledged to protect. Instead, they decided to conduct a campaign of kidnappings and ransoms of the very elite class who, they felt, were oppressing the working class in Italy. Suddenly, rich urbanites were specific and panicked targets of this group's tactic of kidnapping for terror, intimidation, and of course, money. These ransom operations financed other Red Brigade activity and more kidnappings. *Theory Break*: Working on what's called a "cell organization model," five- to ten-person cells with one leader would operate a specific list of terrorist actions, while other cells would be conducting other operations. The value of this model is if caught, one person of the cell can only name the other members of the cell, not the entire organization. This cultural adaptation was learned from urban Marxist organizations broken by informants. The cell formation was a device of control for the extreme tactics of European police forces known to push the boundaries of interrogation. Many Marxist inspired organizations adopted the cell structure and kidnapping model of operations, including the Symbionese Liberation Army that kidnapped Patty Hearst, and rebel groups in Colombia, Ecuador, Peru, Brazil, and the former Soviet republics. The Red Brigade kidnapped and murdered former Italian Prime Minister Aldo Moro in 1978. This event created enough public backlash against the Red Brigade, who had garnered a "Robin Hood" mythology, that police soon had enough credible leads to break up the group. The tactic of abductions worked until Moro's death, then the Red Brigade lost the ideological youth necessary to maintain the cell structure.

The United States has had a long and tainted history with terrorism. Many of our American Revolutionary war heroes were considered godless, lawless terrorists by the English. Men like Paul Revere, Thomas Jefferson, John Hancock, and George Washington were thought of little differently than common criminals by the British, who found a surprising amount of public support for these "terrorists" in the colonies. Engaging in hit-and-run tactics, Washington's men were not considered soldiers by the British, but terrorists, because they rarely wanted to face the seasoned British and mercenary troops in the battle style of the time period—walking in a long straight line towards the enemy in a field.

This was the military culture of the day, but the small beleaguered American forces engaged in their own guerrilla terror tactics, hiding, harassing, and sniping at the larger British army to annoy and confuse it. This tactic also dragged the war out long enough to be expensive and unpopular among the British people and nobility. After winning independence, the British returned the favor of terrorism in the War of 1812 by burning Washington, DC, to the ground.

Most of us today are reluctant to use the word "terrorism" in connection with wartime activities, but that is often a dangerous line of demarcation. It is dangerous because many groups feel that they are "at war" with the United States without the U.S. government fully acknowledging them or the war. These groups develop an entire culture of being "at war with the United States," thus identifying and negotiating with them becomes difficult. If our government labels an organization as "terrorists" then our government can't officially recognize or negotiate with them, despite that in many countries and cities these organizations control much of their territory in question. Defining terrorism, even in the United States, when left to government authorities has been problematic; as an example, city officials at the turn of the twentieth century were quick to label new immigrants, union organizers, anarchists, Socialists, pacifists, or suffragettes as terrorists or agitators. The Haymarket riot of 1886 stands out as an example of urban demonstrators, who were organizing for local unions and ended up being labeled as terrorists. Today, "terrorists" have become synonymous with foreigners, specifically Middle Eastern immigrants in the American lexicon. Linked to the blind Sheik Rahman, an Iranian extremist living in the United States, or Saudi terror leader Osama bin Laden, the public's idea of bombings and terrorist activity being an Islamic Fundamentalist and Middle Eastern preoccupation has become reinforced. American citizens have come to understand that urban areas will be targets because of the large collection of people and symbolic targets located there.

Americans thought that they understood the threat of terrorism as an outside group waging secret bombings on American urban symbols, like the one at the World Trade Center in 1991. Sadly, we were introduced to the threat of domestic urban terrorism by the Oklahoma City attack on April 21, 1995. Timothy McVeigh employed a concoction of diesel fuel and fertilizer in a rented truck to destroy the Alfred R. Murrah Federal Building in downtown Oklahoma City, killing 168 men, women, and children. The immediate reaction to the bombing by news and law enforcement was to suspect Middle Eastern terrorists, and U.S. citizens of Middle Eastern descent were detained and removed from local areas for questioning. That a white extremist would conceive of such an attack on his fellow citizens was slow to dawn on the public, despite the date coinciding with the anniversary of the Branch Davidian tragedy in Waco, Texas. American culture had to change its perspective on urban terrorism and the idea of race associated with terrorism. First, there is no race or ethnicity for terrorism—all ethnic groups are capable of such treachery. Second, no urban area is insulated from such an attack, even those cities in America's heartland.

Urban culture has included the tactic of terrorism as a method of striking fear, redressing grievance, exacting social change, and provoking political change. Yet, in our modern world there seems to be limits to the acceptable use of this tactic at the risk of losing political legitimacy. The PLO found that Jerusalem and the Olympic City were beyond the limits of these tactics, and the Red Brigades found that murdering a former prime minister was likewise unacceptable to the public. The events of September 11, 2001, in New York City were the worst terrorist attacks in world history, and not just on Americans. It was also the worst single loss for British citizens in a terror attack. All of the world's citizens now know that their cities are not safe from terrorism and that the very airplanes that link our nations and our cities can be used as weapons of terror. These tactics were universally denounced by all nations as being unacceptable forms of terrorism. While the United States was recovering the economic and emotional health of its people after this horrible event, the world witnessed the retribution of the U.S. military on the suspected author of the September 11th attacks, Osama bin Laden. Originally trained and equipped by the United States to fight the occupation of the Soviet Union in Afghanistan in the 1980s, the terrorist network al Qaeda, created by Osama bin Laden, resided in the mountains of Southern Afghanistan. The network has connections throughout the Middle East and other parts of the world. Al Qaeda relied on the protection of the Taliban government of Afghanistan for cover from international scrutiny. Oddly, the follow-up to this unfathomable urban terrorist attack led to one of the most remote, primitive, rural areas of the globe in the mountains of the Afghanistan-Pakistan border. The few cities of Afghanistan either surrendered to or were bombed by the U.S. military in retaliation for the September 11th attacks, and the Taliban government was removed. Although driven from their mountain lair by the U.S. military, al Qaeda still remains a potential threat to U.S. cities, from bombings and biological or chemical weapons attacks.

References

EISENBERG, PAUL. 2000. "The Politics of Bread and Circuses: Building the City for the Visitor Class." *Urban Affairs Review.* 35, pp. 316–333.

FIREY, WALTER. 1945. "Sentiment and Symbolism as Ecological Variables." *American Sociological Review.* Pp. 140–148.

GANS, HERBERT. 1962. "Urbanism and Suburbanism as Ways of Life: A Reevaluation of Definitions." *Human Behavior and Social Process.* Albert Rose, ed. Houghton Mifflin: Boston, MA. Pp. 625–648.

GOTTDENER, MARK. 1997. *Theming of America: Dreams, Visions and Commercial Spaces.* Westview Press: Boulder, CO.

GRAMSCI, ANTONIO. 1985. *Selections from Cultural Writings.* David Forgacs and Geoffrey Smith (ed.) Harvard University Press: Cambridge, MA.

GUEVARA, ERNESTO. 1968. *Episodes of the Revolutionary War.* International Publishers: New York, NY.

HOYT, HOMER. 1939. *The Structure and Growth of Residential Neighborhoods in American Cities.* Federal Housing Administration: Washington, DC.

KELLING, GEORGE. 1988. *What Works—Research and the Police.* National Institute of Justice: Washington, DC.

LOGAN, JOHN, AND HARVEY MOLOTCH. 1987. *Urban Fortunes: The Political Economy of Place.* University of California Press: Berkeley, CA.

MARX, KARL. 1859. *A Contribution to the Critique of Political Economy.* Norton: New York, NY.

MOLLENKOMPF, JOHN. 1983. *The Contested City.* Princeton Press: Princeton, NJ.

MUMFORD, LEWIS. 1961. *The City in History.* Harcourt, Brace and World: New York, NY.

RECKLESS, WALTER. 1926. "The Distribution of Commercialized Vice in the City." Publication of the *American Sociological Society* 20.

SHERMAN, LAWRENCE. 1990. "Police Crackdowns." *National Institute of Justice Reports.* April/May 1990.

SHERMAN, LAWRENCE. 1990. "Police Crackdowns: Initial and Residual Deterrence," in *Crime and Justice,* vol. 12 (M. Terry and N. Morris, editors). University of Chicago Press: Chicago, IL.

SIMMEL, GEORGE. 1905. "The Metropolis and Mental Life." Free Press: New York, NY.

SJOBERG, GIDEON. 1965. *The Pre-Industrial City.* Free Press: New York, NY.

VELLING, GEORGE; PATE, TONY; DIECKMAN, DUANNE; AND CHARLES BROWN. 1974. *The Kansas City Preventative Patrol Experiment.* Police Foundation: Washington, DC.

WALLERSTEIN, IMMANUEL. 1974. *The Modern World System.* Academic Press: New York, NY.

WALLERSTEIN, IMMANUEL. 1979. *The Capitalist World Economy.* Cambridge University Press: New York, NY.

WIRTH, LOUIS. 1938. "Urbanism as a Way of Life." *American Journal of Sociology.* Vol. 14, pp. 1–24.

APPENDIX

Urban Culture Methods for Research and Teaching

To properly delve into Urban Culture, a researcher needs to explore both quantitative and qualitative methodologies. While this may be a tall order for many of us, who might be more comfortable with one methodology over another, they are both essential for cultural research. Culture producers and consumers are rarely in easily downloadable databases for quick quantitative procedures, and even if they were, we wouldn't know about these specialized databases without knowing about their art world. The examples I will be using in this Appendix are from my own research projects on Urban Music. One research project is a book *Music in the City: A History of Austin Music* (2000); the other project is from my Master's research on New Orleans's Jazz, which is also being transformed into a book.

My first methodological recommendation is to begin with quantitative data collection, and for me, I always go to the census when I can. The U.S. Census offers a set of numbers that most researchers can agree on for at least initial inquiry into any social phenomena. They aren't perfect, as we will see, but they offer a beginning.

1. Get all available statistics
    a. In my research on Austin music and for my research into Dixieland jazz in New Orleans, I first obtained the available information on musicians and composers from the census from the years in question. The research on New Orleans was a historical query, but I was still able to get a count by race, class, and location of musicians in New Orleans for 1860. And for my research project in Austin, I took a run through the Public Use MicroSample in the census to get a sample of musicians for Austin and the Top 150 cities in America for 1990. Thus, I was able to obtain a count, and demographic, education, and income information on musicians and composers from the census sample.

b. Realizing that the information I was getting was incomplete (which was possible to get only by using qualitative methods, which I'll get to further down the list), the next step was to locate another data set if possible. I contacted the Musicians Union for 1990 numbers on their membership rolls and found them cooperative in obtaining a basic count of current members. A previous researcher's mail-out survey of these musicians, gave an even clearer picture of their demographic information (which the Union was reluctant to give on their current membership for anonymity reasons).

c. Musicians' Union data was also incomplete, which I found out by using qualitative methods. I found a voluntary musicians registry (relatively unique to Austin) hosted by the local alternative culture weekly to further supplement my numbers of Austin musicians. This alternative culture weekly was also an integral part of the local music scene, and it was validated by many musicians, who were seeking others to play with or to get gigs.

d. Next I turned to counting the number of venues that feature "live popular music" on a regular basis. (This definition is important as it sidesteps having to count churches and schools that often have music performance on a regular basis.) A list of these venues was found conveniently in the local alternative culture weekly in Austin. "Regular basis" was determined to mean four nights a week to make a distinction from those clubs and bars that only have music occasionally. I also recommend writing the definitions of terms like "live pop music" and "regular basis" into the narrative, rather than waiting to explain them in a footnote.

2. The researcher should tell each "statistics story" separately to begin with, in order to help your reader. Particularly when dealing with those interested in culture, one's reader will not always be well versed in statistics jargon and process. More so than for other audiences, I recommend explaining the relevance of each statistics category and figure separately *and simply*. Make sure to explain the numbers *and* why they matter to your research point.

a. The census numbers for Austin were used to try to find working musicians and culture producers, but a problem arose—specifically, many professional orchestra members and music teachers were in this category—older, married, employed full time, more affluent and more educated than everyday musicians encountered in direct observations of the live music scene. Again, the importance of balancing quantitative and qualitative methods is essential.

b. Musician union members were another group that didn't match observation of live music performance in Austin. Observation and interviews were able to explain that these musicians were also older, but not as affluent or educated as the census group, due to their work as wedding-band and cover-band members. This realization entailed a working knowledge of the different strata of working musicians (those that played cover music at weddings and planned events and those that played originally written music in clubs) in Austin that has to come from direct or participant observation.

    c. Musician registry members were most often the actual people playing live in the clubs of Austin. Specific bands and players were able to be matched from the musicians' registry to advertised live performances in the city.

    d. Clubs were described through direct observation and counted to make a connection between the availability of musicians and the opportunities to play, i.e., venues/clubs. Without venues, the numbers of musicians in a city become meaningless, because the site of their production doesn't exist.

3. I advocate limiting oneself to descriptive goals with statistics in cultural research (as an example, I found that Austin actually has the highest percentage of musicians in America and one of the highest percentages of live music clubs). Data concerning culture production is often not complete enough to have inferential stats be meaningful; either databases are informal and shoddy or they don't exist at all. And in the case of Austin, which group of numbers does the researcher use? Obviously, the census' older musicians and the Musician's Union's membership seem to overlap. But, do we suspend them completely from one's data report? It is easier to report the data descriptively (warts and all), and let your audience choose from all the available information.

4. One of the last stats of value to obtain is on the economic impact of culture production on the urban environment. For my historical examination of New Orleans and jazz, the economic impact wasn't crucial; however, last year's numbers on tourism, which are obviously linked to New Orleans's development of jazz, show over 300 million dollars attributed to tourism, and the city's largest employer category is tourism. Clearly New Orleans sells its culture image to other cities and tourists that visit the city *because* of its historical culture production. For Austin, city economic impact statements place the value of live music for commerce and tourism at $100 million to the local economy. Thus, culture production can be as integral to the local urban economy as oil and gas or microchips. Culture production is often overlooked, and research endeavors directed at urban culture have the potential to release hidden arts economies in many cities.

5. Situate stats in the social history of the city (including relevant political, social, and economic elements). Constructing an exhaustive and extensive history is not the goal of most urban cultural research, but one must make an attempt to situate the stats and other methods in a historical context. The reason for this is sociology's attempt to place our research and its importance in the city's historical context, as an often undiscovered component of what the urban citizen knows of their city. The value of this historical approach is its ability to demonstrate that while the findings might be new to the reader, the urban culture that they describe has been present all along.

6. Interview key individuals and interview those that compose the labor/direct effect of the cultural phenomenon. The researcher can only hope to get at Becker's "art world" issues by interviewing the human actors themselves in this production. Key musicians, especially big names like Willie Nelson or the Neville Brothers that help define an area musically and are most often successful record-label-signed musicians are obviously at the top of the musician

labor pyramid. Also, the little musician and audience members who participate in the consumption of culture must be interviewed because they are crucial to consumption and sustaining the urban production. Castells warned us about the importance of understanding the consumption component of urban life, and it is the same when examining culture. Key business actors (venue owners, booking agents, record labels, radio operators) also should be considered, as well as key people (Austin and now New Orleans have a music liaison and development official). *NOTE:* Accessing top musicians and music industry personnel can be *very* difficult, particularly if one doesn't have inside contacts. There is a well established set of gatekeepers surrounding these individuals, and without personal contacts this "gate" will be hard to penetrate.

Important life world issues were discovered during the interviews that could not have been discovered through quantitative methods alone or through simple observation alone. Venues are crucial to sustaining music as urban culture, but bars and clubs in Austin face an extreme amount of taxation from the state's Alcohol Beverage Commission, and they receive no tax abatements or other perks regularly circulated to Austin's hi-tech business. This may not be of note except that Austin promotes itself in official tourism and other marketing documents as "The Live Music Capital of the World." Live music has become the city's marketing angle, yet musicians were found to be playing for less than the minimum wage. This occurred often because of various practices at the club like playing for tickets brought in by the audience that have bands making less than $20–30 for a night for the whole band. Having no minimum wage is hurting some musicians, who find it hard to play music and pay rent on meager band profits, but neither the government nor the union seem concerned. The reason for this apathy is because the musicians at the low end of the strata are of no use to the union (which only likes to represent working dues-paying musicians in cover bands or those that have a record deal) or to the government (which only likes to acknowledge big-name musicians and record companies that generate lots of revenue for the city).

7. Observation. Direct and Participant.

   a. Direct Observation of the musicians and the audience is important for the researchers' understanding of the "hows" of production and consumption: How does a band get a gig? How does a band form? What is necessary for a band to be successful? How do audience members select a band to see? How do they keep informed? What elements of identity and social group compose the audience formation? In the end, these are all social and urban questions, because they vary from place to place. How one gets a gig in Austin is *not* the best way to get a gig in New Orleans.

   b. Participant Observation. This methodological recommendation is the most difficult, because it requires special talent, skills, access, and legitimacy within the world of the culture producers. As for me, I was a musician in Austin for some ten years before I started writing about music; this background gave me access to musicians and the world they really participate in that would be difficult for an outsider. It was a regular occurrence for band members to lie to outsiders about money and recording opportunities (usually inflating them) to make the band seem more important than it was. With no musical skills to approach them as legitimate equals, it will be difficult to get factual information from musicians and other specialized culture producers in interviews. This makes participant observations valuable in gauging the validity of interview material, but it will be rare that a researcher will have these skills (since they take years to acquire at times).

8. Combining Qualitative and Quantitative Methods. The modern story of urban culture must be told through both qualitative and quantitative methods for a complete picture to surface. The quantitative information must have the social and historical context offered by qualitative methods if the data is to be interpreted correctly.

9. Review and revise quantitative sources and research assumptions based on qualitative methods. As one is collecting quantitative data, the researcher should also be engaging in qualitative methods as well to ascertain the validity of the data collected. New data sources should be constantly sought, and that information can often come from the human actors and culture producers themselves, who know their art world better than the researcher.

10. Teaching. Urban culture and the examples of music or art or filmmaking have the advantage of holding students' attention to teach them how to employ various methodological techniques. A project I am currently considering in my teaching is to use my Sociology of Music and my Urban Sociology classes in a joint project on the current state of New Orleans music, employing these methods.

Photo Credits

Index

References to illustrations are in *italics*.

B

H

I

J

K

L

M

N

O

P

R

S